SHAKE

AND

VICTORIANS

THE ARDEN SHAKESPEARE

THE ARDEN CRITICAL COMPANIONS

GENERAL EDITORS

Andrew Hadfield and Paul Hammond

ADVISORY BOARD

MacDonald P. Jackson   Katherine Duncan-Jones   David Scott Kastan
Patricia Parker   Lois Potter   Phyllis Rackin   Bruce R. Smith
Brian Vickers   Blair Worden

Shakespeare and Renaissance Politics   *Andrew Hadfield*
Shakespeare and the Victorians   *Adrian Poole*

Forthcoming

Shakespeare and Comedy   *Robert Maslen*
Shakespeare and Language   *Jonathan Hope*
Shakespeare and Music   *David Lindley*
Shakespeare and Religion   *Alison Shell*
Shakespeare and Renaissance Europe   *ed. Andrew Hadfield and*
Paul Hammond

Further titles in preparation

THE ARDEN CRITICAL COMPANIONS

SHAKESPEARE AND THE VICTORIANS

ADRIAN POOLE

The Arden website is at
http://www.ardenshakespeare.com

This edition of *Shakespeare and the Victorians*
first published 2004 by the Arden Shakespeare

© 2004 Adrian Poole

Arden Shakespeare is an imprint of Thomson Learning

Thomson Learning
High Holborn House
50–51 Bedford Row
London WC1R 4LR

Typeset by LaserScript, Mitcham, Surrey

Printed in Croatia by Zrinski

British Library Cataloguing in Publication Data
A catalogue record for this book is available from the British Library

Library of Congress Cataloguing in Publication Data
A catalogue record has been requested

ISBN 1-90343-671-0

NPN 9 8 7 6 5 4 3 2 1

CONTENTS

FOR HESTER

ACKNOWLEDGMENTS

I am grateful to the staff of the following for advice and assistance of various kinds: British Library; Prints Department of the British Museum; Cambridge University Library; English Faculty Library, Cambridge; Sir John Soane Museum; Shakespeare Centre Library, Stratford-upon-Avon; Shakespeare Institute Library, Stratford-upon-Avon; Theatre Museum, National Art Library and Prints Department of the Victoria and Albert Museum; Wren Library, Trinity College Cambridge.

I have many friends and colleagues to thank for advice, suggestions, clues and admonitions. If I have not acted on all of them, this is partly because the topic addressed by this book is even more enormous than I foresaw when I first agreed to write it. I am particularly grateful to the general editors, Paul Hammond and Andrew Hadfield, for their invitation to do so and for their advice along the way. I am indebted to an anonymous reader for helpful comments on the typescript both general and detailed. I would like to thank, for all sorts of assistance, the following: Anne Barton, Jonathan Bate, Gillian Beer, Matthew Bevis, Christopher Decker, Jean Chothia, Stefan Collini, Laura Cordy, Robert Douglas-Fairhurst, Rebecca Edwards, Kelvin Everest, Jennifer Formichelli, Jim Fowler, Rebecca Gowers, Eric Griffiths, John Harvey, Jane Hawking, Boyd Hilton, Jessica Hodge, Peter Holland, Philip Horne, Kevin Jackson, Russell Jackson, Ananya Kabir, John Kerrigan, Nicholas Kneale, John Lennard, Gail Marshall, Ruth Morse, Michael O'Brien, Sophie Ratcliffe, Matthew Reynolds, Christopher Ricks, Peter Robinson, Corinna Russell, Helen Small, John Stokes, Graham Swift, Bharat Tandon, Andrew Taylor, Ann Thompson, Jennie Walton and David Womersley. Finally I must thank my editor, Margaret Bartley, her assistant, Giulia Vincenzi, and my copy-editor, Jane Armstrong, for all their support and co-operation in bringing this book to fruition.

REFERENCES AND ABBREVIATIONS

SHAKESPEARE

All references to Shakespeare are to *The Arden Shakespeare Complete Works*, ed. Richard Proudfoot, Ann Thompson and David Scott Kastan (Walton-on-Thames, 1998). I have not normally commented on deviations between the text quoted (or misquoted) by a Victorian writer and the Arden text. Readers should be warned that the Victorians have an alarmingly variable way of spelling Shakspere's name: these variations have been honoured.

The following abbreviations are used for individual plays:

AC	*Antony and Cleopatra*
AW	*All's Well that Ends Well*
AYL	*As You Like It*
Cor	*Coriolanus*
Ham	*Hamlet*
1H4	*King Henry the Fourth, Part 1*
2H4	*King Henry the Fourth, Part 2*
H5	*King Henry V*
3H6	*King Henry the Sixth, Part 3*
H8	*King Henry VIII*
KJ	*King John*
KL	*King Lear*
MA	*Much Ado about Nothing*
Mac	*Macbeth*
MM	*Measure for Measure*
MND	*A Midsummer Night's Dream*
MV	*The Merchant of Venice*
MW	*The Merry Wives of Windsor*

Oth	*Othello*
R2	*King Richard II*
R3	*King Richard III*
RJ	*Romeo and Juliet*
Tem	*Tempest*
TN	*Twelfth Night*
WT	*The Winter's Tale*

NOVELISTS

Unless noted otherwise, the texts referred to are those in the Oxford World's Classics editions. Given the wide range of editions in which most of the Victorian novels to which I refer can be read, however, I normally cite only chapter numbers (or where appropriate, volume, book and chapter). In chapter four, 'Three Novelists', the following abbreviations are used for works by Dickens, Eliot and Hardy.

AB	*Adam Bede*
BH	*Bleak House*
BR	*Barnaby Rudge* (Penguin Classics, 1997)
DC	*David Copperfield*
DD	*Daniel Deronda*
DS	*Dombey and Son*
FH	*Felix Holt*
FMC	*Far from the Madding Crowd*
GE	*Great Expectations*
JE	*Jane Eyre*
JO	*Jude the Obscure*
L	*A Laodicean*
LD	*Little Dorrit*
M	*Middlemarch*
MC	*Martin Chuzzlewit*
MoC	*The Mayor of Casterbridge*
NN	*Nicholas Nickleby*
OCS	*The Old Curiosity Shop*

OMF	*Our Mutual Friend*
OT	*Oliver Twist*
PBE	*A Pair of Blue Eyes*
PP	*Pickwick Papers*
RN	*The Return of the Native*
SB	*Sketches by Boz* (Penguin Classics, 1995)
SCL	*Scenes of Clerical Life*
TD	*Tess of the D'Urbervilles*
TT	*Two on a Tower*
UGT	*Under the Greenwood Tree*
W	*The Woodlanders*

CRITICAL AND OTHER WORKS

The following abbreviations are used for frequently cited works. Unless noted otherwise, place of publication is London.

ACH	*Jane Austen: The Critical Heritage*, ed. B.C. Southam (1968)
Altick	Richard D. Altick, *Paintings from Books: Art and Literature in Britain, 1760–1900* (Columbus, Ohio, 1985)
BCH	*The Brontës: The Critical Heritage*, ed. Miriam Allott (1974)
Bradley	A.C. Bradley, *Shakespearean Tragedy* (1904)
DCH	*Dickens: The Critical Heritage*, ed. Philip Collins (1971)
Dowden	Edward Dowden, *Shakspere: A Critical Study of His Mind and Art* (1875)
Downer	Alan S. Downer, *The Eminent Tragedian: William Charles Macready* (Cambridge, Mass., 1966)
DPL	*The Pilgrim Edition of the Letters of Charles Dickens*, ed. Madeline House, Graham Storey and Kathleen Tillotson, 12 vols (1965–2002)
ELH	*English Literary History*
Gager	Valerie L. Gager, *Shakespeare and Dickens: The Dynamics of Influence* (Cambridge, 1996)
GEL	*The George Eliot Letters*, 9 vols, ed. Gordon S. Haight (New Haven and London, 1954–78)

HCH	*Hardy: The Critical Heritage*, ed. R.G. Cox (1970)
Hughes	Alan Hughes, *Henry Irving, Shakespearean* (Cambridge, 1981)
MCH	*Meredith: The Critical Heritage*, ed. Ioan Williams (1971)
Memoir	Hallam Tennyson, *Alfred Lord Tennyson: A Memoir by His Son*, 2 vols (1897)
OED	*Oxford English Dictionary* (Oxford, 2000–)
RBCH	*Browning: The Critical Heritage*, ed. Boyd Litzinger and Donald Smalley (1970)
RBP	*Robert Browning: The Poems*, 2 vols, ed. John Pettigrew (Harmondsworth, 1981; repr. 1996)
Ruskin	*The Complete Works of John Ruskin*, 39 vols, ed. E.T. Cook and Alexander Wedderburn (1903–12)
SCH	*Scott: The Critical Heritage*, ed. John O. Hayden (1970)
Shaw	*Shaw on Shakespeare*, ed. Edwin Wilson (1962)
SQ	*Shakespeare Quarterly*
SS	*Shakespeare Survey*
Stoker	Bram Stoker, *Personal Reminiscences of Henry Irving*, 2 vols (1906)
TCH	*Tennyson: The Critical Heritage*, ed. John D. Jump (1967)
TP	*The Poems of Tennyson*, 2nd edn, 3 vols, ed. Christopher Ricks (Harlow, 1987)
Wilde	*Collins Complete Works of Oscar Wilde*, Centenary Edition, ed. Merlin Holland (Glasgow, 1999)
WP	*William Wordsworth: The Poems*, 2 vols, ed. John O. Hayden (Harmondsworth, 1973; repr. 1989)

LIST OF ILLUSTRATIONS

INTRODUCTION

In 1864 Robert Browning was discussing over dinner the proposed arrangements for celebrating the tercentenary of Shakespeare's birth. He was impatient. All those self-important committees. 'Here we are called upon to acknowledge Shakespeare, we who have him in our very bones and blood, our very selves.'[1] It was as absurd as the pronouncement by the Directoire during the French Revolution that men might acknowledge God. Twenty years later Browning mused over the distinction between Shakespeare and God in his enigmatic sonnet, 'The Names' (*RBP*, II, pp. 964–5). Of course there was an absolute distinction between the human and the divine and their power to create. And yet, the poem concludes, 'Shakespeare's creation rises: one remove, / Though dread – this finite from that infinite.'[2]

The Victorians had Shakespeare in their bones and blood, so they liked to believe. He was certainly all around them, on stage and on posters, in paintings and print and cartoons, in the air they breathed, on the china they ate off. As we listen to them now, his words seem always on the tips of their tongues. When Fanny Kemble died in 1893 (she was born in 1809), Henry James commemorated her thus:

> She was so saturated with Shakespeare that she had made him, as it were, the air she lived in, an air that stirred with his words whenever she herself was moved, whenever she was agitated or impressed, reminded or challenged. He was indeed her utterance, the language she spoke when she spoke most from herself.[3]

1

Niece of the great Sarah Siddons and John Philip Kemble, she had been the Juliet of her generation around 1830, before James was born. In his youth he heard her solo readings of *King Lear* and *A Midsummer Night's Dream*. In her last years she was still playing Rosalind, Juliet, Beatrice – to her escorts in the carriage back from the theatre.

Shakespeare sometimes seemed the Victorians' utterance, a language for expressing and explaining themselves and their world, for talking to each other. But what of their own voices? If not a god, Shakespeare was the most powerful of ghosts, and ghosts tend to inhibit at least as much as they inspire and liberate. In dealings between the living and the ghostly, there are always questions of power at stake. Who is using whom? In the course of this book I shall be exploring some of the different kinds of dialogue the Victorians conducted with Shakespeare, as writers, readers, performers, audiences, visual artists and spectators. One of the currently dominant metaphors for the uses to which later artists have put the legacy of Shakespeare is that of 'appropriation'. Yet if we think of what a particular writer such as Dickens owes to Shakespeare, no single metaphor will be adequate to its range and complexity, whether derived from economics, law, physiology, psychology, theology or even literary theory. Think for example (in no particular order) of borrowing, stealing, appropriating, inheriting, assimilating; of being influenced, inspired, dependent, indebted, haunted, possessed; of homage, mimicry, travesty, echo, allusion and intertextuality. All the activities indicated or implied here are important in Dickens's fiction, and his relations to Shakespeare are no less unconfined. It is important to stress this to avoid the often fruitless arguments about the extent to which a particular character or scene or plot should be understood by reference to a Shakespearean source. Pickwick and Micawber are not solely or even perhaps mainly derived from Falstaff; *David Copperfield* and *Great Expectations* are very much more than rewritings of *Hamlet*; the relations between daughters and their fathers (or grandfathers) from Little Nell to Little Dorrit are not modelled solely on those between Cordelia and King Lear. Yet none of these figures or novels would have been what they are without Shakespeare. The same is endlessly true for other Victorian writers and artists.

It is worth reflecting on what is entailed by the two terms of the title. First, 'Victorians'. The mere fact of Victoria's occupation of the throne from 1837 to 1901 does not in itself provide a meaningful way of thinking about all the people who lived through part or all of these sixty-four years. There are all kinds of disputable boundaries in space and in time. Does the Wordsworth born in 1770 who succeeded Southey as Poet Laureate in 1843 and died in 1850 qualify as 'Victorian'? Or the Henry James born in New York in 1843, who settled in London and Rye and took British citizenship shortly before his death in 1917? Are nineteenth-century Americans 'Victorian'? There are good reasons for supposing that they are not, or at least that they are very much less so than the occupants of countries that owed the Queen of that name allegiance. I have excluded sustained discussion of Emerson, Melville, Hawthorne and Poe, yet given the volume of transatlantic traffic in both directions, of performers and lecturers, texts and arguments, it would be impossible to paint a picture of the Victorian Shakespeare without at least glancing reference to Edwin Forrest and Charlotte Cushman, to Emerson and Whitman. The same holds true for the vast topic of 'colonial' Shakespeare, in India, Australia and Canada. Closer to home, there are particular questions about 'Englishness' with which Shakespeare gets increasingly embroiled as the century progresses, especially as they impinge on the *other* island set in the silver sea to the west of the British mainland. Some of these issues are touched on in chapter six.

Nevertheless, it is hard altogether to ignore the impulse to think in terms of chronological phases. The temper of Victoria's reign, for example, can be sharply divided into the twenty or so years before Prince Albert's death in 1861 and the forty afterwards. From a literary and cultural perspective with a particular emphasis on Shakespeare, there are half-truths in contemplating three main phases to the nineteenth century in Britain.

First there is a phase dominated by the Romantic poets, by the novels of Sir Walter Scott, by the performances of John Philip Kemble, Sarah Siddons and Edmund Kean, and the criticism of Coleridge and William Hazlitt. This comes to an end in the early 1830s, with the deaths in quick succession of Hazlitt (1830), Siddons (1831), Scott (1832) and Kean (1833). There follows a long period of consolidation up to the mid-1870s. This sees the proliferation of new editions of Shakespeare aimed at a wider readership, such as Charles Knight's *Pictorial Edition* (1838–42) and Charles and Mary Cowden Clarke's *Cassell's Illustrated* (1864–8). There is quickened interest in Shakespeare's life and times, both what can be known and what can be freely made up when it is not, and there is increasing enthusiasm for Shakespeare's women, nurtured by popular texts such as Anna Jameson's *Characteristics of Women* (1832) and Mary Cowden Clarke's *The Girlhood of Shakespeare's Heroines* (1850–2), of which we shall hear more in chapter three. Key figures in this phase include William Charles Macready (1793–1873), the eminent tragedian, heir of J.P. Kemble, and his leading lady (initially) Helen Faucit (1817–98), but there is also the richly developing tradition of Shakespearean burlesque and the deployment of Shakespeare in new forms of humorous publication such as *Punch* (founded in 1841). Shakespeare infiltrates the imagination of all the major creative writers of these middle decades – Carlyle, Ruskin, Dickens, Thackeray, the Brontës, Trollope, George Eliot, Tennyson, Elizabeth Barrett and Robert Browning, Christina Rossetti – in ways the body of this book will examine.

By about 1875 this phase comes to a close, despite the continuing life and work of some of the figures mentioned here. The Brontës, Elizabeth Barrett Browning, Thackeray and Dickens were all dead and gone; George Eliot issued her last novel in 1876 (*Daniel Deronda*), Trollope's prolific career was beginning to wind down (*The Way We Live Now* was published in 1875), and Hardy's beginning to take off with *Far from the Madding Crowd* (1874). 1875 saw the publication of Macready's *Reminiscences* and the collected essays *On Actors and the Art of Acting* by the leading English drama critic between Hazlitt and Shaw, George Henry Lewes. The sense of a new epoch in the theatre was marked by Henry Irving's first great success as a brooding, controversial Hamlet in October 1874. With help from Ellen Terry and numerous designers, composers, scene-painters and carpenters, Irving's Lyceum dominated Shakespeare on the English stage at least up to 1895, when he became the first actor to be knighted. But in this third phase 'Shakespeare' is fissuring. Voices are being raised against spectacular Shakespeare and in favour of a return to 'authentic' staging. Indeed, voices are being raised against Shakespeare himself as an obstacle to the possibilities of new writing and a new aesthetic, not only in drama and theatre. There were other models both abroad and closer in time, as we shall see in the Epilogue. Even at home, for all his apparent respectability Irving breathed something weird and outlandish into his Shakespearean roles, while Oscar Wilde found dangerous provocation in the sonnets and the boy actors of Shakespeare's own theatre. There were real foreigners too, such as Tommaso Salvini and Sarah Bernhardt, whose flamboyant impersonations of Othello and Hamlet excited and troubled English audiences, as if with the vision of a Shakespeare sailing out of 'our' control into global orbit.

Such temporal maps are at best rough and ready, but this one corresponds to some of the ways in which Victorian writers themselves thought of their relations to Shakespeare. What did this other term, 'Shakespeare', entail? It meant a body of texts, edited, published and marketed with a developing sense of scholarly protocol but also of an expanding readership's diverse needs.[4] It meant an array of stories, characters, speeches and sayings so widely and intimately familiar that readers and auditors could be relied on to recognize them when they were quoted, echoed, mimicked, travestied or transformed. It also meant a whole set of particular images and models through which these Shakespearean 'originals' were mediated. That is to say, through the works of other writers – poets, novelists, dramatists – who had themselves appropriated Shakespeare's words, scenes, figures and plots, such as the Wordsworth who speaks in the 'Immortality Ode' of trembling 'like a guilty Thing surprised' (compare *Ham*, 1.1.48), or the Scott whose David Gellatley made at least one early reader think of the Fool in *King Lear* (*SCH*, p. 70). Nor must we forget the works of the visual artists, the painters, illustrators and cartoonists responsible for imprinting, on the mind of individuals and the culture at large, images of Hamlet and Falstaff, Romeo and Juliet, Lear and Cordelia, Ariel and Caliban – and of their creator. We must allow a special force to the legendary theatrical stars associated with particular roles, often perpetuated by the reproduction of well-known paintings, in illustrated editions of the plays and elsewhere, of Sarah Siddons's Queen Katherine, Kemble's Coriolanus, Kean's Richard III, Macready's Macbeth, Irving's Shylock and Terry's Lady Macbeth.

It was with a mixture of relief, envy and nostalgia that the Victorians looked back at the turbulent half-century preceding the young Queen's accession in 1837. Amongst the great Shakespearean actors of the earth-shaking decades from 1790 onwards, Edmund Kean held a particular fascination for them. In October 1832 the young Robert Browning walked ten miles from Camberwell to Richmond and back again to see Kean in what would turn out to be one of his last performances as Richard III. G.H. Lewes recalled as a small boy having seen Kean in 1825 and again in 1832. He thought him, despite his defects, incomparably the greatest actor he had seen, because of 'the irregular splendour of his power' (p. 2).[5] It was impossible to watch his Othello, Shylock or Richard 'without being strangely shaken by the terror, and the pathos, and the passion of a stormy spirit uttering itself in tones of irresistible power' (p. 3). Kean was irregular and irresistible. Like Rachel across the Channel, he had 'genius', while Macready, whose career overlapped with Kean's, only had the highest form of talent ('one remove – though dread', to borrow from Browning's 'The Names'). In comparing Kean and Macready, Lewes expresses a characteristically Victorian sense of decline from the heady rapture of the Romantics to the steadier, more predictable and conscientious plane of the mid-century. Macready had more flexibility than Kean, more range of intellectual sympathy, but there was no grandeur or splendour even in his best roles: 'They were domestic rather than ideal, and made but slight appeals to the larger passions which give strength to heroes. He was irritable where he should have been passionate, querulous where he should have been terrible' (p. 34). Much the same complaint would in due course be made of Macready's successor as the leading actor-manager of the century's final decades. In Irving's case, however, the contrast did not have to be made with the long-lost Kean. More immediate to hand was the animal vitality of his great contemporary, the Italian Salvini.

If Kean's Shakespearean roles provided a physical intensity, excitement and force for which the Victorians yearned, then for novelists and their readers there was a less intimidating model whom they could look back to – and continue to read. Scott was the first nineteenth-century novelist to provoke comparison with Shakespeare, and he became one of the main conduits through which a certain idea of 'Shakespeareanism' continued to flow until nearly the end of the century. The idea connotes scale, plenitude, multiplicity, an extensiveness and inclusiveness both social and generic, the sense of a 'whole world' in which no person high or low is too insignificant for attention, and no single genre sufficiently elastic to encompass the range of human fortunes, of sorrow and joy. It is exactly what the neo-classic critics had always objected to: Shakespeare's mixing up of the kings and the clowns, the revellers and the mourners, the princes and the grave-diggers.

But for the Victorians Scott was, for all his limitations or even because of them, a helpful model of what it might mean to be a 'Shakespearean' writer. Reviewing Scott's output so far in 1821, Nassau Senior spoke of '[o]ur author's eminent success in the difficult and almost untrodden path of tragi-comedy (few writers before him, except Shakspere, having ever ventured to bring the ludicrous into close contrast with the pathetic)' (*SCH*, p. 231). Other readers admired Scott's ability to portray, like the Shakespeare of the history plays, a large and complex social world. Recalling a great phrase of Montaigne's (*ondoyant et divers*), in 1858 Walter Bagehot praised Scott's representation of 'the undulation and diversified composition of human society' (*SCH*, p. 402). A few years later the young Henry James believed that 'Since Shakespeare, no writer had created so immense a gallery of portraits, nor, on the whole, had any portraits been so lifelike. Men and women, for almost the first time out of poetry, were presented in their habits as they lived' (*SCH*, p. 429). This last phrase, borrowing Hamlet's words as the ghost of his father goes, even now, out at the portal (*Ham*, 3.4.137), was to become a favourite of James's.

But against this there were complaints that Scott's characters lacked the inwardness distinctive of Shakespeare's. Carlyle's judgment was severe: 'your Shakspeare fashions his characters from the heart outwards; your Scott fashions them from the skin inwards, never getting near the heart of them! The one set become living men and women; the other amount to little more than mechanical cases, deceptively painted automatons' (*SCH*, p. 365). Leslie Stephen too thought the novels were addressed to the everyday mind: 'If in his width of sympathy, and his vivid perception of character within certain limits, he reminds us of Shakspeare, we can find no analogy in his writings to the passion of *Romeo and Juliet*, or to the intellectual agony of *Hamlet*' (*SCH*, p. 448). Again, passion and agony seemed to belong to the past.

George Eliot admired Scott, but there was another novelist of an earlier generation, less frequently associated with Shakespeare, who provided an encouraging alternative. In 1843 Macaulay compared Jane Austen to Shakespeare (*ACH*, p. 122), and four years later G.H. Lewes praised her for 'her marvellous dramatic power'. She had just what Scott lacked, 'that singular faculty of penetrating into the most secret recesses of the heart' (*ACH*, p. 215). This sparked a lively exchange with Charlotte Brontë, and when Lewes returned to deliver a fully nuanced judgment on Austen in 1859 (the year *Adam Bede* was published), his enthusiasm was more temperate. She was still 'an artist of the highest rank' whose faculty of characterization was akin to Shakespeare's, but he acknowledged 'her deficiencies in poetry and passion' (*ACH*, pp. 148, 153, 159). Another woman novelist was ready at hand to take up the challenge. To penetrate into the secret recesses of the heart would be one of the ambitions of the author of *Middlemarch* and *Daniel Deronda*. Poets too could be talked of in these terms, especially Robert Browning. And whenever such claims are made about delving into secret recesses, it is the epitome of Shakespearean 'inwardness' that is likely to be invoked.

For if there is a presiding spirit over the Victorian Shakespeare, and what the Victorians made of Shakespeare, it is Hamlet. The Hamlet of whom Ralph Waldo Emerson was thinking when he wrote in 1850 that 'It was not until the nineteenth century, whose speculative genius is a sort of living Hamlet, that the tragedy of Hamlet could find such wonderful readers.'[6] This book will explore some of the wonderful ways in which actors, painters, poets and novelists were fired by Hamlet, and other Shakespearean creatures.

Chapter One

THEATRE

VENUES

L ike most summary accounts of Victorian theatre this chapter will
focus primarily on productions of Shakespeare by a handful of
actor-managers who dominated the London stage, along with a few
leading ladies, from William Charles Macready to Henry Irving, and
Helen Faucit to Ellen Terry. But performance is specific to time and
place. If you lived in early Victorian Hull, the first name on your lips
might well have been that of Ira Aldridge, the African-American whose
Othello was a legend outside London's West End and, from 1852
onwards, across the Continent to the imperial court of St Petersburg.
The experience of Shakespeare in the theatre is always more dependent
on where exactly you are sitting than the experience of reading the
(same) text or seeing the (same) movie.

So we should acknowledge the importance of stories (impossible to
pursue here) about the performance of Shakespeare in Birmingham,
Glasgow and Dublin, in North America, Australia, and India.[1] There is
nevertheless a dominant story to be told through the household names
of their generations such as Macready and Irving, the Americans
Edwin Forrest, Charlotte Cushman and Edwin Booth, the continental
stars Tommaso Salvini and Sarah Bernhardt.[2] To become household
names they had to conquer London, but once they had done so, the
extent of touring across nineteenth-century Britain and Ireland and
North America meant that they became agents and icons of identity,
with and against whom spectators could identify themselves, all the

more powerfully when identity was stamped with the mythic force of Hamlet or Lear, of Juliet or Lady Macbeth. As we shall see in chapter six, Shakespeare carried 'authority' – and exposed it to question. As the nineteenth century progressed, Shakespeare was diffused across the globe not only by the reading of texts but also by the power of performance.

In Britain there was serious money at stake on the national circuit. By 1845 Helen Faucit had established herself on the London stage, but she spent the next six years touring the provinces, where she earned much more than she could have done by staying in the capital. 'The provinces' did not just mean the major theatres in Dublin, Glasgow, Edinburgh, Liverpool and Manchester, but up and down and across the country from Aberdeen to Exeter and Yarmouth to Cork. There was the prospect of even more substantial reward across the Atlantic. Macready made his first trip there in 1826, and a second in the 1840s; Irving the first of eight in 1883. In the other direction, Ira Aldridge sought his fortune in England and found it, even more notably on the Continent; he never returned to America. Charlotte Cushman took London and the British provinces by storm in 1846 with her Romeo, Lady Macbeth and Queen Katherine; Edwin Booth followed suit in 1861–2 and again in the 1880s, most notably with his Hamlet; Ada Rehan excelled as Rosalind, Kate, Beatrice and others from 1884 onwards, and as Viola in 1893 opened a new theatre just off Leicester Square for her boss, the American impresario Augustin Daly.

Daly's was not the only new theatre to open in the London of the 1890s. More important for the story of Victorian Shakespeare was Herbert Beerbohm Tree's Her (in due course, His) Majesty's. Tree and his theatre bring this story to a close, in the sense that they mark the end of a line of succession which in its simplest form begins with Macready's seasons at Covent Garden 1837–9 and at Drury Lane 1841–3. Macready's legacy was taken up by Samuel Phelps at Sadler's Wells from 1844 to 1862, and by Charles and Ellen Kean at the Princess's from 1850 to 1859. There was then something of a hiatus, apart from Charles Fechter's dazzling Hamlet at the Princess's in 1861, and an honourable spell at Drury Lane under the management of

Edmund Falconer and F.B. Chatterton, which saw Helen Faucit's triumphant return to the London stage as Imogen, Lady Macbeth, Rosalind and Juliet in 1864–6. Chatterton is the originator of the mischievous aphorism that 'Shakespeare spells Ruin', so gratefully disproved by Daly and Beerbohm Tree. A new and final phase begins in 1874 with the controversial Hamlet of Henry Irving, the only actor-manager of comparable stature to Macready. He took over management of the Lyceum in 1878, and ruled for a mainly triumphant twenty years. When his Lyceum began to fail in the late 1890s Tree was ready to take up the mantle, though by now reaction was setting in against the distended tradition of spectacular Shakespeare that under Macready had seemed so daringly innovative.

Amongst the several strands making up this reaction were the experiments with 'authentic' staging led by William Poel. He began with a production of the First Quarto *Hamlet* on a bare, curtained stage at St George's Hall in April 1881, then in 1894 established the Elizabethan Stage Society, which for the next ten years furthered his ideals with landmark stagings of *Dr Faustus*, *Arden of Faversham*, *The Broken Heart* and *The Alchemist*, as well as Shakespeare. Poel was not as gifted at putting his ideas into practice as he was bluntly inexorable in their pursuit, but other voices were increasingly raised in the 1890s against Irving and 'the Lyceum style' and then, with more reason, against Tree and Her Majesty's. Shaw was never at a loss for eloquent invective. There was a visionary gleam in the eyes of the young Gordon Craig at the way new technical possibilities (lighting, for instance) might assist the birth of an aesthetic that broke with the long-dominant forms of realism. The combined forces of reaction against Victorian Shakespeare came to full fruition with Harley Granville Barker's productions at the Savoy Theatre of *The Winter's Tale* and *Twelfth Night* in 1912, and *A Midsummer Night's Dream* in 1914.[3]

There were always 'other' Shakespeares, not least outside London. In the capital itself, the two Theatres Royal had an official monopoly on the performance of Shakespeare and other 'legitimate' drama up until 1843, but there was a vibrant life to the alternative, 'minor' or 'illegitimate' theatres. Here you could find all kinds of Shakespeare, both serious and burlesque, alongside the nautical melodramas and pantomimes. But after Covent Garden and Drury Lane lost their monopoly in 1843, Shakespeare was fair game for anyone in the West End or outside it. Covent Garden abandoned the struggle and re-opened in 1847 as the Royal Italian Opera House. Drury Lane remained the grandest stage available for Macready's farewell Macbeth in 1851, Helen Faucit's triumphant return to the West End in 1864, and Salvini's Othello in 1875, though by this time it was best known for spectacular melodrama and pantomime. The Haymarket had enjoyed a limited licence to perform legitimate drama in the summer season, and it continued to be associated with comedy, especially under Ben Webster's management from 1837 to 1853.[4] But after 1843 you could see Shakespeare at a vastly wider range of venues, with names such as Astley's, the Adelphi, the Grecian, the Gaiety, the Marylebone, the Olympic, the Queen's and the Victoria.[5]

'POPULAR' SHAKESPEARE

Most intriguing of all from this distance in time is the whole broad spectrum of 'popular' Shakespeare to be found on stages outside the fashionable West End, such as the Surrey, the Soho, the Standard, Shoreditch, the Victoria (now the Old Vic) and the Britannia, Hoxton. The first numbers of Dickens's *Household Words* in 1850 contain vivid and sympathetic descriptions of these last two.[6] Like the low-life characters and scenes within Shakespeare's plays, in the *Henry IV* plays, *Much Ado* or *Measure for Measure*, this world could cock a wonderful snook at the pretensions of the high-and-mighty. In the 1850s the serious Shakespearean would certainly have wanted to take in Charles Kean's scholarly, even scholastic *Macbeth* at the Princess's. But it might have been more fun to nip over the Thames to Astley's and see William Cooke's equestrian version instead. His brother James Cooke had played Falstaff, Shylock and Richard III on horseback in Hull. Now William followed suit with a *Richard III* where White Surrey fell and played dead with the rest of the stud while above them his master was hacked to death by Richmond. The Cooke family followed these with Garrick's version of the *Shrew*, and a *1 Henry IV* arranged with 'equestrian illustrations'.[7] The writer Theodor Fontane reported admiringly to his German readers on the thrill of the battle scenes at Astley's, the Soho or the Surrey. At a performance of *Antony and Cleopatra* at the Standard, Shoreditch, he found himself between a docker and a soldier. It seemed to him that Shakespeare belonged to 'the people' at least as much as if not more than to the fashionable audience at Drury Lane.[8] 'The people' were not only English. In July 1853 Dickens reported from Boulogne about the hilarious *Midsummer Night's Dream* put on by the Opéra Comique, in which 'a poet named Willyim Shay Kes Peer, gets drunk in company with Sir John Foll Stayffe', and so on – 'the nonsense was done with a sense quite admirable' (*DPL*, VII, p. 119).

There was also the tradition of positive burlesque, from John Poole's *Hamlet Travestie* (1811) onwards, which mocked the pretensions of the Macreadys and Keans and Irvings.[9] In 1874 Irving's Hamlet prompted George Belmore to a burlesque entitled *Hamlet the Hysterical*, and in 1876 the Strand staged *The Rival Othellos*, capitalizing on the current performances by Irving and Salvini (updating an earlier rivalry between Gustavus Brooke and Charles Fechter). One of the later fruits of this tradition was W.S. Gilbert's *Rosencrantz and Guildenstern*, first published in 1874 and performed in 1891 and 1892.[10] Twenty years later in Trieste James Joyce had acquired it for his library and was quoting from it to his students; there is some evidence that it contributes to the use he makes of Shakespeare in *Ulysses*.[11]

We can catch the flavour of mid-Victorian London from the most captivating of burlesque performers, the astonishing Frederick Robson. In 1853 the Keans' *Macbeth* at the Princess's incited him to a burlesque with music 'largely inspired by nigger minstrel tunes' including 'Who's dat knocking on de door?'[12] The diminutive Robson had a remarkable following in his heyday at the Olympic before he drank himself to an early death in 1864. He specialized in abrupt switches from hilarity to horror that sound distinctly appropriate not just for his star turn as Gam-Bogie in *The Yellow Dwarf* (1854) but also for the Macbeth and the Shylock with which he followed it. A few years later he also travestied

Adelaide Ristori's Medea. There were those who thought him the
greatest actor of his generation. Anthony Trollope told G.H. Lewes that
Macready had seemed to him 'a man of supreme intelligence, but with
no histrionic genius', whereas Robson was in the same class as Edmund
Kean and the finest French actors such as Got and Lemaître (*GEL*, IX,
p. 166). Samuel Butler's novel *The Way of All Flesh* (1903) looks back
on this era. The narrator Overton takes the main character Ernest
Pontifex to see Robson and Mrs Keeley at the Olympic on the latter's
first evening out of prison (ch. 70). For Ernest it is a liberating
experience.

> In the scene before the murder, Macbeth had said he could
> not kill Duncan when he saw his boots upon the landing. Lady
> Macbeth put a stop to her husband's hesitation by whipping him
> up under her arm, and carrying him off the stage, kicking and
> screaming. Ernest laughed till he cried. 'What rot Shakespeare is
> after this,' he exclaimed involuntarily.

Overton recalls an undergraduate essay Ernest had published at
Cambridge denouncing the Greek tragedians – 'dull, pompous and
artificial productions' – and praising instead Aristophanes – 'keen,
witty, outspoken' (ch. 46). This last would be an apt description of the
Porter in *Macbeth*, who along with so many of the 'Aristophanic'
elements in Shakespeare's text was normally banished from the
Victorian stage only to pop up again in burlesque.[13]

As we contemplate these diverse theatres and the Shakespeares they
staged, the distinctions between what we have come to think of as
'high' and 'low' culture are far from clear-cut. It was the unfashionable
Sadler's Wells that saw the single most sustained attempt to present the
full Shakespearean canon, under Samuel Phelps's devoted management
from 1844 to 1862. Though there is room for disagreement about
quite how barbaric the North London audience were before Phelps
tamed them (see pp. 202–3), it seems clear that he established an
exceptional rapport between actors and audience. The small size of the
theatre was a help. Phelps was craftsmanlike, personally modest, at
home with an audience whose local core was composed of working

men and women, tradespeople and clerks.[14] Fontane was intrigued by
the Keans' visually lavish productions at the Princess's, especially the
history plays, but his admiration for what Phelps was doing at Sadler's
Wells went deeper. Phelps had nothing like the scenic and technical
resources of the Keans, but this was where you found the real
Shakespeare, so Fontane thought, in a truly 'popular' theatre. It was in
particular the comedy he enjoyed, though this seemed generally true of
English theatres. 'I have yet to encounter a poor clown on any English
stage', he remarked.[15]

As the century progressed the distinctions became sharper, though
even in 1874 Irving's Hamlet was still preceded by a one-act farce
starring the actor who reappeared as the first grave-digger (Henry
Compton). As the fashionable dinner hour became later the bill of fare
became shorter, but back in 1837 it was a lengthy business. Indeed it
comes as something of a shock to read the playbills for Macready's
seasons at Covent Garden and Drury Lane, and to see just how much
else his Shakespeare was mixed up with. In 1833 Bulwer-Lytton had
the hero of his best-selling novel *Eugene Aram* recall the impression
made on him as a boy by an evening at the theatre, when *Hamlet* was
succeeded by an Italian mountebank doing juggling tricks. Shakespeare
delights them, but the mountebank makes them glow with rapture at
his 'mere bodily agility': Aram is cured of the desire for worldly fame
(bk 1, ch. 5).[16] Until later decades a full evening at the theatre required
from its audiences sheer bodily stamina. It lasted some five or six hours,
and consisted of a main piece followed by one or more lighter farces or
comedies. There was a great deal of music. Spectators could skip the
first part of the evening, especially if it seemed too heavy (like *Hamlet*),
and come in at 'second price' half way through. It is true that Elizabethan
audiences enjoyed a good jig as an afterpiece, and fifth-century
Athenians a satyr play after three tragedies. But an early Victorian
who went in for a whole evening's worth of Shakespeare and anything
else must have relished what now seem some pretty rum combinations
(as they did to Eugene Aram then). Here are some examples from
Macready's two seasons in charge of Covent Garden, 1837–9: *Othello*,
followed by Dibdin's comic opera *The Quaker*, and a new one-act farce

The Spitfire (16 October 1837); *Macbeth*, preceded by the overture to Mozart's *Idomeneo* and succeeded by *The Marriage of Figaro* (20 November 1837); *The Tempest*, followed by Reynolds's three-act comedy *Laugh When You Can* (13 October 1838) or Dibdin's comic opera *The Cabinet* (30 October 1838); *Macbeth*, preceded by the overture to Mozart's *Die Zauberflöte* and succeeded by a new one-act farce *Chaos is Come Again; or The Race-Ball* (19 November 1838).[17]

The imagination is particularly stretched by the bill for Thursday, 25 January 1838, announcing the opening night of what has gone down as the historic production of *King Lear*, with Macready in the title-role, Helen Faucit as Cordelia, and the nineteen-year-old Priscilla Horton as the first Fool to be seen on stage since Shakespeare's day. (For the rest of the century the role was usually played by a woman.) One wonders if most members of the first audience were fully apprised of the significance of the occasion. They may well have been there to see Mademoiselle Frederica Fatty-Ma Fantoni as Lady Godiva in the Christmas Pantomime. For it was this that took up the rest of the evening – and a great deal more of the playbill than Shakespeare (see Figure 1). This was, for the twenty-seventh time of asking, the entirely new 'TRAGICAL – COMICAL – HISTORICAL – PASTORAL GRAND CHRISTMAS PANTOMIME, called HARLEQUIN AND PEEPING TOM OF COVENTRY: or THE LADYE GODIVA AND THE WITCH OF WARWICK'. The real star of the evening was the spectacular Diorama by Clarkson Stanfield, later presented on its own, showing a series of views from northern Italy, across the Alps and southern Germany through Flanders to the Channel. Like the increasingly popular Panoramas, the Diorama anticipated the developed technology of the moving image that we have come to know as Cinema. So much for Shakespeare? Yet it is striking that a Shakespearean presence continues to be felt, after the close of the tragedy, not only in the Polonian title of the panto, but in the extraordinary jingling sequence of scenes and actions, a whole story in itself. Suddenly, amidst 'Pursuit – getting into hot water – send for the Doctor', we hear a voice from *Macbeth* (5.3.47): '"throw physic to the dogs"', and again, at the close, this time as unmarked quotation: 'Old King's Head on the road to Fulham. – Inn

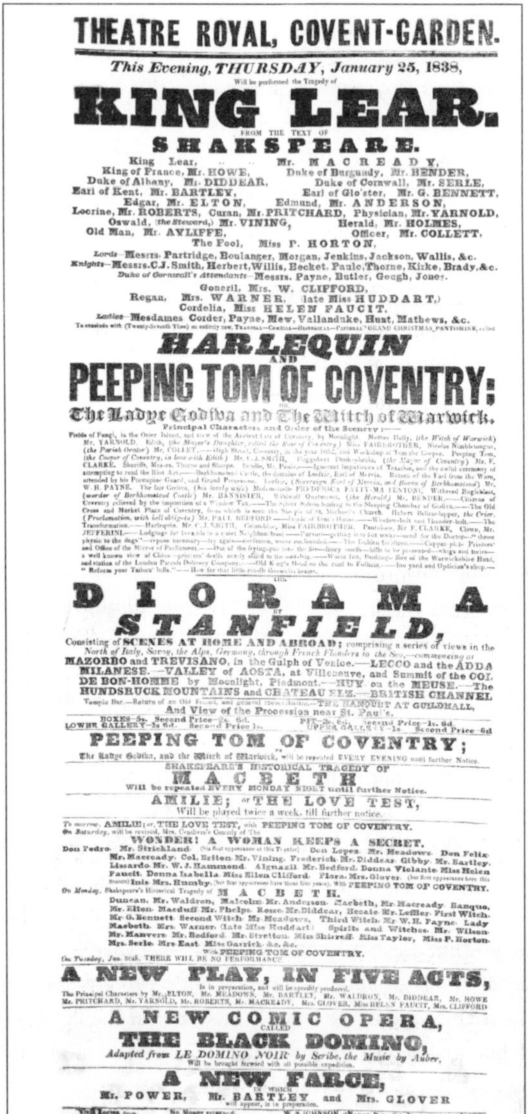

FIGURE 1 Playbill for the first night of Macready's *King Lear* at Covent Garden, 25 January 1838.

yard and Opticians' shop. – "Reform your Tailors' bills." – How far that little candle throws its beams.' These last are Portia's words from *The Merchant of Venice* (5.1.90).

REPERTOIRE

Shakespeare was popular, but some Shakespeares were more popular than others. The sense of stage tradition was very strong, and it took a brave actor or manager to break with it. There was a relatively small number of tried and tested roles in one or more of which any serious aspirant had to make a hit: as Richard III, Macbeth, Othello, Shylock, Hamlet, or as Juliet, Rosalind, Ophelia, Lady Macbeth, Constance. These were roles in which the legendary stars of earlier years had shone – Garrick and Kemble and Kean, Dorothy Jordan and Sarah Siddons and Eliza O'Neill. The pretenders were inevitably measured against them. By the 1830s the plays in which they appeared bore the wounds of over a century and a half of adaptation, many of them handed down from the last decades of the seventeenth century when the re-opened theatres started 'improving' the primitive Shakespearean texts, with William Davenant's *Macbeth* and (with Dryden) *The Tempest*, Nahum Tate's *King Lear* and Colley Cibber's *Richard III*. Throughout the nineteenth century there were calls to rid the stage of these hybrids and return to a pure authentic original, and there were moves in that direction, notably led by Macready and his successor Phelps. These coincided with the proliferation of more scholarly reading editions. But old favourites and habits died hard. Most stagings of *Macbeth*, *A Midsummer Night's Dream* and *The Tempest* would still to our eyes and ears have seemed extraordinarily 'operatic'. Garrick's version of *The Taming of the Shrew* was a hardy perennial. Barry Sullivan was still playing Cibber's version of *Richard III* at Drury Lane the year before Irving played Shakespeare's at the Lyceum in 1877, and in 1861 even Phelps reverted from the Shakespeare he had played at Sadler's Wells in 1845. Tate's *King Lear* was still exerting a powerful influence on what audiences heard and saw when Irving played Shakespeare's – or some of it – in 1892.

Irving's *Lear* has been described as 'a legendary disaster'.[18] If so, it was an exemplary failure. Shaw thought that like almost everyone else Irving murdered the text of Shakespeare. Like Macready and Charles Kean before him, Irving cut the play heavily for performance – an estimated 46 per cent of the original (Hughes, p. 118). He also rearranged things. Following the long tradition from Tate onwards, Irving's Act 1 closed with the cursing of Goneril and the strong curtain-line, 'Away, away!', the operatic climax to a rising sequence of four big speeches. Irving liked to have the last word. Ellen Terry struggled with him over the end of the great scene in *Much Ado* when Beatrice tells Benedick to 'Kill Claudio'. As usual she lost. Irving made her repeat the injunction to create the exit line he wanted: 'As sure as I'm alive I will!'[19] As the dying Tennyson is supposed to have said to Irving himself, of a speech of Wolsey's in *Henry VIII*: 'Shakespeare never wrote that! I know it! I know it! I know it!' (Stoker, I, p. 236). It was not often that Irving was forced to invent; it was usually a matter of deft transposition. When it came to the final scene of *Hamlet*, he divided it in two and closed the first part with a more emphatic sense of Hamlet's resolution than his author provides. Shakespeare gives Hamlet two famous expressions of the stoicism with which he has returned from the sea voyage. The first he utters within a few lines of the opening dialogue with Horatio, concluding with 'There's a divinity that shapes our ends, / Rough-hew them how we will' (5.2.10–11). The second occurs (in prose) some two hundred lines later, after the passage with Osric, and before the entrance of the King and his court (with which Irving began a separate scene): 'Not a whit. We defy augury. There is special providence in the fall of a sparrow. ... The readiness is all' (5.2.218–21). Irving himself believed in providence, as one imagines did most of his audience. Why not unite these utterances to make even more of a credo? His Hamlet therefore chose to follow 'The readiness is all' immediately with the 'divinity that shapes our ends', transported from the beginning of the scene.[20] This suggests the range of what it might mean to remain 'faithful' to Shakespeare's own words. It could mean quietly altering the entire rhythm of a scene or sequence of scenes, and hence their significance, and cumulatively, thus, the 'meaning' of the whole play.

Irving was choosy about the Shakespeare plays he put on, and one of the most striking differences between the Victorian experience of Shakespeare and ours, to speak broadly for the last quarter of a century, is that we enjoy a greater range of plays in performance. This is attributable to the movement which helped to found the Stratford Memorial Theatre in 1879 and to disseminate the concept of a 'Festival Theatre' with which a company such as the Royal Shakespeare Company could be associated. If we owe to Stratford and other festival theatres in the anglophone world the idea of being able to see somewhere sometime every Shakespeare play in the canon, this is an aspiration that should be traced back to Samuel Phelps and his tenure at Sadler's Wells. During his reign at the Lyceum Henry Irving produced twelve Shakespeare plays, but Phelps put on no less than thirty-one, including such rarities (then) as *All's Well That Ends Well*, *Love's Labour's Lost*, *Timon of Athens* and *Pericles* (an astonishing fifty-five performances of this last in 1854–5).[21]

In general terms there has been relatively little change in the level of our admiration for *Hamlet*, *Richard III*, *Romeo and Juliet*, *As You Like It* and *Much Ado*, if not its nature. There has also been less change than one might expect in the standing of *Othello* and *The Merchant of Venice*, plays which troubled and excited then as they do now, albeit that the trouble and excitement are bound to seem like pale premonitions of what are now flagrancies.[22] But there are some distinct differences. We are less intimidated by *King Lear*; we are no longer bewildered by *Twelfth Night*; we relish the emotional and intellectual elusiveness of *A Midsummer Night's Dream* and *The Tempest* as well as their scenic delights. We no longer prize as they did *King John*, *Henry VIII* and *The Merry Wives of Windsor*, a group of plays which minister to an idea of English history and Englishness that seems now largely outmoded. *King John* does not have to be played as the patriotic legend it was for the Victorians, as good modern productions have proved. But for us the English history plays have their main centre of gravity in the troublesome reign of King Henry IV. The Victorians liked Falstaff well enough, but they were as happy to see him at Windsor as at Eastcheap or the battle of Shrewsbury. And for them *Henry V* was a fine but rather simple play, whereas *Richard II* had virtually no stage tradition before the Keans' production at the Princess's in 1857 and Benson's at the Lyceum in 1899.[23] A striking staging of a rarely seen play could stay in the collective memory, such as the productions of *Cymbeline* put on by Macready in 1838 and 1843 and Irving in 1896; Helen Faucit and Ellen Terry both seized the chance these gave them to make Imogen one of their best-loved roles.[24] But as the late plays went in general, *The Winter's Tale* was more frequently to be seen.

Other plays that were comparatively rare on stage, always excepting at the admirable Sadler's Wells under Phelps, included *Measure for Measure* (at the Haymarket in 1876 with Adelaide Neilson as Isabella) and *Antony and Cleopatra*, though around the turn of the century Egypt attracted spectacular treatment focused on Lillie Langtry, Janet Achurch and Constance Collier ('rather over sinuous', murmured the *Manchester Guardian*, of this last in 1906).[25] Fifty years earlier there was no dispute about the reigning Cleopatra – Isabella Glyn. Dickens went to see her in 1849 with Phelps and again in 1855 at the Standard, where a gigantic elderly Octavius Caesar provoked a howl of derision with the line, 'He calls me Boy' (*DPL*, VII, p. 554). Not even Phelps managed *Troilus and Cressida* or *Titus Andronicus*. For its first known staging since Shakespeare's day, *Troilus* had to wait for William Poel's landmark production in 1912. A *Titus* of sorts had been seen on the nineteenth-century stage in a thoroughly improved version for Ira Aldridge as an ennobled Aaron. This played through the British Isles from 1849 to 1860 and in London (but not the West End) in 1852 and 1857, but it was 1923 before Shakespeare's play would be seen in anything like its original form on the English stage, in an Old Vic production by a disciple of Poel's, Robert Atkins.[26]

SPECTACLE

The conventional story about Victorian Shakespeare on stage is that it was dominated or even overwhelmed by spectacle until liberated by Poel and others round the turn of the century. Not all Victorian Shakespeare sought to emulate the production values embraced by

Charles Kean, Irving and Tree, but the dominant ethos would seem as strange to us as it would have done to Samuel Johnson, in the lengths it went to gratify the lust of the eye. Audiences marvelled at the visual splendour of Macready's *Tempest* and *As You Like It*, at the gorgeous pageantry of the Keans' *King John* or the masque in *King Henry VIII*, at the luminous street and canal in their *Merchant of Venice*, at the extraordinary church in Irving's *Much Ado* and the unearthly landscape of his *Macbeth*, at the fantastic landscapes of Beerbohm Tree's *Twelfth Night* and *A Midsummer Night's Dream*. They relished the names of the great scene-painters William Telbin and Thomas Grieve, along with those of artists well known outside the theatre who contributed to the designs of Irving's Lyceum productions, Lawrence Alma-Tadema, Ford Madox Brown and Edwin Abbey. They admired the music, before and between and during the action, familiar by Purcell or Beethoven or specially composed by Arthur Sullivan. There were multitudes of fairies and soldiers, and attendant lords and ladies to fill up the stage. Irving had some sixty witches peopling the wind in Act 4 of his *Macbeth*, and a hundred and sixty-five soldiers for the final scenes. For the closing moments of his *Cymbeline* there were ninety-three people on stage.[27] Nowadays we only see this sort of thing in hit musicals or at the movies.[28]

In fact the birth of cinema at the turn of the century sees a predictable transfer of cultural power. From an English perspective cinema picks up the traditions of Victorian spectacular theatre that culminate with Herbert Beerbohm Tree. In 1897 Tree took over Her Majesty's Theatre and turned it into 'a theatre worthy of a great empire'.[29] He claimed the throne that the failing Irving was vacating when he staged the first of a series of monumental Shakespearean productions that went on up to the outbreak of war. Starting with *Julius Caesar* in 1898, he followed it almost annually with ever more stupendous stagings of *King John*, *A Midsummer Night's Dream*, *Twelfth Night* and others, a total of sixteen. 'Over the top' was a phrase with no meaning for Tree. The intelligentsia sniffed but the Edwardian audiences loved it. Something of a loveable rogue and certainly larger than life, Tree made an unsurprisingly excellent Falstaff. Less predictably, he took a leading role in founding the Royal Academy of Dramatic Art in 1904. It is fitting that the first Shakespeare film ever made should have been of four scenes from Tree's *King John*, released on the same day his stage production opened, 20 September 1899.[30]

There is a great deal of truth to this story. But it is often told with brisk condescension, as if the values of Victorian theatre were simply pernicious and the modernist reaction a clean liberation. The theatre is always vulnerable to condescension, and if we are to understand the real power of performance, we have to slow the story up and delve back in time with informed imagination. Then we can begin to apprehend what it meant to be grasped by the sensory assault of the gorgeous scenery, the insistent music, the charisma of the actors – and to see through it or resist it in the interest of an idea or conception. Doubtless some members of an audience will always lie back and wait to be ravished. But there is sufficient evidence that Victorian audiences contained no less than the usual quotient wanting something more and other, and ready to say so.

Consider this, for example, from John Forster on Macready's *King John* at Drury Lane in October 1842. It is true that Forster was a friend (and writing anonymously), but the loyalty which friendship can inspire need not be solely personal. Just a few years ago, says Forster, you could see this play put on with an English army consisting of seven soldiers and a French army of three.

> What a picture has taken the place of this! There is a line in the tragedy about the alchemist, the sun, which turns with splendour of his precious eye 'the meagre cloddy earth to glittering gold.' Art is such another alchemist: converting to richest use the meagre resources of the stage. The rude heroic forms of the English past; the gothic and chivalric grandeur of the Middle Ages; the woes and wars of a barbarous but an earnest time, with its reckless splendour, its selfish cruelty, and its gloomy suffering: are in this revival realized. ... And above all, in every movement of the tragedy, there is Mind at work, without which wealth of material is nothing.[31]

This begins to capture something of the sheer excitement of 'pictorial' Shakespeare at its first real flowering. It was magic. It was the past brought back to life, revived and 'realized'.[32] It was, said the *Spectator*, in an unwitting prediction of the future, 'an animated picture'.[33]

Of course there were precedents. During his first managerial spell at Covent Garden (1837–9) Macready had begun to develop his idea that the arts of the theatre could be fully integrated, notably in his production of *The Tempest* (1838). More than a decade before there had been the famous antiquarian production of *King John* (1823) by Charles Kemble and J.R. Planché. But it is with Macready's own productions of *King John* and *As You Like It* at Drury Lane in his second managerial stint (1841–3), that these ambitions begin to be realized, and then to extend their influence over the rest of the century. Charles Kean owed a great deal to Macready, including the promptbooks and designs that were passed on to him. So too did Samuel Phelps. Kean went way beyond everyone else in his fanatical pursuit of historical accuracy, whereas Irving after him (like Macready before him) gave priority to artistic effect. (Kean also owed a great deal to his wife, Ellen Tree, who is often elided out of accounts of their reign at the Princess's, though Ellen Terry remembered her as 'at the least, a joint-ruler, not a queen-consort',[34] and the question of such partnerships is an important one to which we shall return.) But allowing for differences of artistic temperament and, no less important, changes in the technical possibilities available to them (lighting, for example), there is a strong sense of continuity from Macready through the Keans to Irving and beyond to Beerbohm Tree. Commentators on the stage history of particular Shakespeare plays invariably speak of this tradition culminating in Tree. But the real climax comes with Irving's Lyceum, after which Tree furnishes a decadent, luxurious epilogue.

The most important sentiment in Forster's praise is the last. The magic is all very well but it does not seek to make us its dupes, so he claims: 'above all ... there is Mind at work, without which wealth of material is nothing'. This was the nub of the matter for the Victorians, as it was for Shakespeare and Jonson, and as it is for us now. The nature of the 'wealth' will vary, as will the way we are showered with it, but the essential dilemma, the drama of drama itself, is constant enough. It is a matter of mind over matter 'in every movement'. This is a tall order, and it would be wrong to suppose that Macready or any of his successors commanded universal applause. Before the start of his second season at Covent Garden, the *Satirist* (2 September 1838) wondered why Shakespeare's works were more than ever *read* and so few people went to the theatre. Because it is all show, of course: 'The eye alone is gratified, while that within a drama, which "surpasseth show," is utterly neglected or grossly caricatured.'

Another clue to the hold that Macready had on his audiences comes from Bulwer-Lytton (with whom the actor was on close terms, along with other writers and artists of liberal political leanings such as Dickens and Forster). When Macready retired in 1851 he was credited with the revival of English drama, especially through the terms of office he had spent in charge of the two great 'national theatres', Covent Garden (1837–9) and Drury Lane (1841–3). These were inspiring years, Bulwer-Lytton claimed, 'when, by a union of all kindred arts, and the exercise of a taste that was at once gorgeous and severe, we saw the genius of Shakespeare properly embodied upon our stage' (quoted in Downer, p. 229). By the 'union of all kindred arts' he meant the resources of visual spectacle, stage mechanics, lighting, and music such as had gone into landmark productions of *The Tempest*, *As You Like It* and others, productions distinguished by the controlling 'idea' of a figure we would now think of as the 'director' (and 'designer'). 'Gorgeous *and severe*', be it noted. There would be many voices raised throughout the rest of the century against a style of production that seemed to be merely gorgeous. In 1882 Henry James complained of Irving's *Romeo and Juliet* that he had converted the play 'from a splendid and delicate poem into a gorgeous and over-weighted spectacle'.[35] When he read the description of Charles Kean's *Winter's Tale*, Macready himself complained that 'the accessories had swallowed the poetry and action' (Downer, p. 251). But it was a charge from which few of the major actor-managers after him would be free until Poel and others tried to sweep the stage bare of all gorgeousness. Macready himself failed to please everyone. And no production can ever be severe enough

for those who believe, to use Bulwer-Lytton's terms, that no
'embodiment' of Shakespeare can ever be proper enough.

Sound was in its way no less important than sight. Irving's Lyceum
had its own regular orchestra, and several leading composers
contributed to his Shakespeare productions, of whom the best
remembered now is Arthur Sullivan. Before working with Irving,
Sullivan contributed incidental music to *The Tempest* (1864), *The
Merchant of Venice* (1867) and *Henry VIII* (1877), all for Charles Calvert
in Manchester, and to two London productions of *The Merry Wives of
Windsor* (1874 and 1889). His most famous involvement was with
Irving's Lyceum *Macbeth* (1888). Typically, this involved an overture
before each act (a total of six, in Irving's arrangement), and passages of
musical accompaniment to the action and dialogue, a wild march to
assist Macbeth's barbarous army across the heath, for example, and
music to bolster the supernatural song-and-dance routines for the
chorus of witches and spirits in Act 4 (Hughes, p. 97). But Ellen Terry's
sleep-walking scene was allowed to take place in silence.[36]

WOMEN AND PARTNERSHIP

Women actors were an unsurprisingly essential feature of the
spectacles mostly managed by male actor-managers. The ways in
which women were needed in performance connect up with their role
in the visual arts and in narrative, and they raise questions about
dependence, independence, agency and complicity that run through
the next two chapters. As regards the theatre, there are particularly
interesting relations between the two most powerful actor-managers of
the age, Macready and Irving, and the great women actors with whom
they were importantly associated: Helen Faucit and Ellen Terry.[37]

It was extremely hard for a woman to achieve independence in the
nineteenth-century theatre. Charlotte Cushman and Sarah Bernhardt
managed it. There were some exceptional figures who made their mark
as managers (in partnership with husbands), Madame Vestris (with
Charles Mathews), Ellen Tree (Charles Kean) and Marie Wilton (Squire
Bancroft), all of whom had excelled in breeches roles. The Keans and

the Bancrofts turned into pillars of the establishment, Squire being knighted in 1897 (two years after Irving). There was the signal case of Fanny Kemble, who abandoned the stage in 1834 at the tender age of twenty-three, reluctantly and briefly returned to it after the break-up of her marriage to an American slave-owner, and then forged a new career for herself in public readings of Shakespeare on both sides of the Atlantic, from 1848 to 1874. In her old age she was escorted to the theatre by the adoring Henry James, who hung on her waspish remarks about the free-and-easy new stars such as Ellen Terry. When Terry's Portia started getting too familiar with Bassanio in the casket scene, Kemble exclaimed (none too softly, one imagines): 'Good heavens, she's touching him!'[38] James's lengthy elegy for Kemble commemorated her legendary one-woman readings of Shakespeare, of *A Midsummer Night's Dream* and *The Merchant of Venice* and others. She did a *Henry V* in which 'Her splendid tones and her face, lighted like that of a war-goddess, seemed to fill the performance with the hurry of armies and the sound of battle.'[39] She played everyone, even King Lear, the whole Shakespearean multitude. We can see in Fanny Kemble an exemplary figure for the actor's power-and-weakness, a paradox sharpened in the female performer unusually freed from dependence on male actor-managers. From one aspect she can seem to assume the creative force of the great author himself, from whom all his creatures receive their voices, while from another she is more than ever exposed as a helpless medium for the god she serves, a Sibyl, a Delphic priestess.

If we leave aside foreigners and managers and the rare soloist, the most interesting cases within our period are those of Faucit and Terry. Both found themselves partnered by powerful male actors who sought to choose their roles, control their appearance, manage their moves. When Ellen Terry sported a blood-red cloak in rehearsals for *Macbeth* it caught Irving's eye, and the next thing she knew it was on his shoulders. Faucit fell under Macready's spell for five of the six years following his assumption of control at Covent Garden, but by 1843 when he left for America she was free of him, professionally at least. From them on she established an exceptional degree of control over her roles and engagements, mainly by touring outside London. The control was unslackened by marriage in 1851, shortly after Macready's retirement, to her long-time admirer Theodore Martin. She made a triumphant return to the London stage in 1864, in what were by then her signature roles of Rosalind (above all), Juliet, Imogen and Lady Macbeth. She retired from the stage in 1871, but in the 1880s she was still exercising her influence, now under the weightier name of Lady Martin, through the publication of her essays on Shakespeare's heroines (see pp. 96–7).

Faucit was over twenty years younger than Macready and seems to have fallen in love with him. When she visited him on his death-bed in 1871 he was asleep on a couch when she entered and she was reminded of King Lear awakening to see his long-estranged daughter restored to him.[40] Her first role at Covent Garden under his management had been Hermione to his Leontes. Ellen Terry did play Cordelia to Irving's Lear (though not Hermione to his Leontes), but she was plagued by no such illusions about her relations with him. It is more conceivable that he was plagued with feelings about her. Unlike Faucit with Macready, however, Terry never escaped far enough from Irving's influence fully to enjoy the roles that Faucit made her own. Terry yearned to play Rosalind, and could only watch in generous envy when Ada Rehan was a hit in the role, at her own Lyceum, in 1890.[41] Terry did play Juliet to Irving's Romeo, but it was not a success; he would never have been young enough for the part. (After the first night his estranged wife Florence wickedly wrote in her diary: 'jolly failure – Irving awfully funny'.)[42] They shared success when she played Portia to his Shylock and Ophelia to his Hamlet, but for her the closest thing to parity was her Beatrice to his Benedick.

The nearest that Terry came to Faucit's independence was as a much-loved Imogen in 1896, and to some extent as Lady Macbeth eight years earlier. These two roles suggest some of the tensions in the great partnership. Imogen is certainly the star of *Cymbeline*, and one of the difficulties for the show in performance, or so it was at least for the Victorians, is the question of which role the male lead should take. Like Macready before him, Irving chose Iachimo rather than Posthumus, whose role was severely reduced. Irving saw Iachimo as a villain-with-a-soul, whose confession and repentance provide the real centre to the final scene. The core of the play became a familiar fable of doomed man redeemed by woman, the Wagnerian versions of which roused Nietzsche to such scorn. As it happens, Vanderdecken, the Flying Dutchman, was one of Irving's most successful roles. No wonder that Shaw wrote such passionate exasperated letters to Terry about Imogen, and many years later rewrote the last act himself (*Shaw*, pp. 39–74).

With Lady Macbeth the case was different. This was partly because of John Singer Sargent. Terry inspired and served as the model for many fine paintings, some of them by her first husband G.F. Watts. Millais painted a Portia inspired by her, though the figure does not bear her features (unlike many of the female characters populating the pages of the Irving Edition, who carry her characteristic jaw-line). But there is no rival to Sargent's magnificent portrait of her as Lady Macbeth, raising the crown above her own head (Figure 2). Or is she taking it off? It is impossible to tell. This lends the portrait a wonderful doubleness. Nina Auerbach reads it as a moment of self-transfiguration, the divine Ellen Terry fusing into the diabolic Lady Macbeth. Shakespeare's queen is displaced by Sargent's, who has no thought of a mate at this supreme moment of self-coronation.[43] Yet it is possible to read it differently. Altick claims that the painting derives from the last moments of the banquet scene, when Irving's production had her left alone on stage: 'The gesture with the crown, not indicated in the text but previously used by Samuel Phelps's Lady Macbeth, Miss Atkinson, in 1857, was devised to portend the darkening future' (Altick, p. 318). Though Terry's notes on the role show her contemplating something like this possibility,[44] there is no evidence that Irving's production adopted it. However, this does not affect the wonderful ambiguity of the pose Sargent created – in collaboration with Terry. On the one hand it celebrates an independence and a triumph such as Terry rarely if ever achieved on stage apart from Irving. On the other it signals the moment of surrender as the great queen uncrowns herself, and looks ahead to the sleepwalking, madness and death that await her. It is a manic pose, a moment of mania, remote from what seems to have been most characteristic of Terry herself, yet deeply true to her situation.

FIGURE 2 John Singer Sargent, *Dame Ellen Terry as Lady Macbeth* (1889).

MACREADY, IRVING AND SELF-CONTROL

The Lady Macbeths of the nineteenth century all lived under the shadow of Sarah Siddons; so did the Constances. For his part Irving was obsessed with Edmund Kean. He owned a malacca cane that came to Kean from Garrick, the knife Kean used as Shylock, and the sword and boots in which he played Richard III. It is fitting, then, that the author of the wonderful little poem 'Memorabilia' should have presented him with Kean's purse. When Browning and Irving got together, the conversation 'usually swerved round to Shakespeare', and others fell silent (Stoker, II, pp. 89–91).

But Kean represented only one aspect of the traditions Irving inherited: the explosive and passionate and physical. Irving could explode but only spasmodically. Stoker speaks of 'the flickering spasmodic power' of his Cardinal Richelieu (Stoker, I, p. 130). The other aspect was a restraint, an intellectuality, even a scholarliness. This comes from Macready, through the intermediary figure of Phelps, to whom Irving confessed that he owed his best work at the Lyceum, both in playing and in production (Hughes, p. 242). Few Victorian actors were as versatile as Phelps. His range extended from Lear and Othello to Hubert and Malvolio down to Christopher Sly and Bottom. He was a good Falstaff, but he also pulled off a fine double act in the rarely performed second part of *Henry IV*, playing the King and Justice Shallow. In 1846 his Falstaff persuaded *The Times* that his particular forte was the pathetic.[45] In 1886, eight years after his death, William Archer thought his best roles had included Malvolio, Bottom, Shallow, Armado and Parolles, and that he might have been the best Shylock since Macklin. But then Archer was no admirer of Irving's.[46]

Another figure to make an impression on the young Irving was the American Edwin Booth (1833–93), with whom he acted at Manchester in 1861. Five years Irving's senior, Booth had a style at once intense, elevated, intellectual; he would prove to be the outstanding Hamlet of his generation on one side of the Atlantic, and Irving on the other. In 1881 they alternated Othello and Iago at the Lyceum, both proving as superb in the latter role as they were all at sea in the former. The other immediate beneficiary of Macready's innovations as director was Charles Kean, and here too there is continuity.

When William Charles Macready joined his father's acting company, England was still at war with Napoleon. Born in 1793, two years before Keats and Carlyle, by the time he was in his early thirties he was being billed as 'That Eminent Tragedian, Mr. Macready', and when Victoria came to the throne he had worked and competed with the Keans and Kembles and emerged as the leader of his profession. Of the forty years or more he spent in the theatre only the last third fell under the reign of Queen Victoria. But he was, his biographer claims, 'born to be a Victorian' (Downer, p. 353).

What does this mean? We know that the young Macready listened to Coleridge lecture, and it is tempting to suppose that his thinking about the unity of a theatrical performance, both the individual actor's and the design of the whole, owed something to that honey-tongued source. In his productions of Shakespeare Macready sought to realize a controlling 'idea' such as we might now take for granted, but in the haphazard theatre of the 1830s and 1840s this was a novelty. Yet it was not Coleridge but Wordsworth to whom the *Theatrical Times* compared Macready in 1847, when it spoke of the 'spiritual tendency' manifesting itself in the poetry of the great Romantics. If Edmund Kean had been the Byron of actors, then Macready was in many respects close to the Wordsworth who died a Victorian even if he was not self-evidently born to be one.

One clue to the contradictions in Macready's 'Victorian' make-up is offered by Alan Downer when he speaks of the combination in him of 'high moral principles and a low boiling-point' (p. 150). Macready took pride in his self-restraint, and there was a great deal to restrain. When in April 1836 his temper got the better of him and he assaulted the manager of Drury Lane, an unprincipled scoundrel called Alfred Bunn, Macready was consumed with remorse. This was not the act of the man – the gentleman – he would like to be; it was more the sort of thing a wild fellow like the late Edmund Kean might have resorted to. Nor was it the kind of actor Macready wanted to be. The same principle of restraint that he believed should govern behaviour back-stage and off-stage was also the secret of effective performance. For the great Shakespearean roles in which Macready excelled – Macbeth above all, but also Othello, Lear and Hamlet – the passion had to be there, but rigorously disciplined. He decided, he says, 'to acquire the power of exciting myself into the wildest emotions of passion, coercing my limbs to perfect stillness'. So he would rehearse on his own the most violent passages from the great tragic roles while keeping his body absolutely undisturbed, lying on the floor or standing against a wall with his arms bandaged or pinioned. He would make himself speak the most passionate outbursts of rage in a whisper. He would stand in front of the mirror and keep the facial muscles unmoved 'whilst intense passion would speak from the eye alone'.[47]

This was very much more than a ruse. Macready possessed himself of an idea and carried it through and passed it on, both to his audiences and to his fellow players. It was an idea of inner passions, both delicate and violent, constantly threatening to break the restraint they are under, whether in violent eruption or more tender expressiveness. We might wish to speak of 'repressed' feelings. But with a more elevated idea of the human will than ours, the Victorians would have preferred 'restraint' or 'control', as a means towards civilized conduct and the mainstay of civil society rather than as the surveillant agencies of a police state. Not that they objected to seeing the passion overwhelm the restraint, for good or for ill – temporarily, safely, on stage. It was essential to feel the full force of pain or passion, that there be a real struggle between the hidden powers of nature and the overt forces of culture, the figurative currents and torrents and volcanoes whose literal power in the external world so fascinated them, along with the possibility – and the limits – of controlling and channelling and predicting them. But for them there was only one desirable outcome to this struggle: conquest not surrender.

Helen Faucit had a merciless mentor in Macready and a gentler one in Charles Kemble, but the line the two men took was very similar. Years later she recalled the advice Kemble had given her:

> on no account to give prominence to the merely physical aspect
> of any painful emotion. Let the expression be genuine, earnest,

but not ugly. ... if pain or death had to be represented, or any
sudden or violent shock, let them be shown in their mental
rather than in their physical signs. ... Under every circumstance
the ideal, the noble, the beautiful, should be given side by side
with the real.[48]

Such an idea seems to have met the deepest needs of her audiences – an
idea of inner elevation, transcendence of the body. But the pain or the
passion that was to be resisted or risen above, this too had to be
rendered with conviction.

In terms of their acting style, both Macready and Irving projected a
strong sense of 'inwardness', both of barely restrained passion and of
restrained spirit or intellect. There were those who thought Irving *too*
intellectual. William Archer remarked, scathingly, that if Edmund Kean
had read Shakespeare 'by flashes of lightning', then Irving read him 'by
the student's midnight oil'.[49] Reviewing his Macbeth in 1875, Henry
James remarked on the meagreness of Irving's 'personal gifts' and
concluded that 'his strong points are intellectual'.[50] Seeking a type with
which to contrast Irving's originality, his house-manager Bram Stoker
summoned the image of the Irish-born Barry Sullivan, 'a purely
traditional actor of the old school ... great strength, great voice, great
physique of all sorts; a well-knit figure with fine limbs, broad shoulders
and the perfect back of a prize-fighter' (Stoker, I, p. 23). Sullivan seemed
a kind of Hercules, as well cut out for the battlefield and sportsground
as for the stage. He was particularly well equipped for the fighting at
the end of *Macbeth*, when he could dash out of the castle gates down to
the footlights and thunder: 'They have tied me to the stake; I cannot
fly.' This is unfair to poor Sullivan, whose young Hamlet had been
admired by the *Athenaeum* back in 1852 for his slender figure and
graceful attitudes even while the deficiency of his vocal organ was
deplored. In 1875 his fifty-year-old Hamlet seemed to a leading New
York critic 'more of the king than the prince, and more of the man of
action than the nerveless dreamer', but he was still described as
'leonine, courtly, graceful, and refined'. As a small boy Shaw had seen
him in Dublin, and looking back some thirty years in 1901 he

considered him 'in his day much further superior in pictorial, vocal, and rhetorical qualities to his next best rival than any actor or actress can easily be nowadays'. In his day: every dog is supposed to have it, and Sullivan's was passing as Irving's dawned. For most of his career Sullivan had never been the mindless Colossus of Stoker's convenient travesty, but his art stood still, as another erstwhile admirer observed. Sullivan got stuck with an image of manliness that came to seem hollow, 'a sort of majestic incarnation of abstract solemnity and magnificence', as Shaw almost ruefully put it.[51]

This sonorous and unreflective manliness was always better adapted to some Shakespearean roles than others. It made Sullivan very effective in a role that came to seem peculiarly difficult for 'Northern' actors in the second half of the nineteenth century: Othello.[52] After Irving's last night as Othello, Terry describes him rolling up the Moor's clothes and saying 'Never again!'[53] The (almost) undisputedly greatest Othello of the age was the Italian Tommaso Salvini, who was everything and had everything that Irving did not: instant physical presence, enormous confidence, the voice of an opera singer. There had been a similar contrast on the American stage between the extrovert Edwin Forrest and the introverted Edwin Booth. In its way it could be thought of as the contrast between a Real Man and a Gentleman, both desirable, but not necessarily at the same time. These intrinsic contrasts had an effect on the roles they played, and the roles people thought they were suited to. One could see a fault-line separating the warrior figures – Othello, Macbeth, Coriolanus, Henry V, even at a pinch King Lear – from the schemers – Hamlet, Iago, Richard III, Shylock.

Irving always found and stressed the intelligence, the intellectuality even, in his characters, distancing them from noise and roar and vulgarity. His Shylock was a gentleman, almost the only one in the play, so he thought. He described his own idea of Richard III:

> Shakespeare's Richard is a Plantaganet with the imperious
> pride of his race, a subtle intellect, a mocking, not a trumpeting
> duplicity, a superb daring which needs no roar and stamp, no
> cheap and easy exultation. Moreover, the true Richard has a

> youthful audacity very different from the ponderous airs of the
> 'heavy man'. In this character, as in Iago, the great element is an
> intrepid calculation.[54]

He was rewarded by Tennyson's admiring growl, 'Where did you get that Plantagenet look?' (Stoker, I, p. 49). He took an interesting line on Iago's youthfulness, 'instinct in all his manhood with the duplicity which belongs to his temperament and his generation'; he should have 'a slight dash of the bull-fighter'.[55] Apart from Richard and Iago, Irving's best Shakespearean roles were Hamlet, Shylock and Wolsey. He particularly excelled at pathos. There was a famous bit of business at the end of the masquing scene in the *Merchant* when his Shylock returned home and knocked on the door of the now deserted house from which Jessica has fled. Ellen Terry reflected: 'For absolute pathos, achieved by absolute simplicity of means, I never saw anything in the theatre to compare' (Hughes, p. 232).

Irving may have striven for Kean's physical intensity but in other ways he was closer to John Philip Kemble. Kean and Kemble, Gielgud and Olivier: there is a traditional kind of opposition here in the perception of theatrical styles which can be too simply described as 'mind' versus 'body', or 'intellect' versus 'instinct'. In the nineteenth-century theatre this opposition seemed to be embodied in the difference between Macready or Booth and Edwin Forrest, between Irving and Sullivan or Tommaso Salvini. There was a certain parallel to be drawn with the theatre of politics. Irving was on excellent terms with Gladstone, who was a regular and privileged visitor at the Lyceum from 1881 to 1895. He came and went through the private door, visited Irving in his dressing-room, and in later years watched the show from what came to be known as 'Gladstone's seat', down-stage right in the OP ('opposite prompt') corner (Stoker, II, p. 27). But for Edward Gordon Craig, Gladstone was the Salvini to Disraeli's Irving. Craig was not alone in detecting a resemblance between Irving and Disraeli.

> Gladstone and Salvini roll their words out, they stride, they
> glare very grandly and are spacious: you want to look and listen

to them. Disraeli and Irving do something quite different. They glide, they are terribly self-possessed, their eyes dart flame: you *have* to look and listen to them whether you want to or not. Rhetoric is for whoever likes to use it – not for Disraeli or Irving. 'He will say something fine' is what listeners would murmur to themselves in the presence of Gladstone or of Salvini – and fine it was. But the same listeners, when watching Disraeli or Irving, would not know where they were, who exactly this being in front of them could be, and would think to themselves: 'What will he say – what will he do now?'[56]

Craig was a partisan – he was Ellen Terry's son – ready to defend Irving to the hilt from all the detractors unimpressed by his awkward gait and eccentric utterance. Even Irving's friends the Pollocks called him 'Crab'. William Archer was no friend: 'He sprawls in his walk and drawls in his talk.' Reflecting on his murderous way with poetic diction, as it seemed to so many, the playwright Henry Arthur Jones compared Irving to Robert Browning – the poet at whom Swinburne sneered: 'You can't sing.'[57] Craig would have none of it. It was the jeerers and fleerers who were blind and deaf; it was not that Irving spoke badly – he was singing; it was not that he could not move smoothly – he was dancing. Perhaps 'self-possession' was not quite the word after all for a man possessed, but by what? Take him for all in all, said Craig, he had been a man with *le diable au corps.*[58]

This would be one way of marking the distance between the two great actor-managers who dominated the beginning and end of Victoria's reign. Both Macready and Irving believed in and practised a kind of 'restraint' with which their audiences readily identified. But there was between them a difference of style that helps to characterize the shift, over the period from the 1830s to the early 1900s, from an 'early' to a 'later' Victorian style and ethos. This extends well beyond the theatre itself, to dominant, emergent and receding ideas about manners, conduct, gentility and Englishness. What was it they were restraining or trying to rise above? For Macready it had been a form of 'passion' with its roots in Romanticism, and the theatre of Kemble and

Siddons and, above all, of Edmund Kean. For Irving it was something more grotesque, sinister, even occult, something with more of a twist to it that suggested the figures of mesmerism and diabolism, the glittering eye of the ancient mariner or the Flying Dutchman. It is not for nothing that Irving was associated with two great new mythic figures who emerge at the end of the century, Sherlock Holmes and Dracula.

A PERSONAL ANTHOLOGY

Macready and Irving enjoyed more control and influence than any other individuals over the Shakespeare experienced by Victorians in the theatre. But theatre can never be entirely controlled, and it thrives on comparison and rivalry. The Shakespeares the Victorians knew were many and various, and as a way of emphasizing this diversity, I shall close this survey by imagining that one might travel through time to a dozen shows in Victorian London. This would be my personal anthology.

1. Madame Vestris's *A Midsummer Night's Dream* at Covent Garden in 1840 (not least for her own performance as Oberon: see p. 56)
2. William Charles Macready's Macbeth at Drury Lane in 1843 ✗ (preferably sitting next to Dickens on 14 June)
3. Charlotte Cushman's Romeo at the Haymarket in 1845
4. Frederick Robson's parody Macbeth at the Olympic in 1853
5. Charles Kean's *King Henry VIII* at the Princess's in 1855 (not for Kean's Wolsey but for the production)
6. Samuel Phelps's Falstaff in *The Merry Wives of Windsor* at Sadler's Wells in 1856 (preferably the same night that Theodor Fontane was there)
7. Helen Faucit's Rosalind in *As You Like It* at Drury Lane in 1865 (though it would have been better to catch her earlier outside London in the late 1840s, in Glasgow, Edinburgh or Manchester, for instance)
8. Tommaso Salvini's Othello at Drury Lane in 1875
9. Henry Irving and Ellen Terry as Shylock and Portia at the Lyceum in 1879

10. Ada Rehan's Katherine in *The Taming of the Shrew* at Daly's in 1893

11. Herbert Beerbohm Tree's *King John* at Her Majesty's Theatre in 1899 (not so much for Tree himself in the title-role but, as with Charles Kean, for the production)

There are some glaring absences from this list. There is no *Richard III*, no *King Lear* and no *Hamlet*. For Lear, one might opt for Macready's instead of his Macbeth, or Salvini's instead of his Othello. But the most serious omission would be a Victorian Hamlet. Again, one might choose Irving for this (and Terry) instead of his Shylock (and Portia). It would be curious to see Charles Fechter's famously flaxen-haired Dane in the 1860s (which so excited Dickens), or Johnston Forbes-Robertson's at the Lyceum in 1897 (which even Shaw admired, not least because it was *not* Irving (*Shaw*, pp. 80–8)). Leaving these aside, the correct choice would probably be Edwin Booth at the Princess's in 1880. As with Helen Faucit, it would have been better to see Booth earlier, and *chez soi* in New York: let us say, to be precise, on 22 March 1865, for the one-hundredth consecutive performance of his Hamlet at the Winter Garden, just over three weeks before his brother would murder Abraham Lincoln. An incorrect but tempting alternative would be to add another notable cross-dressing performance to Vestris's Oberon and Cushman's Romeo: Sarah Bernhardt's Prince of Denmark, at the Adelphi in 1899.[59]

Chapter Two

THE VISUAL ARTS

PERFORMANCE, IMAGE, TEXT

We have seen in the previous chapter what a prominent role the visual arts played in 'realizing' Shakespeare inside the Victorian theatre; they were also busy with Shakespeare outside it. Shakespearean subjects were immensely popular with painters and sculptors, and illustrated editions with readers. Whether on canvas or the printed page, many of these images stay closely attached to what could be seen in the theatre, but others draw the viewer into a world of imagination or fantasy more associated with the experience of reading. In their dealings with Shakespeare the visual arts can be thought of as mediating between the realms of public and private, performance and text, theatre and reading.

To say that Shakespeare was a popular resource for visual artists in the nineteenth century would be an understatement. Literary subjects of all sorts enjoyed a large vogue, and Richard Altick has calculated that in this category of 'literary paintings' Shakespeare accounts for about one-fifth (some 2,300) of all those recorded between 1760 and 1900. Exhibition records show that the comedies and romances were generally more favoured by artists than the tragedies, while subjects taken from the history plays were notably less so.[1] In terms of sheer quantity the high point for all this production was the middle of the century, from about 1830 to 1860. By the 1840s favourite scenes which regularly featured at the annual exhibitions included *Othello relating his adventures to Desdemona and Brabantio, Juliet on the balcony,*

Miranda and Prospero and *Olivia raising her veil to Viola*. Other scenes less familiar to modern readers included *Slender and Anne Page* from the first scene of *The Merry Wives of Windsor* and *Queen Katherine's Vision* from *Henry VIII*. Altick notes that the Falstaff plays drop sharply away from view after the 1860s, and Ashton asserts that, measured by frequency of exhibition at the Royal Academy between 1769 and 1900, the single most popular Shakespearean character was, perhaps surprisingly, Ariel.[2] There is a memorable painting by Daniel Maclise of Priscilla Horton prancing merrily through the jungle: she is showing more flesh than she could have done for real in the spectacular production by Macready by which this vision of winged loveliness was inspired. Ariel was also popular with sculptors, especially in the 1850s, and with the artists of the illustrated editions.

At one extreme these paintings were closely tied to specific productions and actors, though the 'great age' of theatrical portraiture may have been over by mid-century. The inception of the *Illustrated London News* in 1842 heralded a swifter, cheaper means of circulating such images, but near the end of the century stars such as Irving and Terry and Beerbohm Tree were still being painted in character – and also of course, by now, photographed. The work of one of the finest theatrical artists of the time, Charles Buchel, is represented here, showing Irving as Shylock in 1902 (Figure 3). Ellen Terry was frequently painted, as Ophelia (1864) by her first husband, G.F. Watts, and then from the 1880s onwards, as Beatrice, Portia, Juliet, Lady Macbeth and Mrs Page.

Specific artists and paintings could exercise a direct influence on productions which sought to 'realize' them.[3] Irving's 1892 production of *King Lear* owed a direct debt for make-up, posture, characterization and props to Ford Madox Brown's painting, *Cordelia's Portion*. Four years later Edwin Abbey's *Richard Duke of Gloucester, and Lady Anne* had a similar effect on the staging of the wooing scene in his *Richard III*. For a more famous example we can look back to *The Play Scene in 'Hamlet'* by Daniel Maclise, close friend of Macready and Dickens, and depicter of many Shakespearean subjects including *Puck Disenchanting Bottom* (1832) and *The Banquet Scene in 'Macbeth'* (1840).[4] Thackeray called

FIGURE 3 Charles Buchel, 'Sir Henry Irving as "Shylock" at the Lyceum',
Tatler, no. 51, 18 June 1902.

his *Hamlet* 'one of the most startling, wonderful pictures that the English school has ever produced',[5] and Dickens enthused that it was

> a *tremendous* production. There are things in it, which in their powerful thought, exceed anything I have ever beheld in painting. You know the subject? – The play scene in Hamlet. The murderer is just pouring poison into the ear of the mimic King. But what a notion is that, which hoods this murderer's head, as who should say to the real King – '*You* know what face is under that!' What an extraordinary fellow he must be, who so manages the lights in this picture, that on the scene behind, is an enormous shadow of this groupe – as if the real murder were being done again by phantoms! And what a carrying-out of the prevailing idea, it is, to paint the very proscenium of the little stage with stories of Sin and Blood – the first temptation – Cain and Abel – and such like subjects – crying Murder! from the very walls.[6] (*DPL*, III, p. 299)

At least partly based on the design for this scene in Macready's Covent Garden production, Maclise's *Hamlet* exercised considerable influence on subsequent theatrical performance and on illustrated editions. The original painting in Tate Britain seems to have weathered badly by comparison with the sparkling *Scene from Twelfth Night* (1840), also on show there (2003), from which the modern viewer gets a more vivid sense of Maclise's gifts.[7] This shows a delightfully unctuous Malvolio in yellow cross-gartered tights and pink shorts smiling and kissing his hand to a shrinking Olivia, as Maria suppresses her giggles and a small dog looks on impassively. The whole scene is beautifully framed by a massive yew hedge, a perfect theatrical set-up.

The visual imaging of scenes and characters from Shakespeare has a long history prior to this, but it had received a massive fillip at the end of the previous century from the Shakespeare Gallery established in 1789 by John Boydell, an alderman and at one point Mayor of London. The aim of this ambitious venture was to found a British school of historical painting that would use Shakespeare as its main source, and make money through engravings to be sold separately or used in illustrated editions. Though it never realized Boydell's dreams, the enterprise did generate a large number of influential images that held continuing currency throughout the nineteenth century and beyond as advancing techniques lowered the cost of reproduction. Boydell's name will recur. These new techniques also enabled the proliferation of inexpensive pictorial editions which rose in popularity to a high point in the middle decades of the century.[8]

One of the most important was Charles Knight's *Pictorial Edition* (1838–42), with illustrations by William Harvey. (It was the one bought by the young Thomas Hardy.) Here we see how far a visual artist could depart, in one direction, from what might be seen in the theatre. Harvey spends much of his time on views of localities and buildings, coins and coats of arms and, above all, costumes, such that the text is constantly annotated by images drawn from a 'real world' outside it. There are the scenes of Shakespeare's youth, 'May-day at Shottery' and 'Great Hillborough, Barley-break'; we are shown 'the bed of Ware in England' that Sir Toby Belch is thinking of (*TN*, 3.2.46–7), and what a 'Chantry' looks like (*TN*, 4.3.24). If readers of *Hamlet* are stumped to imagine what a 'choppine' looks like, or a 'Danish ship', or a 'pelican', Harvey helps them out. When Rosalind says to Silvius 'I see, love hath made thee a tame snake' (*AYL*, 4.3.70), the reader is offered a distracting vignette of Indian serpent charmers. The whole idiom creates the sense of massive research, such as nowadays one might associate with an expensive theatre programme or television. It imagines readers who cannot imagine much for themselves and certainly do not know enough. It is, in a thoroughly Victorian sense, 'improving'. It creates the illusion that there *is* a world to be known, if only one could know enough, behind or beyond the words on the page.

More distinguished for the quality of its artwork, and much less relentlessly educative, was Howard Staunton's illustrated edition, first issued in monthly parts from November 1857 to May 1860, then gathered in three volumes. Readers got a full-page etching at the head of each play, strong half-page images at the start and end of each act, and a liberal supply dropped in with sufficient frequency that they rarely had to trudge across more than one or two spreads of unalleviated text. The artist was the staggeringly prolific John (later Sir John) Gilbert; he is estimated to have contributed as many as 30,000 pictures over forty years or so to the *Illustrated London News*.[9] Other less resourceful but still impressive editions include the Cassell's Edition by Charles and Mary Cowden Clarke, illustrated by H.C. Selous (1864–8), and the Irving edition (1887–90), with etchings mainly by Gordon Browne. This latter adopts a distinctly 'aesthetic' style characteristic of its time, a more delicate line with lighter cross-hatching, and an alternation of framed and unframed images that lifts them out of the text and sinks them back in (and the reader with them). Further reflection on what it means to 'illustrate' is provoked by the inclusion of coloured plates of well-known paintings, one per volume, including Hunt's *Valentine Rescuing Silvia* and Millais's *Ophelia*, which will be discussed in due course (pp. 59–61, 67–9), and all the way back from Boydell, James Northcote's celebrated *Hubert and Prince Arthur* (*KJ*, 4.1). The principle of illustration survived at least until the emergence and circulation of film and television (and now video) versions. Several of the paintings in Irving were still being reproduced in Ernest Baker's 1949 one-volume edition of the complete works (Waverley Book Co.), for example, along with other old Victorian chestnuts such as Maclise's *Play Scene in Hamlet* and Ford Madox Brown's *Cordelia and King Lear*.

If one of the impulses behind the imagining of Shakespeare in visual form is to release something or somebody from the constraints both of text and performance, another is to solder them more firmly together. Maclise's *Play Scene* was associated in its origins with a production by Macready. Near the end of his life Brown's images from *King Lear* found a home on stage in Irving's 1892 production. Lear and Cordelia loomed large in Brown's imagination, as they did for many Victorian artists and readers.[10] In 1848 he began the painting mentioned above, which shows Cordelia bent in supplication over her sleeping father, moments before their reconciliation, and in 1865 he began his second major *Lear* painting, again from the play's opening scene, entitled *Cordelia's Portion* (now in the Fitzwilliam Museum, Cambridge). Shortly before the artist's death, Irving asked him to provide the designs for his production, and the actor clearly modelled his sense of the role on the king of *Cordelia's Portion*, a white-bearded patriarch with flashing eyes.

RITES OF PASSAGE

Visual artists are drawn to moments of narrative crisis in text and performance, and they can be particularly effective in depicting certain rites of passage, as for example in the relation between parents and children. Such images stay close to the experience of theatre, its gestures, postures, costume and props.

In imagining such rites of passage Victorian artists were conspicuously alive to the significance of hair and hairiness. Must Lear have a beard? (Macready is alleged to have been the first actor to beard up for the part.) The Victorians would have found it hard to imagine a Shakespearean father without any facial hair until near the end of the century. Outside the theatre the actor himself would usually have had to be beardless, and this contributed to his abnormality, as Irving himself observed in 1895.[11] For Victorian artists hair was a crucial resource, as it has always been for actors themselves, from the First Quarto's lyrical stage direction for the mad Ophelia's entrance (*Ham*, 4.5) onwards: 'playing on a Lute, and her haire downe singing'. For a Victorian Touchstone or Malvolio funny hair was a must, and Bottom of course does not have much choice.

In some of the illustrators' most memorable images the conflict between generations is represented by bearded male and smooth-faced youth, of either sex. This can be the matter of fun and fantasy, as it is in *A Midsummer Night's Dream* and *The Tempest*, where the hairiness of Bottom and Caliban is set off against the blemishless skin of androgynous fairies and spirits. David Scott's disturbing *Ariel and Caliban* (1837) anticipates many later contrasts between ethereal spirit and brute body – 'dream and nightmare', as Nicola Bown puts it.[12] In the years after Darwin's *Origin of Species* (1859), the opposition of smoothness and hairiness took on increasingly 'evolutionary' implications, such as Stevenson would famously draw on in *The Strange Case of Dr Jekyll and Mr Hyde* (1886). But where fathers are concerned –

Cordelia's, Jessica's, Miranda's, Desdemona's, Imogen's – there is also a continuing 'theological' suggestion that their beards express the force of God the Father (or in Jessica's case, the opposite). Consider Gilbert's fine frontispiece to *Romeo and Juliet* (Figure 4). This is a weightier and more dignified Capulet than we would normally expect nowadays, one perhaps with more right on his side than the petulant girl on her knees at his feet, asking to be excused from marrying Paris on Thursday. She seems more of a Goneril or Regan than a Cordelia, more like Dickens's angry Tattycoram than docile Little Dorrit. And what is she doing with her own hair, if not expressing an aggressive sexuality she shares with the stony naked bust above her?

There is a contrasting story about parents and children which can be read in concentrated form in Selous's frontispiece to *1 Henry IV* (Figure 5). This tells the other story of the child who returns, like Cordelia and Perdita, to redeem the father. But in this case the youth is a boy, or to be precise, he is a young man whose rite of passage into manhood we see being enacted before us. In this complicated design, Henry IV lies helpless beneath 'the insulting hand' and poised sword of the Douglas, his own sword shamefully broken and his legs entangled with his fallen horse's. Prince Hal steps forward to save his father and redeem his 'lost opinion' (*1H4*, 5.4.47). It is a classically heroic pose, like that of Ajax saving the Greeks from Hector's terminal assault. Not that there is much hide or hair to be seen when men are clad cap-a-pé in complete steel. An armoured knee is a good way of asserting your manhood (as Holman Hunt's Valentine also demonstrates (see Figure 9, p. 60) and only a scurrilous eye would pause to reflect on the symbolic position of the King's left arm.

The relations between youth and age cannot always be so frankly figured, nor the passage from innocence to experience. Shakespeare's plays are full of great crises in which girls and boys defy or submit to their fathers (and less often, mothers). They must save them or slay them to claim their own adult identity, and their own certain gender. The comedies allow more licence to the uncertainties of gender than the tragedies and histories, and *A Midsummer Night's Dream* and *The Tempest* in particular permit an exploration of erotic fantasy of which

Act III. Sc. 5.

FIGURE 4 John Gilbert, frontispiece to *Romeo and Juliet*, in *The Plays of Shakespeare*, ed. Howard Staunton (vol. I, 1858).

FIGURE 5 H.C. Selous, frontispiece to *1 Henry IV*, in *The Plays of Shakespeare*, ed. Charles and Mary Cowden Clarke (Cassell's Illustrated Shakespeare, vol. II, 1864–8).

Victorian artists took eager advantage. But there is also a troubled strain of interest in the young children of the history plays, the young princes of *Richard III* and Prince Arthur in *King John*. These and all children's roles were played by girls or young women on the Victorian stage: Ellen Terry was Charles Kean's Arthur in 1858, having made her debut as Mamillius in his *Winter's Tale* two years before.[13]

Victorian nerves were particularly touched by the scene between young Arthur and his guardian Hubert (*KJ*, 4.1), who has been charged with putting out the lad's eyes. Arthur yearns for a father to love and be loved by: 'I warrant I love you more than you do me', he says (4.1.29), sensing Hubert's extreme discomfort at the betrayal of trust, let alone the physical violence, that he is required to perpetrate. When Arthur discovers the truth he pleads for mercy, and Hubert eventually relents, though the struggle is painfully protracted. It was a scene that had appealed to painters at the end of the previous century such as James Northcote. Indeed, faced with such a familiar subject by W.F. Yeames in 1882 (Figure 6), the *Spectator* was inclined to yawn. The modern viewer might be less inclined to yawn at Yeames, best remembered now for the historical costume painting *And When Did You Last See Your Father?* (1878). Where Northcote had given his Hubert an attitude of active agony, Yeames sinks his potential child-abuser in a melancholy that his vaguely monastic or criminal cowl, the altar-like table behind him, and the dark red bench beneath him do nothing to relieve. The child knows nothing. He could be the agent of redemption, and this would be true to the Shakespearean source in which the boy does indeed 'save' Hubert. But it is hard not to feel the stirring of more trouble here than Shakespeare provides, the kind of sexual trouble on which Henry James would draw for his governess's fevered tale in *The Turn of the Screw* (1898).

FEMININITY, FAIRIES, FANTASY

In all such visual translations of a written text there is both collaboration and rivalry. The relationship takes on an interesting new form with the development of images that turn away from the

FIGURE 6 W.F. Yeames, *Prince Arthur and Hubert* (1882).

conditions of performance towards a realm of their own. There was a particular attraction in the possibilities for fantasy afforded by the representation of women and fairies.

The Shakespeare Gallery, first issued by Charles Heath in 1836–7, represented a new kind of challenge to Boydell. The Boydell images were always of scenes from the plays. Heath's were of characters – and specifically of female characters – whose relation to the scene and play from which they are drawn is interestingly ambivalent.[14] The great majority are young and pretty, and there is not a lot of difference between them. Enormous eyes, rosebud lips, large forehead and Roman nose: this is the basic model, equally adaptable to the sportive-to-vixenish such as Beatrice, Maria and Kate, and to the victims and weaker vessels such as Lavinia, Ophelia and Virgilia. They are mainly distinguished by costume and attitude, particularly the aspect of head and eyes – righteously uplifted for Cordelia, coquettishly angled for Cressida and Cleopatra, scowlingly averted for Kate. On the face of it this is just a little lexicon of female body language. But each engraving is accompanied by an act and scene reference and preceded by an appropriate passage of text. For all their apparent independence these young women are still attached to the scene from which they derive and from which they have only been partly liberated. Both the first and last women in the volume are in fact listening to someone else's words: Miranda is preceded by Prospero's words to her (*Tem*, 1.2), and Desdemona by Othello's great wooing speech to the senate (*Oth*, 1.3). Once the viewer realizes that these women are not just beautiful icons who have floated out of dense particular scenes into white space, they are instantly re-animated. The piously hand-clasping Isabella recovers the appeal she risks losing when we realize that she is involved in a fraught scene with Angelo (*MM*, 2.2). Mariana is not alone but with the Duke (*MM*, 4.1). Cordelia is not frozen into righteous abstraction but praying to the kind gods (*KL*, 4.7). It is important to recognize here in one of its starker forms a kind of drama with which nineteenth-century readers and artists were obsessed. We shall return to it in the next chapter. It is a drama in which 'character' tries to free itself of circumstance, context, scene and plot, to realize itself as pure selfhood and essence. And fails, as it must, this side of paradise.

FIGURE 7 Charles Baxter, *Olivia* (1862).

These widely diffused images were known as 'Keepsake Beauties'. They often served as secularized icons for Protestant homes in the Victorian cult of woman-worship (Altick, pp. 86–7). Yet their iconic force can be complex; so can the cult that they serve. One of the most popular images was that of Olivia unveiling herself to Viola in *Twelfth Night* (1.5). Charles Baxter's *Olivia* (1862) is a fair example (Figure 7).[15]

This Olivia unveils herself not to Viola but directly to the viewer. Unveiling is the sign with which the bride presents and offers herself to her husband. Yet brides do not have a monopoly on this gesture, and it is just as well that we are told the identity of Baxter's woman, otherwise we might have taken her, like Shakespeare's most notoriously deluded husband, for a whore of Venice. The claim to a Shakespearean provenance makes her respectable – or pretends to. A viewer who took it seriously would have to think of himself or herself as Viola, and this too might be slightly disturbing – and exciting. Whichever way one looks at her this 'Olivia' is unnerving, half her face still buried in darkness. Put Olivia back in the scene with a Viola to whom she can direct her offer and the threat-and-promise becomes distanced, comical. Yet what may be the last painting of the prolific Charles Robert Leslie shows a woman in mourning who seems to suggest, as she raises her black veil, 'a figure of wisdom revealing secrets from the other side of the grave'.[16] Eros and Thanatos, the Bride and the Whore: it is not untrue to the darker undercurrents of Shakespearean comedy to suggest such confusion, however temporarily.

These images minister to fantasies in which an element of the erotic is rarely if ever entirely absent, whatever the viewer's inclinations. The opportunity for another kind of erotic interest is provided by the astonishing fairy paintings for which A Midsummer Night's Dream and The Tempest were a frequent inspiration. The genre enjoyed a distinctive heyday in the late 1830s and 1840s with such striking Shakespearean examples as Richard Dadd's Come Unto These Yellow Sands (1842), and Millais's Ferdinand Lured by Ariel (1849). Poor deranged Dadd was confined to Bethlem Hospital after killing his father, but with encouragement from an enlightened doctor he went on to complete several extraordinary paintings before being transferred to the newly-opened Broadmoor in 1864. These include Contradiction: Oberon and Titania and the stylistically related The Fairy Feller's Master-Stroke. The latter is a thronged enigmatic fantasia located, as it were, on the far side of Shakespeare's wood, an uncharted brink where creatures once human are doomed and light is the colour of lead.[17]

'But we are spirits of another sort', says Shakespeare's Oberon (*MND*, 3.2.388), and most artists promoted a blither vision of the fairy world. They were encouraged by influential productions of the *Dream* and *The Tempest*, and they could exert reciprocal influence on theatrical production, which had in any case always been inclined to maximize the opportunities the two plays afford for singing and dancing. In 1838 Macready gave *The Tempest* an unprecedentedly lavish production, which opened with an astoundingly realistic storm. In 1857 Charles Kean followed with a 'sumptuous revival' which suggested the 'dangerous affinity with the shifting and dissolving scenes of pantomime'.[18] His no less exotic *Dream* would have done nothing to disown this affinity, boasting more fairies in heaven and earth than philosophy could dream of. The watercolours which commemorate the scenic designs for this and other productions of the 1850s are ravishingly pretty. (They are preserved in the Charles Kean Collection at the Victoria and Albert Museum.) The other influential precedent was the landmark production of the *Dream* in 1840 at Covent Garden with Eliza Vestris as the Fairy King.[19]

In *Martin Chuzzlewit* an aristocratic patron of the theatre complains that Shakespeare is an infernal humbug. '"There's a lot of feet in Shakspeare's verse, but there an't any legs worth mentioning in Shakspeare's plays, are there, Pip? Juliet, Desdemona, Lady Macbeth, and all the rest of 'em, whatever their names are, might as well have no legs at all, for anything the audience know about it, Pip'" (ch. 28). What a lot the poor Viscount was missing: Rosalind, Viola, Julia, Portia, Imogen – and Oberon. Madame Vestris had excellent legs and she took every opportunity of showing them off (unlike poor Helen Faucit who argued unavailingly with Macready about the costume for Imogen/ Fidele). Like the Ariel so appealingly played by Priscilla Horton in Macready's production, the role of Oberon was marked off as officially ungendered or at least de-phallicized. This applied to the whole fairy domain – and all children: the young Ellen Terry was Charles Kean's Puck and her elder sister Kate his Ariel. Ethereal and unearthly, they conformed to an idea of women and children as beyond or outside gender, like angels. It was men who had gender (preferably men with beards, to be sure). For a woman to play Oberon was somehow to inoculate the role against (male) sexuality. Something similar happened when Charlotte Cushman played Romeo and Sarah Bernhardt played Hamlet, but theirs were more exceptional cases, whereas the female Oberon was entirely conventional. Shakespeare seems to sponsor this gender confusion with all the boy/girl cross-dressers from Julia to Imogen, the respectable married woman. Basking in this legitimized 'innocence', the actress could gaily flaunt the normally tabooed – those shapely legs. Spectators could close one eye to look with the other and then, as it were, deny that they had done so.

There was a great deal of naked flesh to look at, far more on canvas or page than in the theatre, where even a Vestris would hesitate to bare as much as the Oberons (and Titanias and Ariels) of the illustrated editions. To see how far Victorian visual artists could go in the deployment of nudity, we can look to the two remarkable paintings inspired by the *Dream* by Joseph (later Sir Joseph) Noel Paton: *The Reconciliation of Oberon and Titania*, exhibited at the Royal Scottish Academy in 1847, and *The Quarrel of Oberon and Titania*, shown there two years later (Figure 8).[20] Together they constitute the nearest thing to an orgy to be found in Victorian art. Lewis Carroll saw the *Quarrel* in Edinburgh and counted one hundred and sixty-five fairies. This is an impressive total, yet the number of different things they are up to seems more to the point: the aerial acrobatics, the flight-and-pursuit, the hide-and-seek, the owl-riding, the intimate caresses. Not everyone is being gratified, it is true, least of all the pretty Oberon with the golden curls, pink flying cloak and intriguing diaphanous tunic; he is being defied by the flawless white queen with her mischievous Indian Cupid. There is the odd disappointed satyr, and a wicked little red-capped gnome with a gang of deformities up to no good. This realm has not been entirely purged of conventional male sexuality even if Oberon is not contributing much towards it, for all his two long spears. The Puck set to dive on a teasing nymphet is a real enough wild boy, and there are youths with less feminized bodies and postures than Oberon. More disturbing is the presiding stone divinity at the right, the bearded and lecherous Pan. He looms in the background to the *Reconciliation* also.[21]

FIGURE 8 Joseph Noel Paton, *The Quarrel of Oberon and Titania* (1849).

These paintings present a remarkably rich sense of the erotic possibilities inherent in Shakespeare's play. They do not exclude the darker, more violent elements, but they give pride of place to pleasure, excitement, mirth and absurdity. Thomas Sinclair thought the *Dream*'s fairies personified flowers, 'for no objects play, and rightfully, so large and beautiful and emblematic a part in the history of high free racing chasing human love as they'.[22] There are fungi, foliage, tree trunks and water in Paton's paintings as well as flowers, but 'high free racing chasing' is a fair way to characterize the bacchanalian energy that courses through them. As for the creatures themselves, drawn from so many different mythologies, Greek and Roman and Teutonic, Henry Maine was moved by the *Reconciliation* to see in them 'the veritable "good people" (to use the timid old euphemism) ... hanging loosely on the confines of existence, annually recruited from mankind, and annually tythed by Satan'.[23] He had noticed the goat-god.

SEX, REALISM AND THE PRE-RAPHAELITES

Paton was a lifelong friend of John Everett Millais and supporter of the Pre-Raphaelite Brotherhood (founded in 1848), of which Millais was a leading member. The Pre-Raphaelites were particularly interested in Shakespeare and sex. They were also interested in 'realism', and Millais's *Ferdinand Lured by Ariel* (1849) is a solitary, purposively grotesque excursion into the 'fairy' genre. Between them the Pre-Raphaelites produced more than sixty illustrations from Shakespeare.[24] In general they sought situations of emotional and psychological complexity in both comedies and tragedies, though mainly the latter. At the outset their paintings created scandal, attracting accusations of ugliness and vulgarity. In 1850 *The Times* called Millais's *Christ in the House of His Parents* 'revolting', and Dickens was no less rude about the kneeling Mary. A few years on Hunt's Claudio was disparaged as a vulgar lout and Isabella as a homely creature (Altick, p. 227).

We get a sense of how well Victorian artists expected their viewers to know their Shakespeare from the painting exhibited by William Holman Hunt at the Royal Academy in 1851 (Figure 9). The catalogue confused things by calling it *Valentine receiving Sylvia from Proteus*, a mistake repeated by the *Athenaeum*.[25] *The Times* called it *Valentine receiving Proteus*. Who is receiving whom? And who is the fourth figure not receiving anything from anyone, but anxiously fingering a ring behind her (is it her?) back? Who are those people in the distance? Suppose that 'receiving' were corrected to 'rescuing'. This would mean that the powerful man with the dark moustache and shining armour is saving, or has saved, the kneeling floral woman from the younger blond man who has lost his hat and is nervously feeling his neck. But it still looks as though the presiding man could be going to join their hands together, so that this would indeed be an act of giving and receiving we are about to witness – along with the bewildered bystander.

The artist helped his audience by inscribing on the spandrels of the frame some lines from the climactic scene of *The Two Gentlemen of Verona*. Even here there is some confusion. Valentine is given the line: 'Who should be trusted now, when one's right hand / I've perjured to

FIGURE 9 William Holman Hunt, *Valentine Rescuing Sylvia from Proteus* (1851).

the bosom?' But the 'I've' is a mistake for 'Is'. The perjury should belong to the kneeling man he is addressing, Proteus. In the play Valentine rushes on in the nick of time to prevent his best friend from raping his own girl Silvia. He is watched in horror and then relief by Julia, Proteus's abandoned sweetheart, now disguised as a boy. Valentine bitterly accuses Proteus, who begs forgiveness and receives it along with – and this is the shocking thing – Silvia, just to prove that the men are real friends. Julia promptly passes out, comes round, reveals her identity, and Proteus decides to have his first girl after all. Silvia's father – who is leading the party approaching in the background – arrives to withdraw the paternal curse and bless the two unions. Silvia is speechless. George Eliot was disgusted by the scene.[26]

On stage all this can happen at the speed of dream or nightmare. But the nineteenth century saw few performances of this play and it inspired comparatively few paintings.[27] The denouement scene had been painted before, but no one had delved as deeply into it as Hunt was moved to. He froze the lovers at the moment of maximum ambivalence, when the story could still go more than one way, along with their passions and loyalties. There is no knowing for sure who will end up with whom, whether received or rescued. Hunt had first thought of showing Valentine repelling Proteus, but in the finished painting he moved the scene on a frame to the moment of forgiveness just before Valentine tries to make a gift of Silvia, or so we suppose from the hint of complacency in her expression. She will get a terrible shock when he removes his arm from behind her head to put her right hand in Proteus's. Nor will the tree supporting the unsteady Julia save her from collapsing in a heap among the withered leaves. The *Examiner* was unimpressed by the women, calling Silvia 'a hard-featured faded specimen of stale virginity' and accusing Julia of 'lounging in the attitude of a sulking lubberly schoolboy' (quoted in Altick, p. 263). (This last is a memory of Slender's disappointment at the end of *Merry Wives*, in another forest, when the Anne Page he had thought to marry turns out to be 'a great lubberly boy' (5.5.182).) But in a letter to *The Times* Ruskin praised 'the contending of doubt and distress with awakening hope in the half-shadowed, half-sunlit countenance of Julia' (Ruskin, XII, p. 325). The contention is still unresolved, like her gender. So too is the genre of the story to which she seems to hold the key.

The Pre-Raphaelites were drawn to the moodiest aspects of Shakespearean comedy, notably in *As You Like It* and *Twelfth Night*. But Hunt's other finest Shakespearean painting (Figure 10) is drawn from a comedy neglected by the Victorian theatre, though not outside it by writers and readers. If ever there were a Shakespeare play to bring a blush to the cheek of the young person, *Measure for Measure* was it. Given her provenance in seedy Vienna, Isabella was as popular a heroine as could be expected – Shakespeare's only saint, said Ruskin – and her great lines about 'man proud man' were frequently quoted out of context. But as with the scene from *The Two Gentlemen* Hunt saw an opportunity here for the staging of sexual turmoil. Isabella looks appealingly but uncertainly at her brother and presses two strong healing hands to his heart.[28] Claudio turns his shadowed head away, in

FIGURE 10 William Holman Hunt, *Claudio and Isabella* (1850).

distraction rather than rejection, a simmering young man with difficult hair; his left hand grips her wrist, while his right fingers the heavy iron shackle chaining his leg to the wall. Like Julia, Isabella's expression is suspended between hope and doubt; like Julia, Claudio gazes on vacancy and displaces his unresolved passion onto a ring behind him, his reddish tunic and purple leggings repeating some of her colours.

But everything is darker and more introverted. Where Julia and her ring look ahead to the future, Claudio and his shackle point back to the past, to the sexual passion for which forgiveness cannot be so lightly sought and granted. The tree trunks of the scene in *The Two Gentlemen* have been replaced by iron bars; beyond them there is blue sky, apple blossom and a church spire, a world from which Claudio may be forever shut out. Yet as with the earlier scene the moment is charged with possibilities. The frame carries Claudio's words 'Death is a fearful thing' and Isabella's response 'And shamed life a hateful'; the catalogue for the 1853 Royal Academy exhibition carried an extract from Claudio's great speech 'Ay, but to die, and go we know not where' (*MM*, 3.1.117–30). We know that in performance the scene will shortly explode into recrimination, shame and mistrust. Yet in the painting there is hope, embodied in Isabella's forceful hands and steady posture no less than in her habit of faith. There is at least ambivalence in the lute with red ribbons hanging on the wall. This may point back to the sensual pleasures Claudio has enjoyed, but it may also look ahead to the song associated with Mariana at the turning-point of the play.[29] Above all there is an even-handedness to the painting's sympathy for what this moment means to both brother and sister, an impartiality that rebukes the tendency of many readings to disparage her religious conviction in favour of his creaturely passion and weakness. The power with which the ambivalence is realized, the doubt and distress no less than the hope, enable the modern viewer to enter its drama more easily than some of the other paintings through which Hunt expressed his moral and religious beliefs, such as *The Awakening Conscience* (1854).

Something of the sexual and emotional tension in Hamlet's dealings with the women in his life can be found in Dante Gabriel Rossetti's pen and ink drawing of Hamlet and Ophelia (Figure 11), now in the British

FIGURE 11 Dante Gabriel Rossetti, *Ophelia Returning the Gift to Hamlet* (1858?).

Museum. Not much privacy is afforded the youngsters by the cramped little oratory to which Ophelia has retired with the devotional book her father has given her. Polonius and the King would not have much difficulty overhearing young Hamlet's abusive rant, when she gives him back his remembrances (*Ham*, 3.1.93). Her averted head and limp left hand express a desolate acquiescence, while he tears a rose tree to shreds and partly mimes a crucifixion. His legs have oddly disappeared

– he is presumably kneeling on the seat – while an outsize sword extending to the floor, more like a walking stick, takes their place. His youthful awkwardness makes him mistakable for Romeo, but the shaming frustration brings the young couple closer to the world of *Measure for Measure*. Little hope of escape is offered by the intricate stairs and passages outside and above the oratory. This little enclave is thick with uncomforting religious symbols, most notably the Old Testament carvings on Hamlet's right. On the wall is paradise lost, guarded by angels with flaming swords; the serpent coiled round the Tree of the Knowledge of Good and Evil ends in a crowned head, apparently confirming the Ghost's story that 'sleeping in my orchard, / A serpent stung me' (1.5.35–6). Beneath there is an enigmatic misericord depicting a recumbent or falling male figure with arm extended to touch a little structure topped by the sun and guarded again by two winged figures. The name 'Uzzaus' identifies him as the man who touched the Ark of the Covenant and died: another great instance of a primary taboo, and its violation. One might take these to refer to the crime (or crimes) of Hamlet's uncle (and mother), which have desecrated the world and thwarted the future that should have been embodied in the youngsters. But Rossetti himself described them as 'symbols of rash introspection',[30] as if they were warnings to young Hamlet, and it was his own self-absorption that was to blame for the loss of the future he might have had with Ophelia. This minatory or even punitive perspective on Hamlet is reinforced by lines from the Apocryphal *Ecclesiasticus* (ch. 6). Along with quotations from the play, these frame the drawing with: 'thou shalt eat up thy leaves, and lose thy fruit, and leave thyself as a dry tree' (v. 3), and 'extol not thyself in the counsel of thine own heart, that thy soul be not torn in pieces' (v. 2). Not for the first time in a Victorian work of art, this leaves one feeling sorry for the human figures assaulted by a moralizing authority with which the artist seems to conspire. Yet the artist has written himself into the two young victims as well as the forces seeking to destroy or save them.[31]

Ford Madox Brown was another notable artist who produced several Shakespearean paintings, especially of Lear and Cordelia, as noted

FIGURE 12   Ford Madox Brown, *Romeo and Juliet* (1870).

earlier (pp. 46–7). When Henry James reported on the posthumous exhibition of 1897, it was however not the *Lear* paintings that caught his eye and prompted his pen so much as the *Romeo and Juliet* (Figure 12). Juliet and her balcony had been a favourite with painters throughout

the century. Put a pretty girl on a balcony and you could call her 'Juliet'
as surely as a woman in white with flowers near a stream was
'Ophelia'. There was more drama to be had by adding a Romeo,
whether wooing her from below (2.2) or parting at dawn (3.5),
especially the latter when the young man could look athletic on a rope-
ladder. It was exactly the awkwardness that James admired in Brown's
curious but unforgettable version. James wrote:

> In the 'Romeo and Juliet', painted with a childlike *gaucherie*,
> the motion as of a rope-dancer balancing, the outstretched, level,
> stiff-fingered hand of the young man who, calling time, tearing
> himself away in the dovelike summer dawn, buries his face in his
> mistress's neck and throws his ill-shaped leg over her balcony –
> this little gesture of reason and passion is the very making of the
> picture.[32]

As one first reads this it is unclear for a moment whether 'the motion as
of a rope-dancer balancing' refers to the lover's pose in the painting or
continues the thought about the artist's 'childlike *gaucherie*'. It is the
former, we realize, yet the reason and passion James admires here
belong no less to the artist than to the lover. Juliet's pose is almost as
memorable as that of the perilous acrobat she is trying to restrain. Her
arms are clasped round him to save him from the world of risk beyond
the balcony. It is a vain effort, as her monumental head and shoulders
seem to know, in anticipation of their next meeting in the tomb. James
called it 'intensely queer and intensely charming', but it is more gravid
than this, a good example of the way artists can arrest a moment of
crisis from the onward movement of text and performance.

A WORLD ELSEWHERE

Visual artists were often tempted by scenes that are not or cannot be
represented on stage, such as Paton's *Oberon and the Mermaid* (see
n. 20). The most celebrated example from the Victorian era is John
Everett Millais's painting of Ophelia (1852, Figure 13). It remains the
most famous of many nineteenth-century attempts to 'realize' the great

FIGURE 13 John Everett Millais, *Ophelia* (1852).

speech given to Gertrude in performance: 'There is a willow grows
askaunt the brook' (*Ham*, 4.7.166–83). This is the one moment when
the Queen holds centre-stage, and in so far as she expresses a sense of
solidarity with the dead girl, it creates a temporary community of
shared female grief equivalent to the willow song scene in *Othello*
(4.3).[33] The conventional thing was to show a pathetic waif on the way
to the water or poised on a willow bough, self-adorned with her
fantastic garlands. Millais's master-stroke was to suspend her in the
stream, at once sinking and floating, 'like a creature native and indued /
Unto that element' (*Ham*, 4.7.179–80). The two halves of her body
seem to be separating, as her lower, limbless being takes on a death of
its own, but the horizontal pose reduces what might otherwise have
been the elevating implications of this fission. The painting echoes the
suspended quality of Gertrude's speech. The curious rivalries of light,
colour and texture begin to find visual equivalents for its verbal
complexity – the obscure and the lucid, the evanescent and the spiny-
sharp. The words the artist is translating have already gone some way
towards turning the dead girl into an aesthetic object. These seek to

mourn her, to acknowledge and to mask Gertrude's own sense of complicity in the girl's death, to soothe the potential rage of her brother Laertes and distract his desire for revenge. But the painting's indebtedness to its dramatic source is no more powerful than the independence it asserts. This is a liberation, though it is inevitably incomplete. Ophelia has been rescued from Elsinore, from Shakespeare, from words. She floats forever in an English country stream, in paint, in Tate Britain, in infinite reproductions, including this one.

My second example is less well known. It is by James Clarke Hook, an artist who exhibited at the Royal Academy first in 1839, and then continuously from 1844 to 1902.[34] Part of the beauty of his painting of *Othello's Description of Desdemona* (c.1852, Figure 14) is that it draws on our associations of Desdemona with music. Yet it is not the willow song scene that is being depicted here. Instead this painting illustrates Othello's memories of Desdemona, whom he describes as 'an admirable musician. O, she will sing the savageness out of a bear! of so high and plenteous wit and invention!' (*Oth*, 4.1.185–7). These exclamations come from the terrible scene in which Iago steels Othello to strangle Desdemona in bed, just before Othello hits her in public and storms off muttering 'Goats and monkeys!' (4.1.263). The artist has seized on this moment of respite, which is all the more painful for our knowledge of what is so promptly to come. The painting shares with us the tormented man's memory, while also suggesting or predicting the gulf between the two figures. It is suffused with the melancholy recognition that however admirable the woman's music, it will not sing the savageness out of this bear. William Pressly notes the Biblical model for music's power to soothe the savage breast in David's singing to Saul. But he concludes: 'As with this Old Testament subject, the spellbinding music can only postpone, rather than cure, the eruption of crazed violence.'[35]

FROM THE CRADLE TO THE GRAVE

These two paintings depict scenes in a world elsewhere that seems closer to what goes on in a reader's imagination than in performance

FIGURE 14 James Clarke Hook, *Othello's Description of Desdemona* (c.1852).

on stage. The visual art of the cinema screen extends such possibilities, as Kenneth Branagh's 1996 film of *Hamlet* demonstrates, with its relentless translation into the visual of just such off-stage scenes and memories. But some of the things we can do with words are particularly resistant to such translation. For the Victorians, this issue was focused in Jaques's speech on 'The Seven Ages of Man' from *As You Like It* (2.7).

It was a tempting topic for artists.[36] In 1840 John Van Voorst put out what we would now call a coffee-table book, *The Seven Ages of Shakespeare*, with original woodcuts by leading artists including William Mulready, C.R. Leslie, John Constable, David Wilkie and Edwin Landseer (whose 'lean and slippered pantaloon' has a delightful white poodle at his feet, solemnly contemplating himself in the looking glass). Daniel Maclise exhibited a painting of the subject at the Royal Academy in 1848, and in 1851 the Art Union published a set of etchings by E. Goodall after his designs. In 1849 a little album came out entitled *Man: from the Cradle to the Grave. Being Shakspere's Seven Ages of Life*, illustrated with seven original designs, and with an introduction by William Bridges. In a later Victorian household you could even eat off Shakespeare, if you bought the plates made by Minton's Art Pottery Studio, illustrated with 'The Seven Ages' by Henry Stacey Marks (1873).

Few speeches from Shakespeare are as easily extracted from their dramatic context as Jaques's. In performance Duke Senior and the other courtiers can greet it as an old familiar friend, a regular *tour de force*, though even so it may carry a chill in its close such as they had not quite bargained for (nor the speaker himself, for that matter). One can see how it might appeal to the sense of 'moral narrative' by which nineteenth-century readers set such store. No wonder that visual artists were attracted to it. But there is more than one difficulty. The Shakespearean source does not speak a Victorian idiom. There is an alarming rift between the bleak trajectory of Jaques's speech and the sense of progress on which most Victorian models of narrative depend. What *are* Jaques's 'seven ages'? At their barest, they are the infant, the schoolboy, the lover, the soldier, the justice, the pantaloon and – strictly speaking, a state of being rather than a character – 'second childishness'. This is not a triumphant advance. And where does it culminate? It does not rhyme with most Victorian ideas of what constitutes a satisfactory narrative.[37] This is made painfully evident by *Man: from the Cradle to the Grave*, which begins with Jaques's fifth age, an impressive justice, well-bearded, sensual, a touch of Henry VIII to him, exempt from the quiet mockery in 'Full of wise saws and modern instances'. He is the nearest thing to culmination that the Shakespearean source can provide.

Or rather, as William Bridges's revealing introduction describes it, it is the nearest thing to 'Consummation'. More troubling than this relatively slight adjustment of the Shakespearean body to its Victorian clothes is the difficulty presented by the parallel required to the 'History of the World's Life'. For according to Bridges, the Consummation of that must be the advent of Christianity 'amid the throes of barbarism struggling with the intellectual dawn'. But then there is a blatant contradiction between the decay and death of the individual represented by Jaques's consolation-less story and the continued progress of civilization. This latter is ensured by amongst other things the printing press which 'has preserved and secures an eternal validity to all that went before; and, spite of the perils of this our period of fiery transition [this is the end of the turbulent 1840s], the last scene of all, that ends this "strange eventful History", shall of a surety be the lasting reign of "Peace on Earth and Good-will towards Men"'. One turns with curiosity from this voice of desperate piety to the etchings that depict the problematic last phases of the Seven Ages. And one finds a suggestive solution to the yawning gap which separates Jaques's pagan oblivion and Bridges's Christian triumph. A lean and slippered pantaloon is almost run down in the street by some bright young things on horseback, but he is accompanied and perhaps saved by a child, who might well be Little Nell or Little Dorrit. Last scene of all shows him being tended by the daughter into whom the child has presumably grown up, while in the corner her own daughter, his granddaughter, plays on the floor. So the story does continue, unlike Jaques's, if not thundering on to the new Jerusalem, then more modestly on to the next generation.

FIGURE 15 William Mulready, *The Seven Ages of Man* (1837).

The most complex treatment of this teasing topic is by the Irish-born painter and draughtsman William Mulready, close friend of David Wilkie, admirer of Dutch and Flemish genre painting, honoured by Thackeray and others for his 'brilliant, rich, astonishingly intense and luminous colours', supplier of nudes to Victoria and Albert.[38] His ambitious painting *The Seven Ages of Man* (Figure 15) was prompted by the much less refined drawing he had done for the Van Voorst volume. It was exhibited at the Royal Academy in 1838 and praised by M.A. Titmarsh (Thackeray's *nom de plume*) who crowned him 'KING MULREADY ... in double capitals'.[39] But others found it over-ambitious. Ruskin admired Mulready's technical ability, but he thought the subject simply could not be painted: 'In the written passage, the thoughts are progressive and connected; in the picture they must be co-existent, and yet separate; nor can all the characters of the ages be rendered in painting at all' (*Ruskin*, XII, p. 364). Even Thackeray conceded that 'the thing [was] better done in Shakspeare'.

Ruskin puts his finger on what is exciting and disturbing about Mulready's painting. Visual art gives bodies to thoughts and makes them co-exist, but it can puzzle the desire for connexions between them and complicate the idea of progress. This is where the Mulready exemplifies a radical tension in the relationship between narrative and visuality. Things would be easier if the seven ages were separately imagined, like chapters of a book, as they are in *Man: from the Cradle to the Grave*. But as Thackeray perhaps too blithely enthused, 'there they are, all together'. In what sequence could or should one describe the seven ages in this image of Mulready's? Thackeray's choice is revealing in the way it crosses the painting from left to right and back again: 'the portly justice, and the quarrelsome soldier; the lover leaning apart, and whispering sweet things in his pretty mistress's ear; the baby hanging on her gentle mother's bosom; the school-boy, rosy and lazy; the old man, crabbed and stingy; and the old, old man of all, sans teeth, sans eyes, sans ears, sans every thing'. But it is worrying that the lover with the ballad sighing like furnace seems distinctly pretty himself, that the soldier beating the fellow on the ground cannot also be shown seeking the bubble reputation even in the cannon's mouth, that it is hard to see why the old man on the right courteously doffing his cap deserves to be called 'crabbed and stingy' and looks neither lean nor slippered. Who are all these other people – the man drinking madly in the right foreground, the boy with his back to us rebuking him, the grand lady distracted from her failing charge by the lovers behind her, the dogs for that matter? What is that white-shrouded shape on horseback disappearing through the town gates? The viewer's eye is first drawn to the faces we can see most fully, the big bearded justice and the dying man in the chair, and most vividly of all to the sombre reflective boy in the centre, whose own eyes turn away from the wise saws of the justice towards the dying man, and us. There is a movement which asks the viewer's eye to be swept forward in a curve 'down-stage', as it were, from the mother with child in the mid-background on the left to the young lovers elevated on the right. This would be one way of reading the ages of man as a story of love and the sexual drive ensuring that life goes on, as you like it. From behind the justice's right shoulder the schoolboy's eye is yearningly drawn towards the young lovers. But like the mother-with-child to his right they are not centre-stage. This position is taken, however reluctantly, by the *other* boy with the sad bright face and the anxious hands, to whom our own eyes keep returning. It is tempting to suppose that his name is Jaques.

CREATOR AND CREATURES

It is a short step from here to the idea of a brooding figure who is Shakespeare himself, a type of the creative artist. Perhaps even *the* type, save that such claims are rarely uncontested. For the Victorians there was always Dante; on occasion there might be Milton.

When the weekly penny magazine *Great Thoughts* started running a series on 'Great Teachers' in January 1888, it began with Shakespeare. The list of his successors in following weeks makes slightly bizarre reading: John Ruskin, Dr James Martineau, Madame De Staël, Jean-Jacques Rousseau, Rev. T. Binney, Beaumont and Fletcher, Matthew Arnold, Gottfried Ephraim Lessing, Linnaeus and Lord Byron. And so the list went careening on. But at the end of the year readers were rewarded, for the increased expense of 6*d.*, with a bumper Christmas issue which included free with each copy a colour plate entitled 'The Genius of Shakespeare' (Figure 16). It shows the writer brooding by the fireside, as he dreams up some of his most famous creations: starting at the top left, Othello with Desdemona and Brabantio, Portia pleading with Shylock in court, Hamlet holding Yorick's skull in the graveyard, King Lear on the heath in the storm, Romeo and Juliet on the balcony, Falstaff being stuffed into the buck-basket by the Merry Wives, and Macbeth meeting the witches. This format owes something to the frontispieces of editions of the *Works* throughout the century, and to elaborations of the image of Shakespeare between Tragedy and Comedy, such as Henry Howard's *Vision of Shakespeare* (1827, now in Sir John Soane's Museum). But by the 1880s the image of the author conjuring up his fictional characters is particularly associated with Dickens. The design for the frontispiece of *Martin Chuzzlewit* in 1843 by 'Phiz' (Hablot K. Browne) shows Tom Pinch at the organ surrounded by the

FIGURE 16 *The Genius of Shakespeare*, chromo-lithograph presented with *Great Thoughts* Christmas number, 1888 by W. Hobbs and Son.

novel's other characters, as if dreaming them up.[40] From here it was a short step to the picture in words drawn by John Hollingshead in 1857 of the author 'surrounded by those delicate and beautiful creations of his fancy, that ideal family, the children of his pen' (*DCH*, p. 377), and to the now famous picture of 'Dickens's Dream' by Robert W. Buss, left unfinished at the artist's own death in 1875. Dickens himself spoke of the magical life of Shakespeare's characters: his birthday was an occasion 'to celebrate the birthday of a vast army of living men and women, who would live for ever with an actuality greater than that of the men and women whose external forms we saw around us'.[41]

The editorial line on 'Shakespeare's Genius' attributed to him the supernatural powers normally associated with divinity: 'The writer stands like a magician above the race, and penetrates with one glance into all the depths, mysteries, and perplexities of human character' (8 December 1888, *Great Thoughts*, p. 360). It is all the more striking to find this single note of qualification, for the editors confess that they are offended by *The Merry Wives*. They recall Dean Farrar's judgment, that when it comes to the comparison between Shakespeare and Milton, the latter has to be admitted as 'the rarer and lordlier soul'. Why? Because, say the editors, 'Milton could not have conceived such a character as Falstaff. For that "foul-gray-haired iniquity," he would have had no bursts of inextinguishable laughter, but only the glance of a noble scorn' (p. 362). So much the worse for Milton, one might think, and all upwardly mobile subscribers to this improving magazine.

A few weeks before this, on 10 October 1888, Falstaff had enjoyed more honour at the unveiling of the Shakespeare Monument in Stratford-upon-Avon behind the Memorial Theatre. In 1933 it was moved to its present site in the Bancroft Gardens and the disposition of the figures slightly altered. The century abounds in busts and portraits of Shakespeare, and the tercentenary of 1864 had sparked moves for a memorial which had never come to fruition. Lord Ronald Gower conceived his own idea for an elaborate sculptural group in the summer of 1877 and worked on it in Paris with Luca Madrassi for the next ten years or so before its inauguration in Stratford. In his seven years as a Liberal member of parliament he had spoken only once, when he quoted Malcolm's lines on the execution of the Thane of Cawdor in a debate on the Scottish reform Bill of 1868.[42] He was more interested in Shakespeare (and Joan of Arc, and Marie Antoinette) than in the House of Commons, and his private life could be pursued more safely in Paris than in London. Some have supposed that he served as the model for Lord Henry Wotton in *The Picture of Dorian Gray*. This is dubious, but it is certainly the case that Oscar Wilde delivered a eulogy at the Stratford unveiling. It is unlikely that there was anyone there from *Great Thoughts*.

Falstaff is one of the four Shakespearean characters chosen by Gower as a guard of honour encompassing the central rotunda on which their author is regally perched looking out. The other three are Hamlet, Lady Macbeth and Prince Hal. Gower seems to have thought of them as the personification of tragedy (Lady Macbeth), comedy (Falstaff), history (Prince Hal) and philosophy (Hamlet).[43] This idea is assisted by the individuated quasi-antique masks on the decorated consoles with which the four figures are associated, though the thongs restraining the open mouths, or holding them open, lend a touch of discreet sado-masochism characteristic of the *fin de siècle*. There are also appropriate quotations inscribed above them, though the one for Prince Hal is less predictable than the others: 'Consideration like an angel came / And whipped th'offending Adam out of him' (Canterbury's words, *H5*, 1.1.28–9). The total effect is intriguing. It has been said of the Memorial that it represents an important liberation from 'the classic "ideality" of high Victorian sculpture'.[44] The figures may represent 'ideas', but they have been liberated into bodies with real appetites, desires and pains, the stuff of new forms of fantasy more readily associated with Paris and Vienna than with Stratford-upon-Avon. The very names of the collaborators inscribed on Gower's monument testify to a new cosmopolitan ethos: Madrassi, Tassel, Graux and Marley, De Cauville and Perzinku. Meanwhile the writer sits like a therapist above his patients seeking to plumb the depths, mysteries and perplexities of the human psyche.

Who else could one choose instead of these four? A daughter perhaps? Other possible candidates tend to come in pairs. In 1879 Gower had thought about adding four couples: Lear and Cordelia, Romeo and Juliet, Antony and Cleopatra, Othello and Desdemona. But this came to nothing. His chosen four could exist on their own, for better or worse, yet put them together like this and they make an ideally dysfunctional family – bad mother, bad father, two difficult sons. Yet in so far as the positioning of the figures hints at a story, it is one which now firmly puts the two tragic figures behind their author, and Falstaff and Hal out in front.[45] Of these two it is the young prince over whom the figure of Shakespeare himself is angled to brood, paternally and/or lovingly. Hal is an image of young adolescent beauty. Gower would have liked him stark naked but Mrs Grundy would not have allowed it; at least the artist could ensure that the costume was skin-tight. This English prince is very much younger than his Danish sibling. Hamlet looks down at a skull while Hal lifts the crown over his head, in the same pose as John Singer Sargent's Lady Macbeth, charged with erotic vitality.

Once Shakespeare's characters are liberated from their dramatic contexts – into other media, into other words – there is no knowing what they may help to unleash. One may recognize a contrary impulse to gather them all together, the whole extended family, say for a christening. This is how George Cruikshank imagined *The First Appearance of William Shakespeare on the Stage of the Globe with Part of His Dramatic Company in 1564*, exhibited at the Royal Academy in 1867. (In 1564 there were still another thirty-five years to run before the Globe would be built.) Under the motto over the proscenium (another comical anachronism), 'All the World's a Stage', the cradle of the newborn Shakespeare is surrounded by a host of the characters he will go on to create, from the comedies and romances on one side, and from the tragedies and histories on the other – including an alarming Lady Macbeth with daggers raised. It has justly been called a 'whimsical extravaganza' (Altick, p. 145).

The whimsy is less blatant, if not the extravagance, in John Gilbert's *Apotheosis of Shakespeare's Characters* (1871, Figure 17). This reworks an earlier but more horizontally designed painting of Gilbert's from 1850. Both draw on a tradition going back to the beginning of the century, particularly associated with a frieze by Thomas Stothard, *Shakespear's Characters* (1813). The verticality of the 1871 image is striking, but many of the characters and groups are repeated, as one would expect. One can readily identify (even in reproduction) the infant Perdita and the shepherds, Lear and the Fool, Hamlet and Ophelia, Shylock and Portia, Othello and Desdemona and Iago, Falstaff being manhandled by

FIGURE 17 John Gilbert, *Apotheosis of Shakespeare's Characters* (1871).

the Merry Wives, Prospero and Ariel and Caliban and Miranda, Bottom and Puck, Henry VIII and Cardinal Wolsey, Prince Arthur and Hubert, Petruchio and Katherine. We recognize some more easily than others, as happens at large family gatherings. We realize that not everyone has been invited. There are no Romans nor Egyptian queens; there are no Macbeths.

Who is the figure high up on his own in the centre? He looks distinctly unhappy. It seems to be Henry IV, as it certainly was in the 1850 painting, the sad guilt-ridden usurper, most honourable type of all the tormented kings in whose roles the great actors liked to be painted, from Garrick's Richard III to Beerbohm Tree's King John. One might have expected Gilbert to put Shakespeare himself there, where many similar compositions place him. Perhaps in a sense he has. We shall see in chapter six some of the contradictions embodied in this figure of supreme authority, the dream of triumphant near-divinity and the anxieties attendant on such terrible power: King Shakespeare.

Chapter Three

CHARACTER, STORY AND PLOT

ESCAPING THE PLOT: THE CASE OF FALSTAFF

It is no wonder that Shakespeare has been called 'novelistic' when his characters have such complex being-in-time. In their own minds they live in imagined pasts and futures as well as here and now on stage. And the reader's and spectator's sense that they have, as we say, 'a life of their own' is reinforced by belief in the other worlds they inhabit off-stage – not just an inner world of memory and desire but the real space and time that they share with others. These other worlds (past, future, elsewhere) create the sense that both characters and stories enjoy a certain 'freedom of movement', but we also recognize this liberty to be curtailed by something else called plot. This chapter explores a few exemplary ways in which Victorian writers developed the relations between character, story and plot by reference to some Shakespearean models.

The conditions of 'the Shakespearean stage' are notoriously unlike their classical (and neo-classical) counterparts in permitting the story to move freely from one place and time to another. As an audience we can never be certain we know where we are or will find ourselves next: Eastcheap, the Court, Gloucestershire, a battlefield; Rome, Egypt, Sicily, Parthia; Sicily now, Bohemia sixteen years later. Characters disappear and never return, like France and Burgundy in *King Lear*, or Brabantio in *Othello*, or Donalbain and Fleance in *Macbeth*, or Sextus Pompey in *Antony and Cleopatra*. Others do come back, like the Ghost in *Hamlet* or Hermione in *The Winter's Tale*, or suddenly appear for the first time, like

Marcade in *Love's Labour's Lost* or Mariana in *Measure for Measure* or Hymen in *As You Like It*. There are stray characters like Claribel in *The Tempest* or Marcus Luccicos in *Othello* whom we hear of in passing but never get to see. Yet who knows? We might. The world is so full of stories – old stories, new stories, other stories.

Falstaff is full of stories but he does not have much interest in plot. Indeed one might say that he tries to escape from plot into myth. The four fictional characters sculpted by Gower for his Shakespeare Monument all have claims to mythic status. Such works of art as Gower's Monument help them to escape the plot in which their dramatic and narrative sources try to embroil them. They rise above it; they stand alone. But this is more certainly true of Falstaff and Hamlet than of Lady Macbeth and Prince Hal/King Henry, and in some ways it is more true of Falstaff than of Hamlet because the former has less plot to escape from. In this respect Falstaff is an exemplary figure for the concerns of this chapter with the possibility of escaping and contesting plot. As we shall see, the old rogue differs from the young Shakespearean women who inspire so much Victorian writing in that he is not interested in making a new story of his own. Falstaff comes to typify for Victorian writers and artists an idea of 'freedom' that belongs largely to the past. This is in contrast to the models of liberation, or attempted liberation, embodied in Shakespeare's young women.

What does Falstaff stand for? 'Good times' might be one answer. Good times can be here and now in performance on stage, and this sense of presence can be re-created in narrative, most notably in characters who seem to live as they speak. This is the mark of Dickens's genius. But storytelling leans towards the past, and sooner or later this is where the sense of good times will end up, somewhere back there and then, in the good old days, merry England, once upon a time. For writers of the generation of Thackeray and Dickens, born respectively in 1811 and 1812, it was tempting to identify these good times with the years of their own childhood and adolescence, the Regency and the 1820s. For them and their readers this was the era with which Falstaff, a figure of conviviality and (male) clubbability, was particularly associated.

If you were looking for a Victorian Falstaff you would have been most likely to find him in the offices of *Fraser's Magazine* or *Punch* (established in 1830 and 1841 respectively). One of the founders of *Fraser's*, William Maginn, wrote a fine essay on Falstaff for Dickens,[1] while one of the founders of *Punch*, and its long-serving editor, Mark Lemon, played Falstaff in Dickens's production of *The Merry Wives*.

Thackeray wrote for both *Fraser's* and *Punch*, and he liked eating almost as much as he liked drinking. He stood six foot three, and in his late thirties went up to sixteen stone.[2] In *Vanity Fair* (1848) he drew Jos Sedley as a Falstaff entertained by Becky Sharp's Doll Tearsheet. But it is in his next novel, *The History of Pendennis* (1850), that we find the character most fully associated with the Fat Knight. Major Pendennis plays Falstaff to the Prince Hal of his nephew Arthur ('Pen', the novel's main character). The Major is principally opposed by Pen's manly, upright friend Warrington, who takes Pen to task in a key passage of dialogue in chapter sixty-one, 'The Way of the World'. Warrington accuses Pen of being in thrall to his uncle's worldly ambitions. Pen responds with spirit that he is not Prince Hal or Hamlet, nor was he meant to be: 'I say, I take the world as it is, and being of it, will not be ashamed of it. If the time is out of joint, have I any calling or strength to set it right?' He proceeds with an eloquent lament for the quiescence of youthful idealism, the acquiescence in things as they are, that seems to draw on some of Thackeray's own deepest feelings. 'Perhaps I am a coward', Pen admits, again dissociating himself from the Hamlet who asks 'Am I a coward?' (2.2.572). But Warrington's judgment is as stern and authoritative as one could wish from a true mentor or father (like the Lord Chief Justice in *2 Henry IV*).

> You are six-and-twenty years old, and as blasé as a rake of sixty. You neither hope much, nor care much, nor believe much. You doubt about other men as much as about yourself. Were it made of such *pococuranti* as you, the world would be intolerable; and I had rather live in a wilderness of monkeys, and listen to their chatter, than in a company of men who denied everything. (ch. 61)

'I would not have given it for a wilderness of monkeys': these are Shylock's words when he discovers that his daughter Jessica has exchanged his wife Leah's turquoise for a monkey (*MV*, 3.1.114–15). Here Warrington redeems the great phrase to suggest the real and everyday hell that threatens Pen.

But Pen continues to follow his uncle's worldly plot by preparing to take a seat in parliament and marry a scheming and faithless young woman, Blanche Amory. His friend Warrington asks which party he will belong to: 'And under which king does Bezonian speak or die?' This is Pistol's challenge to Justice Shallow, near the end of *2 Henry IV*, at the news that Prince Hal is now King Henry V (5.3.114). The Shakespearean model closes in on the relationship between nephew and uncle and comes to a climax in a great and painful scene (ch. 70, 'Fiat Justitia'), when the heavens fall on the Major's wretched intrigue and Pen effectively says to his Falstaff, 'I know thee not, old man.' But it is worth noting how Thackeray's lenience towards the old, infirm and defeated gives the end of the scene a charitable turn. (Dickens would have simply twisted the knife.) The old man is allowed to cushion the blow by invoking for himself a grander model than Falstaff. He covers his nakedness with some of Cardinal Wolsey's famous last words from *Henry VIII*, not quite exactly remembered.

> 'I have done my best, and said my say; and I'm a dev'lish old fellow. And – and – it don't matter. And – and Shakespeare was right – and Cardinal Wolsey – begad – "and had I but served my God as I've served you" – yes, on my knees, by Jove, to my own nephew – I mightn't have been – – Good-night, sir; you needn't trouble yourself to call again.' (ch. 70)

The scene leaves the Major looking 'very much oldened', a word for which Thackeray had a peculiar tenderness (as he did for the word 'darkling').[3]

There is certainly room for a Falstaff figure in a story about the oldening of a young man with great expectations, like a Hal or a Hamlet, at least for writers of the generation of Dickens and Thackeray. But by the time of Thackeray's death in 1863 at the age of fifty-two,

Falstaff was in comparative eclipse. Up until the 1850s, he was a popular figure on stage, both in *1 Henry IV* and *The Merry Wives*. They were roles in which Phelps excelled, from 1848 at Sadler's Wells up to 1874 at the Gaiety. Towards the end of the century Falstaff was particularly associated with the always extravagant Beerbohm Tree, from 1888 onwards in the *Merry Wives* and 1896 in *1 Henry IV*. In 1906 his production of *1 Henry IV* prompted *The Times* reviewer to remark how dull the history scenes were by comparison with 'the rich glowing world' of Falstaff and his cronies. So far from the worlds of the Boar's Head and the Court reflecting on each other, they seemed quite separate; we would readily forget the latter for the sake of the former, so the writer thought. Thomas Hardy copied it into his notebook.[4] Four years earlier Tree had put on a celebrated production of the Windsor play, starring Ellen Terry and Madge Kendal. This was aimed to coincide with the assumption of the throne by the monarch known as 'fat Edward' and 'Edward the Caresser', who had waited for decades as a bored Prince of Wales, devoted to uniforms and the pleasures of the flesh. No wonder the satirists and cartoonists had associated him with the story of Hal and Falstaff, most notably in the 1876 verse drama *Edward the Seventh* by Samuel Beeton and some henchmen.[5] Recalling the new King Henry V's pivotal speech about turning away his former self, his recent biographer reflects that this was exactly what the Victorian Prince failed to do when he ascended the throne.[6]

Round the previous turn of the century the *Henry IV* plays had taken a more dangerous role in political satire and caricature.[7] The then Prince of Wales was a Hal surrounded by Falstaffian scoundrels, otherwise known as Whigs. Or even worse, he was himself a Falstaff, with the laws of the kingdom almost at his command. With a mad king on the throne, *King Lear* was a play much on people's minds at the time, though not on the stage. So too, with all the fears about his successor protracted over so many years, were Shakespeare's great plays about the education of the Heir Apparent. From 1790 to 1820 Britain was in violent turmoil at home and abroad, and we should never underestimate the time it took for the memories of these thirty years to subside. They were continually being re-ignited, at least until mid-century. In 1853 the parallel between Prince Hal and the Prince Regent was still vivid in the mind of a writer in *Blackwood's Magazine*, meditating on the moment in the 1790s when the Prince had had to break with the life of pleasure and his Whig associates, and assume power and responsibility. Shakespeare had foreseen it all: 'The scene between Henry the Fifth and Falstaff has been acted in every court of Europe, where the acquaintance began in the tavern.'[8]

Amongst visual representations of Shakespearean characters Falstaff had been a dominant, perhaps *the* dominant, figure since featuring in the frontispiece to *The Wits* in 1662.[9] But by 1860 there has been a radical change. After this date, the Falstaff plays 'virtually disappear from the exhibitions' (Altick, p. 260). By the late 1850s Falstaff seemed an object of nostalgia, the vanishing symbol of a risky, roistering 'good time'. This was how a writer in the *Athenaeum* described him in 1857: 'an Epicurean gentleman, shrewd, careless, witty, suspicious of too much virtue, and a moral cosmopolite, sociable from his birth, – a character grown impossible since taverns have become extinct'.[10] By 1857 the suspicion was widespread that it might be impossible to have too much virtue. In Trollope's novel of the following year, *Dr Thorne*, the alcoholic Scatcherds, father Sir Roger and son Louis, both rouse a glancing memory of Falstaff. The good doctor reminds the former that 'A man can die but once' (ch. 9), and the narrator remarks of the latter that he had been 'living cleanly and forswearing sack for what was to him a very long period' (ch. 28). The resolution of the plot depends on both father and son drinking themselves to death.

This is the context in which to read the Falstaff of a major artist who lived and worked through this transition. Born in 1792, George Cruikshank has been described as 'the principal graphic artist transmitting Hogarth to a new century'.[11] He became a prolific illustrator of periodicals and books, and in due course teamed up with the young Dickens for *Sketches by Boz* (1836) and *Oliver Twist* (1837–9). They remained good friends until falling out over drink, when the artist's fanatical devotion to the temperance movement produced the moral narratives in woodcut, *The Bottle* (1847) and *The*

FIGURE 18 George Cruikshank, *Herne's Oak from 'The Merry Wives of Windsor'* (c.1857).

Drunkard's Children (1848). At Dickens's death in 1870 Cruikshank is supposed to have said, 'One of our greatest enemies gone.'

This did not stop him turning a sympathetic hand to the great Shakespearean model of intemperance. In 1857 Cruikshank conceived the idea for an illustrated *Life of Falstaff*, with text by Robert Brough, a popular writer of burlesques and humorous essays. He also exhibited an oil painting of *Herne's Oak from 'The Merry Wives of Windsor'* (Figure 18). Artists had often portrayed Falstaff being stuffed into the buck-basket by the merry wives or tipped into the Thames by their servants, and the Herne's Oak scene had been represented in the 1790s, but it gained a new currency in the mid-Victorian years.[12] Cruikshank's painting may well have been part of a belated attempt in the 1850s to establish himself as a 'serious' artist. If so, there is a distinct pathos to his choice of Falstaff's humiliation at the hands of the fairies, the instruments of his bourgeois tormentors. It is a terrible come-down for the knight who had consorted with royalty, as admirers of the figure he cuts in the *Henry IV* plays have regularly complained, from Hazlitt onwards.

The Life of Falstaff was not a success. The old man's star was on the wane. But in any case there was something perverse about trying to retell his story in this way. Brough's narrative is relentlessly humorous without ever being funny. How could anyone compete with the voice Shakespeare gives the old rogue?[13] Falstaff lives for performance, and any life he might have off the stage will need to rival this sense of live presence. The case is very different with the young women whose stories Mary Cowden Clarke so successfully retells (see pp. 92–6); they yearn for more presence than their plays allow, and hence for more 'story'.

There are two final points to be made. The first is that it is Rosalind who supplants Falstaff in the second half of the nineteenth century as *the* typical, typifying figure of Shakespearean comedy. Great mythic figure that he is, Falstaff survives, but in the late-Victorian and Edwardian years he becomes increasingly associated with a myth of Merrie England – and correspondingly stuck in it. His 'Englishness' becomes pronounced and *The Merry Wives* a particularly patriotic play.[14] The second is that musical elaboration was always prominent in theatrical performance of *The Merry Wives*, and this provides a clue to the major imaginative extensions enjoyed by Falstaff – in music. There is a sense in which music provides Falstaff with the extended space and time that the Shakespearean women find in their 'alternative' stories.[15]

It is not in story itself that Falstaff seeks or needs other lives. In his mythic aspect he lives in an eternal present, as he does on stage in performance, whether supported by music or not. He can *tell* tales for ever. But in so far as he is ever *in* one, he faces towards and belongs to the past. For Shakespearean characters who incite new fictions, we must look to younger and more feminine figures, such as Rosalind – and Hamlet. Like Falstaff they are mercurial, resourceful and witty, but they are fired by passion, they dream of the future, and for better and worse, in all sorts of ways, they are undecided. This makes them good models for artists who want to tell old stories in new ways.

RETELLING THE STORY OF
SHAKESPEARE'S WOMEN

The story of how the Victorians made stories out of Shakespeare begins with Charles and Mary Lamb, whose *Tales from Shakespear: Designed for the use of Young Persons* (1807) was endlessly reprinted throughout the century. Together with Henrietta Bowdler's edition of *The Family Shakespeare*, published in the same year under her brother's name, they represent a first assault, benignly wreathed with the best of intentions, on the Young Reader. As the century progressed there were editions such as Caroline Maxwell's *The Juvenile Edition of Shakespeare: Adapted to the Capacities of Youth* (1828), and a stream of what we would now call 'novelized' versions of the plays for pre-adult readers of various ages.[16] These introduce the young reader to an idealized world from which moral and psychological complexity has been largely expunged. The Lambs' volume, for instance, begins with an account of *The Tempest* which eliminates Stephano, Trinculo and Sebastian, removes any shadow from Antonio's final repentance, and trims Prospero of his less affable features by, for example, giving the responsibility for his harsh treatment of Caliban to Ariel. The play, says Megan Lynn Isaac, 'becomes a reassuring fable of the triumph of good over evil and the farsighted wisdom of conventional authorities – both fathers and kings'.[17] Charles Lamb took the tragedies and his sister Mary the comedies, and there is a case for reading Mary's contributions with a more sympathetic eye to the constraints under which both writer and her female characters labour together. She begins, albeit gingerly, the process of sympathetic identification with the beleaguered and resourceful heroines of the plays, especially the comedies, on the strength of which her successors will more boldly elaborate.[18]

The Lambs' pleasantly written tales are sophisticated by comparison with some of their progeny, such as Mrs Valentine's *Shakespearian Tales in Verse* (1881), a typical product from much later in the century, which retells with coloured illustrations *The Winter's Tale*, *The Tempest* and *The Merchant of Venice*. This last climaxes with a full-page image of Shylock on the quayside, his keys at his feet and the caption 'ALONE':

So thus the wicked Jew was caught,
   In the same net that he had laid
To kill the good Antonio –
   And had himself to death betrayed.

But as a Christian must forgive,
   And mercy to the wicked show,
Antonio for Shylock pleads,
   And begs the Duke to let him go.

His prayer was heard; old Shylock's life
   They spared, but took his wealth away,
And a poor, broken-hearted man,
   He went with heavy heart away.

This does credit to everyone's feelings, but it is pure wish-fulfilment. In Shakespeare's play neither Antonio nor anyone else pleads for Shylock's life. Portia suggests that he begs for himself, Gratiano makes a vicious joke and the Duke spares him before he has time to ask for pardon. No one mentions forgiveness, however much one might wish them to.[19]

Following the Lambs, the next significant figure in the tradition of 'retelling' Shakespeare is Anna Jameson, whose *Characteristics of Women: Moral, Political, and Historical* (1832; later known as *Shakespeare's Heroines*) enjoyed at least eighteen editions up to 1925.[20] Jameson's polemical intent can be gauged from the words she gives her spokeswoman Alda in an introductory dialogue with her male friend Medon.

It appears to me that the condition of women in society, as at present constituted, is false in itself, and injurious to them, – that the education of women, as at present conducted, is founded in mistaken principles, and tends to increase fearfully the sum of misery and error in both sexes. (I, p. 8)

Jameson takes Shakespeare's women to be exemplary of the range of female capabilities, grouping them under four categories, 'Characters of Intellect', 'Characters of Passion and Imagination', 'Characters of the

Affections' and 'Historical Characters'. There is enthusiastic celebration of Juliet who is 'love itself' (I, p. 185), sympathy for Ophelia, 'facile to every impression, fond in her simplicity, and credulous in her innocence' (I, p. 265) and appreciation of Cleopatra's contradictions, 'fused into one brilliant impersonation of classical elegance, Oriental voluptuousness, and gipsy sorcery' (II, p. 123). But the most memorable writing is incited by the women of intellect, above all by Portia.

> A woman constituted like Portia, and placed in this age, and in the actual state of society, would find society arm'd against her; and instead of being like Portia, a gracious, happy, beloved, and loving creature, would be a victim, immolated in fire to that multitudinous Moloch termed Opinion. With her the world without would be at war with the world within; in the perpetual strife, either her nature would 'be subdued to the element it worked in', and bending to a necessity it could neither escape nor approve, lose at last something of its original brightness; or otherwise – a perpetual spirit of resistance, cherished as a safeguard, might perhaps in the end destroy the equipoise; firmness would become pride and self-assurance; and the soft, sweet, feminine texture of the mind, settle into rigidity. Is there then no sanctuary for such a mind? – Where shall it find a refuge from the world? – Where seek for strength against itself? Where, but in heaven? (II, pp. 95–6)

These questions receive a great creative echo in the pages of Victorian novelists such as the Brontës and George Eliot, for whose protagonists the world without is indeed at constant war with the world within. No sanctuary, but perpetual strife – and striving.

Jameson's more direct successor in the tradition of women's appropriation of Shakespeare was Mary Cowden Clarke, who exercised great influence over nineteenth-century reading and interpretation of Shakespeare's plays.[21] She compiled the first concordance to the plays (1845), an idea suggested to her by the Lambs; she edited the *Works* by herself in 1860 and again with her husband Charles, in *Cassell's*

Illustrated Edition of 1864–8; she published *The Shakespeare Key* (1879, again with Charles), and contributed many articles on Shakespeare to journals and magazines. How many editors of Shakespeare have played Mistress Quickly? She took the role in Dickens's 'amateur' production of *The Merry Wives* in 1848; he addressed her as 'My dear Concordance' (*DPL*, IX, p. 239).

But it is for *The Girlhood of Shakespeare's Heroines* (5 vols, 1850–2) that she is best remembered. One wonders how many of the twentieth-century critics who have poured scorn on them have actually read these fifteen tales. If we suspend our sense of superiority to the Victorians' boundless appetite for story, we can begin to appreciate why they were so phenomenally popular throughout the second half of the nineteenth century, on both sides of the Atlantic, going through several editions and enjoying in 1879 a skilful abridged version by her sister Sabilla Novello. It is true that the writing can be extravagant, moralistic, theatrical. The restoration of the young Ophelia to her mother Aoudra prompts a paean to 'Holy mother-love! nearest semblance vouchsafed to mortals of Divine protection! Benignest human symbol of God's mercy to man!' (II, p. 219). For the Lammas Eve that gives birth to the white dove of Verona, every Italian fruit, flower, tree and scent one can think of adds 'voluptuous weight to the torpid atmosphere' before exploding into 'storm and devastation' (II, p. 347). It is much the same with the olde Englisshe feast at the christening of the merry wives of Windsor, as they will grow up to become: 'there was double beer, double-double beer, mum, and dagger-ale; there was the popular huffcap ale, dear to the common lip by such familiar titles as "mad-dog", "angels' food", and "dragon's milk"' (I, p. 382). There is not much call for understatement, under-eating or under-anything, when 'double-double' is the rallying cry.

Yet the appetite on which these tales draw and which they generate is consistently compelling. This is because there is so much more we want to know or more fully imagine about many of Shakespeare's characters, especially about the women whose roles in the plays themselves are generally so much fewer and shorter than the men's.[22] Some independent-minded women can hold centre-stage or share it, such as Juliet, Rosalind, Portia, Isabella, Lady Macbeth and Cleopatra. But in every case they remain at least partly dependent on their men. Wealthy, beautiful and independent, Portia is particularly important for the later Victorians as at once the most desirable role model and prize.[23] And it is this problem of dependence, independence and interdependence that intrigued the Victorians, as it affected women both on the page and off it.

The strength of Cowden Clarke's formula is that it draws on exactly this question. Her tales are dependent on the 'parent' texts provided by Shakespeare, and she provides many anxious diligent notes to prove the tales' factual (and often verbal) correspondence with the details of their source. But every tale is strictly limited by the rule that it must finish with the first words spoken by the heroine in the Shakespeare play. This is the plot in which they are confined. So Isabella's tale ends with her asking, 'And have you nuns no farther privileges?' (*MM*, 1.4.1), Ophelia's with her reproach to her brother, 'Do you doubt that?' (*Ham*, 1.3.4), Olivia's with her command to 'Take the fool away' (*TN*, 1.5.36). The tale can say that like a good daughter it is bound to the parent play according to its bond, no more nor less. It never oversteps the boundary by imagining a different future from the one so adamantly prepared for it by Shakespeare's play. Indeed quite often it calls attention to this unalterable future, and the inexorable moral to be drawn from it. There are many grim premonitions of the fates that lie ahead for the tragic victims. Poor Ophelia gets used to the idea of young women dying for love: both the peasant girl Jutha with whose family she spends her earliest years and, later, a lady of the court called Thyra are betrayed by a rascal called Eric. Desdemona absorbs similarly dire lessons about the mortal consequences of passion from her maid Barbara and her lover Paolo. But there are also more heartening anticipations of the strength that will allow others to survive, in, for example, Portia and Isabella, who are blessed with good surrogate parents or mentors.

Alongside this submission to plot, there is also a space for free play which mirrors the time and space of licence accorded the young lovers in the comedies, especially in *A Midsummer Night's Dream* and *As You Like It*. It is then curious to see the fantasies that begin to blossom, especially in the darker tales. Almost all the girls are in some sense orphaned. Many have lost their mothers, either in childbirth, like Portia and Gruoch (the future Lady Macbeth), or before they are out of girlhood, like Helena (in *All's Well*), Isabella, Desdemona, Ophelia and others. Some find surrogate mothers, notably the young Isabella who escapes from the feckless Madame Leerheim ('Empty Home') to the good sister she finds in the nunnery next door. Or there are strong bonds of friendship, between Meg and Alice, Rosalind and Celia, Beatrice and Hero. More troublesome and therefore productive are the relations between these daughters and their unsatisfactory fathers. When Portia's mother dies in childbirth, her father Count Guido promptly goes missing for seventeen years, confiding her to the charge of uncle Bellario, from whom she receives a good education. Ophelia's father goes off with his wife to a posh job in Paris and leaves her with peasants in the country. Gruoch's father is feeble, milky and lily-livered, while Desdemona's is severe and scary. In almost every case, it is the deficiency of these fathers that shapes the fantasy of the Other Man, the good, true, real male. Sometimes he is an uncle like Portia's Bellario or Desdemona's Gratiano. Sometimes he is a nearby he-man like the mountainous man-at-arms called Grym, against whom wee Gruoch measures everyone else.

It is not always as grim and grisly as this, at least for the comic heroines. One good reason for liking and admiring and even wanting to *be* Rosalind is that whatever else she is, she is triumphantly not Ophelia. Beatrice is also an attractive role model. She enjoys an extravagant holiday from Messina when she is sent with Hero on an excursion to visit their terrible great-aunt in her castle up in the mountains. This is to escape Shakespeare and plunge into a novel by Mrs Radcliffe. The old virago rather takes to the undauntable Beatrice, but Hero is scared out of her wits. Fortunately the castle burns down. Beatrice escapes in the nick of time (though the great-aunt does not) only to be captured by bandits; they too are charmed by her feistiness. Again she escapes, though not before she has given them a lecture on liberty and good manners.

There is a heartening variety to these fantasies. Just as there is a dynamic and diverse relationship between the daughter story and the parent plot, so too there is an unpredictable tussle, unique to each tale, between 'nature' and 'nurture'. The first is given, like your biological parents, or the script whose words you will find yourself speaking. But the second is a matter of the mentors, nurses, patrons and tutors who fall in your path (as with poor Ophelia), whom you seek out (like the resourceful Isabella), or to whom you stand up (like Beatrice). The tales ask us to read them not only as if we were heroines, but also as (surrogate) parents with an eye to the ways we can fail our impressionable daughters. (Don't send them away to peasants in the country! Don't be too stern! Don't be too soft!) They encourage readers with good thoughts about our daughters' appetite for knowledge, their capacity for friendship, their resilience and wit.

The actress Helen Faucit was in her heyday when Cowden Clarke's tales were published. Some thirty years later, in 1880, she was prompted to start writing about some of the roles she had played by her friend Geraldine Jewsbury, who was dying of cancer. She went on to write essays on Ophelia, Portia, Desdemona, Juliet, Imogen, Rosalind, Beatrice and Hermione that were gathered together in the volume *On Some of Shakespeare's Female Characters* (1885).[24] Faucit follows her predecessors in imagining the 'pre-dramatic' life of her characters. But she also expresses a desire to continue their stories into the future, especially in the cases of Portia and Imogen. Unlike Cowden Clarke, she explicitly challenges the finality of the Shakespearean plot. She confesses that 'I could never part with my characters when the curtain fell and the audience departed. As I had lived with them through their early lives, so I also lived into their future' (p. 39). Faucit is in a sense quite rightly disturbed by the unresolved tensions in the plays' conclusions. Her Portia is still troubled by Shylock and the state in which he has been left. So she starts to visit him and care for him as no one has cared for him since the death of his beloved wife Leah, until he can turn his own life into story and give it to a sympathetic listener. She associates herself with Tennyson's 'Isabel' (a glorified version of the Shakespearean Isabella), and plays the Desdemona to his Othello, giving him 'a world of sighs'. There are several Shakespearean scenarios being played out here. She reminds the reader of Paulina supervising Leontes's long penance. She makes Shylock imagine 'the smell o' the blood' he would have had to live with, like the Macbeths, if he had used the knife on Antonio. In due course the old man is ready to be reunited with his chastened daughter Jessica, who has herself had time to reflect on the injuries she has done him. The great model behind all this is Lear and Cordelia. But here it is only the father who has to die, and it is on an angel of mercy rather than a real errant daughter that his last looks fall.

Faucit does something similar with Imogen, but the ending to *Cymbeline* requires slightly different treatment. In the case of Imogen and her husband Posthumus, the question that Faucit cannot get out of her head is how exactly this marriage is supposed to succeed with such a backlog of hurt and guilt to work off. Perhaps Imogen can forgive the man who has accused her of being a whore. But can Posthumus forgive himself? 'No! I believe, never,' Faucit exclaims (p. 221). For all Imogen's angelic tenderness, she has simply suffered too much from Shakespeare's plot to endure. There is the heart-wound of her husband's letter, the days and nights of exposure and starvation, the discovery of his headless corpse (as she thinks). Faucit imagines this Imogen wasting to death, ethereally and always forgivingly. One cannot help feeling with Faucit's recent biographer that Imogen's death will be the ultimate punishment to her widower.[25] It is interesting to note the dissent provoked by these imaginative excursions: Browning and Ruskin remonstrated with her over Portia, and Tennyson over Imogen.

Tennyson was not alone in his idolization of Imogen. As the iconic figure of the Loyal Wife she is in a class of her own amongst Victorian heroines. It is no wonder that she attracted particular hostility from the rabidly iconoclastic George Bernard Shaw, especially when he discovered she was going to be impersonated by his beloved Ellen Terry. The correspondence between them over the role makes for amusing and instructive reading (Shaw, pp. 39–74).[26] Shaw's passion is more than a personal eccentricity. He is articulating all the growing aggression towards the earlier Victorian idealizations of women, an aggression which finds expression towards the end of the century in the 'New Women' who erupt both in art and life, slamming the front door as they leave home, reading John Stuart Mill, smoking cigarettes and campaigning for the vote. None of these are causes which Shakespeare's Imogen could be imagined as supporting.

Desdemona is also a loyal wife, and *Othello* is a much more fertile play than *Cymbeline* when it comes to inspiring other writers. So far we have been considering the comparatively sunny models provided by young lovers such as Rosalind and Portia. But Victorian writers were also stimulated by darker models of passion, courtship, marriage, jealousy, madness and murder. The most significant Shakespearean women concerned here are Ophelia, Desdemona and Lady Macbeth, and the most important play is one that moves beyond comedy, courtship and the defiance of fathers into its aftermath, marriage. The passions which come to violent fruition in Shakespearean (and Greek) tragedy do not often take the same form in the modern world. This is why the Victorians were so thrilled and appalled by *Othello*. It provided models of marital jealousy for many nineteenth-century novels, including Scott's *Kenilworth* (1821), Trollope's *He Knew He Was Right* (1869)[27] and more faintly – think of poor short-sighted Dorothea–Desdemona – George Eliot's *Middlemarch* (1872). We shall now look, in a certain amount of textual detail, at a series of novels by three writers that draw explicitly on *Othello* and other Shakespeare plays for their exploration of marriage.

MARRIAGE AND MURDER 1: THACKERAY

The relationship between Falstaff and Hal is not the only Shakespearean model invoked by Thackeray in *Pendennis*. An intriguing role is also played by *Othello*. When young Pen falls unsuitably in love with an actress, his mother enlists her brother-in-law the Major to persuade the impressionable lad out of his precipitate engagement. The Major's tactic is to open Pen's eyes and ears to the fashionable world in which he himself moves. He tells anecdotes about royalty and all the eligible matches with society dames that the young man is forgoing: 'These things to hear did young Pendennis seriously incline' (ch. 9). This is a wittily twisted allusion to the way Othello describes his wooing of

Desdemona with tales of exotic adventure (1.3.146–7). It makes of Pen a Desdemona who needs to be disenchanted of his crush on a mere actress and re-enchanted with visions of a high social sphere more congenial to his family. The Major succeeds.

This casts a slur on Pen's masculinity which is deepened when the Shakespeare play returns in the form of a vignette which shows Othello murdering Desdemona (ch. 24). The significance of the allusion is not immediately clear. The chapter begins by telling us a good deal about the shady colonial background of the young adventuress to whom Pen has now become attracted, Blanche Amory. Christened Betsy, this young woman has renamed herself to insist on her 'whiteness', for there is a hint that her mother is the illegitimate daughter of an English merchant father and a native Indian 'wife'. (Thackeray himself had just such a half-Indian half-sister, whom he described as 'black'.) John Sutherland may well be right in supposing that it is Blanche's 'black' mother who puts the writer in mind of *Othello*.[28] Nevertheless, the idea of murderous Shakespearean jealousy invoked here is not applied to the potential young lovers, Pen and Blanche. It is Pen's mother Helen on whom the green-eyed monster preys. She does not trust Blanche, quite rightly, and she watches the two of them 'with that anxiety with which brooding women watch over their sons' affections – and in acknowledging which, I have no doubt there is a sexual jealousy on the mother's part, and a secret pang' (ch. 24). What is more, Helen's sexual jealousy is repeated in the person of Pen's quasi-sister, Laura Bell, the orphan adopted by his mother and destined in her ambitions to be his wife.

What has this to do with Othello killing his wife? Like the epigraphs with which George Eliot heads the chapters of her later novels, Thackeray's vignettes cast an oblique light over the tale-telling they herald. Here the violence of the Shakespearean scene stands in stark contrast to the modern world of civilized feeling. It belongs to the past, to fiction, to a world elsewhere (like India). In any case, who would want to murder whom? Yet the taint of sexual jealousy lingers, as something which the women have difficulty in acknowledging. But as Othello himself says: 'It is the cause' (*Oth*, 5.2.1).

In all this Pen continues to find himself more like Desdemona than any of the male figures in Shakespeare's tragedy. It is the possessive family women, his mother and adopted sister, who take Othello's position. This inversion of the Shakespearean model is carried further when yet another sexual rival appears on the scene in the shape of young Fanny Bolton. She is infatuated with Pen, who falls into a near-fatal fever out of 'discipline and self-denial', as he tries to drive her image 'out of his inflamed brain' (ch. 51). His mother arrives to take possession of him, and with Laura's help she hustles poor Fanny away. It is at this point that the narrator recalls the great lines that Iago speaks in triumphant anticipation of his master's fate (*Oth*, 3.3.333–6).[29]

> There is a complaint which neither poppy, nor mandragora, nor all the drowsy syrups of the East could allay, in the men in his time, as we are informed by a popular poet of the days of Elizabeth; and which, when exhibited in women, no medical discoveries or practice subsequent – neither homoeopathy, nor hydropathy, nor mesmerism, nor Dr Simpson, nor Dr Locock can cure, and that is – we won't call it jealousy, but rather gently denominate it, rivalry and emulation in ladies. (ch. 52)

There is no need for these women to smother Pen–Desdemona as s/he lies in bed. They have him all to themselves again, having cast the *other* woman, Fanny, as the jealous loser. This is made explicit in the heading to chapter fifty-four: 'Fanny's Occupation Gone', which recalls Othello's famous *cri de cœur*, 'Othello's occupation's gone' (*Oth*, 3.3.360). Meanwhile the play that Laura reads to Pen in 'a low sweet voice' as he lies in his sickbed is not *Othello* but *Cymbeline*, another play about sexual jealousy in which the accusation against the woman turns out to be false. But in this case the story ends in her restoration to husband and father. So with Pen, who finds himself yet again in the woman's position, returned safely to – mother and 'sister'.

Othello is the great archetypal play about the man who murders his wife, and the horrific scene in which he does so is a prime source for Victorian representations of murder. Bill Sikes's killing of Nancy in *Oliver Twist*, for example, owes a great deal to it (ch. 47). But where is its complement, about the wife who murders her husband? There are various likenesses between Greek and Shakespearean tragic figures, most notably between Orestes and Hamlet. But in this respect there is an interesting mis-correspondence. The Greeks provide models for the wife who kills her husband – Clytemnestra of course, but also the Danaids who slay their husbands on the wedding night. The Greeks do not, however, bequeath a great model for the story of the husband who kills his wife. Shakespeare in turn does not do the story of the wife who kills her husband: Hamlet's mother is no Clytemnestra. Shakespeare does give us murderous women from Tamora and Queen Margaret to Goneril and Regan and Cymbeline's Queen. But Lady Macbeth is in a class of her own, the nearest thing to a Clytemnestra – save that she is fiercely loyal to her husband. Yet Thackeray imagines the way these two figures might blend together as he develops the character of Becky Sharp in *Vanity Fair*. The Clytemnestra she plays in the charades at Gaunt sounds very like Lady Macbeth: 'Scornfully she snatches the dagger out of Aegisthus's hand' (ch. 51). It is as if Becky were picking up the scattered allusions to the dowager Lady Southdown looking like Mrs Siddons (chs 40, 41), to Lord Steyne's wife being as gay as Lady Macbeth (ch. 48), to the 'Lady Grizzel Macbeth' who is so much more respectable than her great ancestor (ch. 51). In the novel's closing moments Thackeray famously brings Becky's Clytemnestra back to threaten poor Jos Sedley or predict his end at her hands (though not before a vignette has cast her as the Doll Tearsheet to his Falstaff (ch. 55)). Becky is nothing if not versatile, a figure for female performance through whom all sorts of danger can be expressed. Thackeray has blurred the murderous wives in Aeschylus and Shakespeare into the single figure of a woman with a knife in her hand.

For murder-in-marriage Shakespeare seems only to provide the model of Othello and Desdemona (and, less directly, its shadows in *Much Ado* and *The Winter's Tale*). Yet everyone knows that wives can kill their husbands or might want to – and that husbands can fear that they might. Everyone knows that the modern world still contains Lady Macbeths, even if they do not have to murder sleeping kings to prove it. Anna Jameson reminded her readers of this when she asked: 'are there, therefore, no Lady Macbeths in the world?'[30] What if Desdemona were infused with the spirit of Lady Macbeth? Better still, what if the bride were disappointed in love, like Ophelia, then married off to the wrong man, a Juliet forced into marriage with the County Paris? This is not a character or a story Shakespeare ever exactly creates, of passionate female desire that is thwarted and turns to violence, yet one can readily see how someone else might do so, out of the components he provides. The story might be called 'Love's Madness'.[31]

There is indeed a fictional figure whose story fills for the nineteenth century the gap that Shakespeare left. It is Walter Scott's Lucy Ashton, the Bride of Lammermoor, who (like one of the Danaids) stabs her unwanted husband to death on their wedding night. Her story was hugely popular, and the mad murderous bride took on the force of a modern myth. In the hundred years after its first publication in 1819, Scott's novel generated more than twenty-five stage plays, melodramas and operas, performed all over the western world, including the operatic version that has now eclipsed the novel itself, Donizetti's *Lucia di Lammermoor* (1835).[32] Lucy Ashton is an Ophelia forced into the wrong marriage – as Juliet might have been – who then finds a Lady Macbeth in herself. We can imagine Hamlet reading Scott's novel and thinking that *this* is what Gertrude should have done to Claudius.[33]

MARRIAGE AND MURDER 2:
CHARLOTTE BRONTË

Charlotte Brontë wrote *The Professor* in 1845–6, before *Jane Eyre*, but it was not published till 1857, two years after her death. Her earliest prose, in the 1830s, had been suffused with Shakespearean quotations, almost as many as the Biblical; particularly favoured plays were *Othello*, *Macbeth* and *A Midsummer Night's Dream*.[34] *The Professor* contains a number of passing allusions to Shakespeare, but the most arresting is an explicit reference to *Othello* made by the main female character, Frances Henri, the beloved Anglo-Swiss pupil of the narrator, William Crimsworth. Frances is having a heated argument with a difficult friend of Crimsworth's called Hunsden. This man is thoroughly obnoxious to

Frances, taunting her about William Tell and Wellington. Frances is finally roused to ask if he is married. No, he says: 'I should have thought you might have guessed I was a Benedick by my look' (ch. 24). This flirtatious move casts Frances as Beatrice, and implies that the passage of arms just past has been coloured by unavowed sexual feelings. Crimsworth himself has been looking on with amusement. The spirited Frances ripostes with a warning that Hunsden had better not marry a Swiss girl and start being rude about William Tell. If he does, he might find himself smothered one night, like Desdemona. This is to turn the air blue, or blueish, which the men seem rather to enjoy.

> 'I am warned,' said Hunsden; 'and so are you, lad,' (nodding
> to me); 'I hope yet to hear of a travesty of the Moor and his gentle
> lady in which the parts shall be reversed according to the plan
> just sketched – you, however, being in my night-cap. Farewell,
> Mademoiselle!' He bowed on her hand, absolutely like Sir Charles
> Grandison on that of Harriet Byron, adding; 'Death from such
> fingers would not be without charms.' (ch. 24)

This is not like Samuel Richardson's Grandison at all. It is much closer to the Lovelace of his *Clarissa*, or another Byron altogether. What is going on with these Englishmen? 'Mon Dieu!' murmurs Frances, as well she might, taking refuge in French.

It is hard to imagine what charms there might be in death at the hands of the mad wife in *Jane Eyre* (1847). With her blackened, swollen face, Bertha Mason subsumes a travesty of the Moor and his gentle lady (and the sexual union between them). When she invades Jane's room in the middle of the night dressed all in white and bearing a candle, she turns into Lady Macbeth with a vengeance. Rochester can dress up as an old gypsy woman and playfully invoke King Lear as he steps out of disguise with 'Off, ye lendings!' There is nothing playful about his wife's embodiment of murderous marriage. She is its living ghost: 'do not forget' that the story that begins in romantic courtship can end like *this*.

Othello is explicitly invoked in *Jane Eyre* on a couple of occasions. The first is when Rochester gets Jane to recount her unromantic tale of childhood misery at Lowood. She tells him how much the girls disliked Mr Brocklehurst for cutting off their hair, and buying them bad needles and thread. 'And was that the head and front of his offending?' asks Rochester, facetiously (ch. 13). Is he conscious of using Othello's proud confession to the Venetian senate, as he launches into his round unvarnished tale, that he has indeed taken away the old man's daughter and married her, and that this is 'The very head and front of my offending' (1.3.81)? Does he want Jane to recognize it? A few chapters on, as if responding to Rochester's cue, Jane herself recalls the same speech of Othello's. Victorian writers are as fond of citing as artists were of painting the (imagined) scene in which Othello captures with his stories Desdemona's eager impressible ear and heart. Thackeray's Glorvina O'Dowd, for example, lays siege to Dobbin in India, 'ready to listen and weep like Desdemona at the stories of his dangers and his campaigns' (*Vanity Fair*, ch. 43). In her invocation of the Shakespearean Othello's romantically affirmative note Jane Eyre affects a clear-sighted realism. Now that she has met the beautiful Blanche Ingram, she realizes the futility of her own hopes of romance with Mr Rochester. She reflects to herself:

> Reason having come forward and told in her own quiet way, a plain, unvarnished tale, showing how I had rejected the real, and rapidly devoured the ideal; – I pronounced judgment to this effect: –
>
> That a greater fool than Jane Eyre had never breathed the breath of life ... (ch. 16)

But there is an irony in her memory of Othello's 'round unvarnished tale ... / Of my whole course of love' (1.3.91–2), which Jane does not entirely control. This romantic fantasy will turn out to be true for her, after all.

The significance of these allusions keeps on spiralling, for there is a further Shakespearean twist to Jane's thoughts. She tells herself to make two pictures, one of her indigent plebeian self and the other of the magnificent Blanche, so that whenever she is tempted to suppose that Rochester might think well of her, she will take the two portraits out to remind her of the absurdity. This recalls Hamlet with his mother, confronting her with the pictures of her two husbands (3.4.53). Jane congratulates herself on her self-admonition. Her story will not be the 'whole course of love' but a self-imposed 'course of wholesome discipline'. The passions that require such discipline are unruly, but so too are the literary allusions through which they are figured. For this is not the last we hear of the scene between Hamlet and his mother. Rochester returns to it when he seeks to reassure the anxious Jane that she may marry him without causing pain to anyone else. He is lying.

> 'That you may, my good little girl: there is not another being
> in the world has the same pure love for me as yourself – for I lay
> that pleasant unction to my soul, Jane, a belief in your affection.'
> (ch. 24)

This is an ominous misquotation, a travesty of Hamlet's good counsel to his mother not to lay 'that *flattering* unction to your soul' (3.4.147). A line or so later Hamlet is speaking of ulcerous places, of rank corruption and unseen infection – figures for the violent and diseased passions which Rochester is trying to ignore.[35]

Like Jane Eyre and most of her first readers, Charlotte Brontë believed in wholesome discipline. It is one way of thinking about what Rochester is made to endure before he becomes a fit mate for Jane. Discipline, passion and punishment are closely intertwined in the study of courtship and marriage that owes the most explicit debt to Shakespeare in Brontë's work. Her second published novel *Shirley* (1849) makes remarkable use of *Coriolanus*.[36]

Caius Martius Coriolanus may seem a surprising choice for a romantic hero. But the play and the role had acquired high currency in the decades of revolution and war after 1789, the year in which John Philip Kemble first performed it at Drury Lane with his sister Sarah Siddons as Volumnia.[37] For William Hazlitt in 1816 the play had been too close for comfort, inciting him to an extraordinary tirade against the collusion of poetry and political power, all too reminiscent in its violence of Caius Martius himself, if diametrically opposed in its political loyalties.[38] Several Victorian novelists draw on the play, notably

Catherine Gore in her popular *Mrs Armytage, Or Female Domination* (1836, reissued in 1848). The title-character is a wealthy, petty Yorkshire Volumnia, with more of Caius Martius in her than her feebly rebellious son Arthur. She tyrannizes over her children, destroying a wilting lovelorn daughter and cowing Arthur until he can stand it no longer. Arthur bursts out with the dreadful secret that he is the rightful owner of the family estate, and promptly collapses at his mother's feet to beg forgiveness. There are numerous Shakespearean chapter epigraphs that climax, for the big family showdown (III, ch. 16), with the famous lines 'O mother, mother! / What have you done?' (*Cor*, 5.3.185–6). Some aspects of the novel anticipate George Eliot's far more substantial *Felix Holt* (1866), which also deploys some important references to *Coriolanus*. Lady Volumnia Dedlock's name proclaims her pedigree in Dickens's *Bleak House* (1852–3), while in *Hard Times* (1854) Mrs Sparsit is endowed with a 'Coriolanian style of nose', both the oppressive employer Mr Bounderby and the nobly isolated factory 'Hand' Stephen Blackpool bear a resemblance to Shakespeare's hero, and the novel partly rewrites the play's ending when the former is exposed by his unacknowledged mother (Gager, pp. 200–1).

The young Charlotte Brontë admired the Duke of Wellington as '*le moderne Coriolan*'.[39] In *Shirley*, however, the admiration is severely qualified. The equation is explicitly made between Shakespeare's Roman warrior and the central male figure, the autocratic Yorkshire mill-owner, Robert Moore, who refuses to bow to the Luddites determined to smash his new machinery. Caroline Helstone chooses the play for the two of them to read together. She is more than half in love with Robert, but rightly thinks he has something to learn about how to deal with the working classes.

> 'Your heart is a lyre, Robert; but the lot of your life has not been a minstrel to sweep it, and it is often silent. Let glorious William come near and touch it; you will see how he will draw the English power and melody out of its chords.' (ch. 6)

Glorious William duly rouses Robert to identification with the title-character, but this is too easy: the play simply reinforces his prejudices.

Hazlitt would have shrugged: what else do you expect? Caroline naïvely supposes that Robert will recognize the moral of the story, that he will see himself in the Roman autocrat and become less tyrannical towards his workfolk. Robert brushes aside the 'little democrat'. He chooses something for her to read in return, a passionate poem he knows she admires, 'La Jeune Captive', the lament of a young woman for her own lost life as she stands under sentence of death, by the doomed André Chénier who was himself executed in 1794 at the age of thirty-two. This performance allows Caroline to express a truth about herself and her longings for the future, but the exchange of readings has not helped her or Robert learn anything about themselves. They have simply swapped a couple of stereotypes.

Yet like all the craftiest uses of Shakespeare in Victorian fiction, this scene sets many questions in motion. If Robert Moore is going to be a feasible partner for young Caroline, his Coriolanus will need to be re-educated. Shakespeare's version (and Plutarch's) does a good job of humbling Coriolanus but it ends in tragedy. What is the alternative? It is not only Coriolanus who needs redeeming from all that Romanness; it is also his poor wife, 'my gracious silence' (*Cor*, 2.1.175). Has Caroline grasped what it might mean to embrace the Roman code for women, to which Virgilia tries to submit under the beady eye of her mother-in-law? In the following chapter it is the voice of Volumnia with which the narrator addresses her (and the reader), chastising her (and our) youthful fantasies. There are terrible rites of passage ahead: 'The heart's blood must gem with red beads the brow of the combatant, before the wreath of victory rustles over it' (ch. 7). 'Oh Jupiter, no blood!' exclaims Shakespeare's Virgilia (*Cor*, 1.3.38). This is as nothing compared to the grim message that the Volumnia–narrator will shortly deliver.

> You expected bread, and you have got a stone; break your teeth on it, and don't shriek because the nerves are martyrized: ... You held out your hand for an egg, and fate put into it a scorpion. Show no consternation: close your fingers firmly upon the gift; let it sting through your palm. Never mind: in time, after your hand and arm have swelled and quivered long with torture,

the squeezed scorpion will die, and you will have learned the
great lesson how to endure without a sob. (ch. 7)

The bread, stone and scorpion may come from the Gospels, but this is
scarcely a comfort. The narrator promises a 'convenient stoicism'
drained of all faith, hope and charity. Much later on, Caroline reflects
on the separate spheres for modern boys and girls: all the brothers in
business or professions, all with something to do, while 'their sisters
have no earthly employment, but household work and sewing; no
earthly pleasures, but an unprofitable visiting; and no hope, in all their
life to come, of anything better' (ch. 22). She finds herself thinking of
the Roman Lucretia, 'spinning at midnight in the midst of her maidens'
(ch. 22). Lucrece, Virgilia, the Portia and Calpurnia of *Julius Caesar*, the
Octavia of *Antony and Cleopatra*: these are not inspiring prototypes for a
young woman.

Fortunately Caroline can call on other resources. When they are
reading the play together, Robert is no good at the comic scenes, so she
does them for him with spirit, which is encouraging. The narrator goes
on to remark that her conversation this evening was

> as of something untaught, unstudied, intuitive, fitful; when once
> gone, no more to be reproduced as it had been, than the glancing
> ray of the meteor, than the tints of the dew-gem, than the colour
> or form of the sun-set cloud, than the fleeting and glittering
> ripple varying the flow of a rivulet. (ch. 6)

In other words, she sounds like a natural actress. But there are some
particular other words in play here.

> *Medon*:   Analysing the character of Cleopatra must have been
> something like catching a meteor by the tail, and making it sit for
> its picture.
> *Alda*:   Something like it, in truth; but those of Miranda and
> Ophelia were more embarrassing, because they seemed to defy all
> analysis. It was like intercepting the dew-drop or the snow-flake
> ere it fell to earth, and subjecting it to a chemical process.

This is from Anna Jameson's Preface to *Characteristics of Women* (I, pp. 60–1). Glancing as the references to the 'meteor' and the 'dewgem' in *Shirley* may be, they establish an affinity with Jameson, who is drawing on an idea of the volatile, liquid, fluent, mercurial and metamorphic 'nature' of women to which Shakespeare's own plays give such powerful expression.

The 'Cleopatra' of *Antony and Cleopatra* is the name for all that Roman women are not. One wonders what would have happened if Caroline had proposed *this* as the play for them to read together. But for obvious reasons Cleopatra made most Victorians nervous. In Trollope's *The Way We Live Now* (1875) she features as one of Lady Carbury's *Criminal Queens*. In *Jane Eyre*, St John feeds himself in fancy with the 'delicious poison' of Rosamond Oliver's charms (it is Cleopatra's phrase, *AC*, 1.5.27–8), but he knows there is 'an asp in the garland' (ch. 32). In *Villette*, Lucy Snowe comes face to face with Cleopatra in a picture gallery. She is not impressed: 'very much butcher's meat ... affluence of flesh ... no business to lounge away the noon on a sofa ... this huge, dark-complexioned gypsy queen' (ch. 19). Paul Emanuel is shocked to find her looking at this monster and escorts her to the other side of the room where she can contemplate four angels representing *'La vie d'une femme'*, all 'grim and gray as burglars, and cold and vapid as ghosts'.

Caroline needs help, but a Cleopatra is not the answer. The answer in this novel is the astonishing invention of the title-character, Caroline's friend Shirley Keeldar, the transvestite heiress, a blend of Rosalind and Portia (of Belmont, not Rome). As an heiress she is a Portia, but as a dazzling cross-dresser and a good friend, she is the Rosalind to Caroline's Celia. *The Times* reviewer grudgingly conceded her originality but did not much like it, and tried to class her with Katherine and Beatrice, the Shrews, before sarcastically concluding that really she was just beyond belief: 'a more subtle metaphysician, a more acute reasoner, a finer talker, and a more skilful tactitian [*sic*], never existed than the lovely Miss Keeldar, and the portrait, so accordant with all that we see and hear of in every day life, is complete' (*BCH*, p. 150). Brontë was distressed by this, but Shirley was meant to cause mischief or even havoc, what with a radical theology that puts

Milton and Genesis in their places to insist that 'Eve is Jehovah's daughter, as Adam was His son' (ch. 18). Shirley is drawn from the world of Shakespearean comedy to contest all the grim assumptions on which the Roman history plays (and conventional Christian piety) are founded. She draws Robert Moore out of himself and his world, until he knows hunger and want and exposure at first hand. A broken Coriolanus, Moore survives attempted murder to be united with the faithful Caroline and perhaps put his newfound sense of compassion to good social use.

Brontë had difficulties in winding her story up, and indeed, throughout the novel, in controlling the dizzying conflict of genres it appeals to. Along with Shakespearean history, tragedy and romantic comedy, there are paradigms drawn from scripture of personal conversion and global apocalypse that threaten to overwhelm all others and make the accommodation of mere individual lives and loves relatively trivial. Yet the novel remains amongst other things a resourceful and spirited challenge to the Shakespearean model it explicitly invokes.

MARRIAGE AND MURDER 3: MARY ELIZABETH BRADDON

Shakespeare was also an essential resource for the woman who spent three years on the stage under the name of 'Mary Seyton' before turning herself into a full-time writer in 1860. Two years later Mary Elizabeth Braddon made her name with *Lady Audley's Secret*, following it up a year on with the scarcely less successful *Aurora Floyd*, and establishing herself as 'Queen of the Circulating Libraries'.[40] The two 'sensation novels' by which she is best known both demonstrate an artful use of Shakespearean allusion. There is not much precedent for bigamy in Shakespeare, but where 'crime' and 'women' are joined together there is an inevitable model, and sure enough, it is with Lady Macbeth that the murderous Lady Audley is associated. *Aurora Floyd* conducts more elaborate negotiations with *Othello*. Various characters are associated with Desdemona, Othello, Iago and Cassio, and even

with Emilia, Roderigo and Brabantio. There is a Caliban too. Braddon
had not wasted her time on the stage, nor her reading.

Lady Audley fascinates everyone, inside the novel and out, not
because she is a murderous bigamist but because she is an actress. She is
pretty, blonde, delicate, more like a Keepsake Beauty modelling for Anne
Page than the super-shrew or virago we might expect. She conforms to
an idea of Lady Macbeth to which some actresses were attracted, even or
especially when it was at odds with their own physicality. Ellen Terry, for
instance, thought of Lady Macbeth as 'a delicate little creature, with
hyper-sensitive nerves'. In this she was following Mrs Siddons's idea of
the character as 'fair, feminine, nay, perhaps even fragile'.[41] Both Helen
Faucit and Ellen Terry presented a Lady in whom the elements of
conventional 'femininity' were prominent. They might have been hard
put not to, given the 'loveable' associations so firmly embedded in the
minds of their audiences by their previous roles.

The self-possession of Lady Audley's performance exasperated some
readers, such as this reviewer:

> The nerves with which Lady Audley could meet unmoved
> the friend of the man she had murdered, are the nerves of a Lady
> Macbeth who is half unsexed, and not those of the timid, gentle,
> innocent creature Lady Audley is represented as being. ... Her
> manner and her appearance are always in contrast with her
> conduct. All this is very exciting; but it is also very unnatural.[42]

Braddon must have been delighted. This is exactly what she was out to
excite: the reflex belief that there *must* be an art to find the mind's
construction in the face. Lady Audley provides a clue to the invisible
depths within her when she plays Beethoven on the piano. 'It was one
of the many paradoxes in her character, that love of sombre and
melancholy melodies, so opposite to her gay, frivolous nature' (I, ch. 11).
But her antagonist, and the novel's other main character, Robert
Audley, is on the track of this paradox. Essential to the whole genre of
'sensation fiction' is the fearful thought that there may be no
correspondence whatever, or none to be read, between the tranquil
everyday world of appearances that we think of as 'natural' and the

truths that lie behind it. Yet even as Robert expresses his scepticism, the Shakespearean allusions in his speech suggest a circuitous route to the truth. It is a key passage.

> 'What do we know of the mysteries that may hang about the houses we enter? If I were to go to-morrow into that common-place, plebeian, eight-roomed house in which Maria Manning and her husband murdered their guest, I should have no awful prescience of that bygone horror. Foul deeds have been done under the most hospitable roofs, terrible crimes have been committed amid the fairest scenes, and have left no trace upon the spot where they were done. I do not believe in mandrake, or in blood-stains that no time can efface. I believe rather that we may walk unconsciously in an atmosphere of crime, and breathe none the less freely. I believe that we may look into the smiling face of a murderer, and admire its tranquil beauty.' (i, ch. 18)

'Foul deeds' and 'the smiling face of a murderer' are from *Hamlet*; the 'murdered guest' and 'blood-stains that no time can efface' are from *Macbeth*. Robert is doing what he is saying, as he looks into Lady Audley's smiling face and admires its tranquil beauty. She is the perfectly domesticated, self-controlled murderess, whose secret can only be read with the help of Shakespeare.

As he becomes convinced of her guilt Robert tries to make Lady Audley conform to her Shakespearean role model and rouse the sense of guilt that will erupt into Lady Macbeth's 'madness'. But when he finally puts all the evidence together, the guilt of which she is convicted is an external matter, and the madness she alleges is indistinguishable from just another performance. Confined to an asylum on the Continent, she impresses her French doctor as a 'beautiful devil' and orders him from the room with a gesture 'worthy of "the Mars"'. That is to say, Mademoiselle Mars, the great French actress of the first half of the nineteenth century, to whose crown Rachel would succeed. This reference brings to a head the opposition in the novel, of immense importance throughout the nineteenth century, between French and English models of theatricality, especially those associated with tragic women. For all the references to Shakespeare here, they are outweighed by those which point across the channel, to Dumas *fils*, Paul de Kock and others.[43] Here 'France' provides Braddon with a world elsewhere to which Lady Audley's unnervingly brilliant, and therefore in the end distinctly un-English, performing skills can be finally consigned. Robert has wanted to see Lady Audley turn into Lady Macbeth for real and go mad in English. She eludes him by going mad in French, where perhaps she has always belonged.

'Canst thou not minister to a mind diseas'd?' Macbeth asks the Doctor (5.3.40). Robert tries this line on Lady Audley, but she bravely snaps back: 'Who said that my mind was diseased?' (II, ch. 11). *Aurora Floyd* (1863) is a complement and antidote to its predecessor. Like Lady Audley, Aurora is 'diseased' by bigamy, but her 'crime' has more extenuating circumstances, and when the first husband reappears she does not, like her predecessor, tip him down a well-shaft. She is altogether more troubled by conscience than Lady Audley, even though the latter looked so unimpeachably English. Aurora carries an aura of foreignness, at once Irish and Mediterranean, with her 'great, brilliant, black eyes, and so much of the south in her beauty' (ch. 4). She is however sufficiently well read in her Shakespeare that when a man she might marry asks her if she needs a doctor, she replies that 'There are diseases that cannot be ministered to' (ch. 8).

There are moments at which Aurora's snaky Medusa locks associate her with Cleopatra, and the 'crime' involved by her first marriage to the rascally groom certainly carries more sexual implications than did Lady Audley's. But the Shakespearean role model by whom Aurora is most threatened is Desdemona. She is a Desdemona who really *has* had an affair with, or, according to the Victorian rules about how such liaisons are acknowledged, been 'married' to Cassio. There is worse to it than this, however, for the Cassio to whom she is sexually linked – her first husband, a groom named James Conyers – also turns out to be Iago. He has competition for this role from Aurora's villainous paid companion, 'the ensign's widow', Mrs Powell, who by rights should be playing Emilia. But this is exactly the trouble and fun with Shakespearean analogues, that they never quite fit, or scarcely fit at all.

Early on Aurora has a passionate admirer in Captain Talbot Raleigh Bulstrode, who compares her to all sorts of alluring women including Nell Gwynne, Lola Montes, Charlotte Corday and Cleopatra. He cannot stand the idea of her having a secret past and refuses to marry her without knowing what the secret is. When he finally breaks with her, he casts her as Desdemona and himself as the honourably deceived Othello: 'this woman whom he loved, so far from wisely, yet fearfully well' (ch. 9). The 'fearfully' is a bit deflating, but Bulstrode is passing on the role to his old friend and schoolmate, a bluff, extrovert Yorkshire squire named John Mellish. Mellish dotingly marries the guilty Desdemona and finds himself saddled with the role of Othello for which, in his thoroughly English way, he is superbly unsuited. One wonders if he knows the play at all, despite having been educated at Rugby School. He knows that his wife has a secret but he refuses to believe that she is 'really' guilty. The narrator is aghast.

> Ah, how weak and imperfect a passion is this boundless love! How ready to sacrifice others for that one loved object, which *must* be kept spotless in our imaginations, though a hecatomb of her fellow-creatures are to be blackened and befouled for her justification! If Othello could have established Desdemona's purity by the sacrifice of the reputation of every lady in Cyprus, do you think he would have spared the fair inhabitants of the friendly isle? No; he would have branded every one of them with infamy, if he could by so doing have rehabilitated the wife he loved. John Mellish *would* not think ill of his wife. (ch.26)

In other words he is a fool, or a mischievous inversion of Shakespeare's jealous husband.

At the crisis of her fortunes, Aurora gazes into the mirror and thinks: 'I look like a woman who could cut her throat in such a crisis as this' (ch. 28). But this is a modern English novel, not a French one. Nor is it a Shakespearean tragedy, for all that it flirts with the likenesses. On the contrary, it is a model for the conversion of *Othello* into contemporary English melodrama. The villains are concentrated together (Mrs Powell,

Conyers and a Caliban figure nicknamed 'the Softy'). Desdemona is given three lovers in an ascending sequence progressively purged of sexuality and danger (the lascivious Conyers, the simmering Bulstrode and the hearty Mellish). It is important to recognize that the key figure in this sequence is Bulstrode, to whom Aurora returns at the crucial point for judgment and forgiveness. The scene is crucial because it requires the old sexual attraction between the two to be kept firmly at bay, otherwise who knows what might happen. But that would be another story – a French one. Braddon is playing all sorts of witty games with old Shakespearean stories and modern French alternatives, and inviting her readers to join her.

We began this chapter with Falstaff, a character who escapes from plot into myth. As the nineteenth century progressed, the old man increasingly seemed to belong to the past. More inspiring for Victorian writers were the Shakespearean women apparently trapped in their plots yet restless with unfulfilled stories, with desire and need for a different future. The comic heroines such as Rosalind and Portia were encouraging models up to a point, but beyond that point there were modern stories that asked to be told about the darker aspects of passion in marriage and family life, for men and women alike. In the next chapter we shall look in some detail at the uses to which both Shakespearean comedy and tragedy were put in the pursuit of such stories by three of the greatest Victorian novelists.

Chapter Four

THREE NOVELISTS:
DICKENS, ELIOT, HARDY

SHAKESPEARE IN MODERN ENGLISH

All three of the novelists to be discussed in this chapter were compared to Shakespeare by their contemporaries. At the outset of his career the author of *The Pickwick Papers* reminded readers of Hogarth, 'except that he takes a far more cheerful view, a Shakespearian view, of humanity', said Mary Russell Mitford (*DCH*, p. 36); at the end of it, Trollope spoke for many when he claimed that 'no other writer of English language except Shakespeare has left so many types of character as Dickens has done' (*DCH*, p. 324); even in disparagement they were yoked together, by the Shaw who scorned their lack of 'philosophy' (Shaw, pp. 213–16). Theodore Martin described the characters in *Adam Bede* as 'Shakespearean in their breadth of sympathy' (*GEL*, III, p. 42), Herbert Spencer hailed their author as 'the female Shakespeare' (*GEL*, v, p. 463), and Alexander Main prefaced his anthology of *Wise, Witty, and Tender Sayings in Prose and Verse Selected from the Works of George Eliot* (Edinburgh, 1872), with the assertion that 'What Shakespeare did for the Drama, George Eliot has been, and still is, doing for the Novel' (p. ix).[1] Hardy's rustics were endlessly compared to Shakespeare's clowns (Joseph Poorgrass was particularly popular), Tess was deemed 'fit to set in the gallery of Shakespeare's women' (*HCH*, p. 234), and Siegfried Sassoon thought her author 'the nearest thing to Shakespeare I should ever go for a walk with'.[2]

'Shakespearean' was the highest term of praise any novelist could attract. Towards the end of the century George Meredith drew frequent comparisons with Shakespeare, especially for his women. W.E. Henley thought the eponymous heroine of *Diana of the Crossways* (1885) like Rosalind, 'pure woman', and George Gissing called the novel 'Shakespeare in modern English'; Meredith had 'drawn more portraits and characters of true women than any other Englishman, but Shakspere and Browning', said Lionel Johnson; and for Robert Louis Stevenson the last interview between Lucy and the title-character in *The Ordeal of Richard Feverel* (1859) was simply 'the strongest scene, since Shakespeare, in the English tongue' (*MCH*, pp. 259, 363, 521, 523). As for women writers, they might hope to be lauded as Shakespeare's younger sister, at least after a decent interval, as Jane Austen was by G.H. Lewes in 1851 (*ACH*, p. 130), and Emily Brontë by Angus Mackay in 1898 (*BCH*, p. 446). The only way of topping this was to be hailed, like George Eliot, as the female Shakespeare herself.

CHARLES DICKENS

If there is a single idea with which Shakespeare is associated for Dickens, both on the stage and on the page, it is that of transformation. This was true for him of the theatre in general, but the theatre and Shakespeare could not be thought of for long without each other. Behind the scenes in 'Private Theatres' (*SB*), he admires the real people who will turn into Lady Macbeth ('she is always selected to play the part, because she is tall and stout, and *looks* a little like Mrs Siddons – at a considerable distance'), and Duncan ('a boy of fourteen who is having his eyebrows smeared with soap and whitening'). If there is a prevailing mode in which Shakespeare figures in Dickens it is playful. This is not the whole truth, as we shall see, but in terms of the sheer quantity of references, quotations and allusions explicit and implicit, Shakespeare provides Dickens and his readers with an indefinite supply of fun and games.[3]

In private Dickens produced for family and friends in 1833 a burlesque of *O'Thello* (the Irish version, with tunes).[4] His letters abound in facetious allusions, as for example when he complains to Macready with help from Jaques that he is getting old and grey: 'My hat a world too wide for my shrunk locks' (*DPL*, p. v, 486). To describe his restlessness on starting a new novel, he confessed to Leigh Hunt that he was 'as infirm of purpose as Macbeth, as errant as Mad Tom, and as rugged as Timon' (*DPL*, VII, p. 608). For his Christmas book *The Chimes* (1844), he borrowed from Falstaff's 'We have heard the chimes at midnight, Master Shallow' (*2H4*, 3.2.215). For his weekly magazine *Household Words* (1850–9), he lifted the title from Henry V's speech before Agincourt (*H5*, 4.3.52), and – after unwisely toying with 'Household Harmony' (from *3H6*, 4.7.14) at a time when it might have attracted comment on the chaos of his private life – he adapted for its successor *All the Year Round* some words from *Othello* ('the story of our lives from year to year' (1.2.130–1)). He took endless pleasure in the associations of Gad's Hill Place, the house near Rochester he bought in 1856 and the only home he ever owned. He wove it into one of his finest non-fiction pieces, 'Travelling Abroad' (1860), where he meets his own younger self looking wistfully, like a young Pip, at the great house his older self will one day – now – occupy.[5] In *Pictures from Italy* he reports from Verona that the House of the Capulets now boasts 'a grim-visaged dog, viciously panting in a doorway, who would certainly have had Romeo by the leg, the moment he put it over the wall' ('By Verona ... into Switzerland'). In the last letter he wrote, on the day of his fatal stroke, as if by the sort of inadvertent premonition he had employed in his own fiction, he quoted Friar Laurence's prediction: 'These violent delights have violent ends' (*DPL*, XII, p. 547).

Whatever it means to know a writer by heart, this was how Dickens knew Shakespeare. Words and phrases and scenes are so deeply rooted in his imagination that there is no telling when they may break the surface of his writing. This raises important questions about control, complicity and recognition that will be one of the main themes of this chapter. It is one thing for writer and reader to share their recognition of an allusion to Shakespeare, but where does this leave the characters who stand as it were between them? Think of those who raise a laugh by the way they mangle immortal verse into mundane prose. Sampson Brass imagines Quilp coming before his eyes 'like the Ghost of Hamlet's father, in the very clothes he wore on work-a-days'

(*OCS*, ch. 49). Mr Micawber praises his father-in-law: 'Take him for all in all, we ne'er shall – in short, make the acquaintance, probably, of anybody else possessing, at his time of life, the same legs for gaiters' (*DC*, ch. 12). Montague Tigg reflects: 'As Hamlet says, Hercules may lay about him with his club in every possible direction, but he cannot prevent the cats from making a most intolerable row on the roofs of the houses, or the dogs from being shot in the hot weather if they run about the streets unmuzzled' (*MC*, ch. 4). These examples are all from *Hamlet*, the great model for such redundancy, digression, not getting on with the plot, being carried away by words, words, words. We enjoy recognizing the Shakespearean source through the obliqueness, inversion or travesty perpetrated by these distorting lenses.

It is different when it is the narrator in charge, brandishing his ingenuity. Think of the 'milk of human kindness' (*Mac*, 1.5.16). It is not just that so many Dickensian characters are devoid of it (unlike Macbeth, who has too much of it, so his wife alleges). There is the false benevolence of Pecksniff, who 'rather looked as if any quantity of butter might have been made out of him, by churning the milk of human kindness, as it spouted upwards from his heart' (*MC*, ch. 3). This is in contrast to the true benevolence of Gabriel Varden, whose jovial humour is 'a sight to turn the vinegar of misanthropy into purest milk of human kindness' (*BR*, ch. 80). It is as if the literary allusion were bound to be churned in the process. There is a certain competitive element in all this. If Dickens is paying homage to Shakespeare, it is not exactly cap-in-hand deference.

In these instances the fictional character is excluded, and the reference shared between writer and reader. There is an important distinction between performers who know themselves to be performing and know that their audience know and want them to know they are both in the know, and those who do not. When Dickens speaks in his own voice to a private correspondent or makes a public speech, it is clearly the former. But when he is narrating a fiction, the allusion to Shakespeare is likely to have a different effect, for it raises the question of how far if at all the fictional character(s) may be party to the knowledge connecting the narrator and reader. Sometimes they cannot possibly hear it, when the allusion is in a chapter heading, for instance, or the descriptive headlines added by Dickens to the 1867 edition, such as the three references to 'Cleopatra' in *Dombey and Son* (chs 30, 40, 41) or to 'The Funeral Baked Meats' in *Martin Chuzzlewit* (ch. 19). There are innumerable instances of allusions of which the character is quite unaware. Miss Tox attracts a memory of Banquo's Ghost (*Mac*, 3.4.93–4) when she is adorned with a locket 'representing a fishy old eye, with no approach to speculation in it' (*DS*, ch. 1). Lady Dedlock comes up from her place in Lincolnshire '[w]ith all her perfections on her head' (*BH*, ch. 2), at once like and unlike the Ghost of Hamlet's father (*Ham*, 1.5.79). Such sly allusions pass over the heads or behind the backs of characters who do not know they are being mocked. Not that we need to feel sorry for them, when they travesty the Shakespearean ideals to which they ludicrously aspire, like Mrs Skewton.

> The Serpent of old Nile (not to mention her disrespectfully) was reposing on her sofa ... and Flowers the Maid was fastening on her youthful cuffs and frills, and performing a kind of private coronation ceremony on her, with a peach-coloured velvet bonnet; the artificial roses in which nodded to uncommon advantage, as the palsy trifled with them, like a breeze. (*DS*, ch. 37)

As so often in Dickens, the mortal thrust is held back till the end – the palsy.

Yet there can also be the sense of a middle ground where character and writer might meet and converse. Think for example of Helena's beautiful speech at the start of *All's Well* about her hopeless love for Bertram: ''twere all one / That I should love a bright particular star / And think to wed it, he is so above me' (*AW*, 1.1.86–8). Compare the absurdity of Miss Tox's forlorn hopes of marrying Mr Dombey, with whose world she now has nothing to do:

> Exacting and harrassing as ever, it goes on without her; and she, a by no means bright or particular star, moves in her little orbit in the corner of another system, and knows it quite well, and comes, and cries, and goes away, and is satisfied. (*DS*, ch. 51)

This is less vindictive an allusion than it might be because 'she knows it quite well' – not the phrase itself but the forlornness it connotes. The poetic allusion touches the character gently, almost ruefully, as if it is a shame that she cannot hear it or voice it herself.

This brings us back to fictional characters who *do* quote or allude, not bunglingly but skilfully and effectively – like their creator. Think of Squeers, railing about Smike: 'What's come of my milk of human kindness? It turns into curds and whey when I look at him!' (*NN*, ch. 38). Or Jenny Wren on her hopeless alcoholic father, Mr Dolls: 'I wish I had never brought him up. He'd be sharper than a serpent's tooth if he wasn't as dull as ditch water' (*OMF*, bk. 3, ch. 10). Perhaps she has heard Lear's famous curse on stage (1.4.280–1). Sam Weller certainly owes to some evenings in the theatre his famous injunction: 'Business first, pleasure arterwards, as King Richard the Third said ven he stabbed t'other king in the Tower, afore he smothered the babbies' (*PP*, ch. 25). When cheerful Tommy Traddles says of his obstinate hair that 'I am quite a fretful porcupine' (*DC*, ch. 41), he may know he is quoting the Ghost in *Hamlet*, but we scarcely pause to ask. We warm to these speakers at such moments (even Squeers), because we recognize a magic circle within which they are enclosed, for the moment: we are all in the same theatre enjoying the same performance – the writer, the reader, the character.

These are glancing, apparently artless allusions, but the case is more complex with people who set themselves up as performers, characters more continuously animated by their self-importance or self-pity, intent on being admired, not least by themselves. Such as Mr Turveydrop, recalling Macbeth: '"For myself, my children," said Mr. Turveydrop, "I am falling into the sear and yellow leaf, and it is impossible to say how long the last feeble traces of gentlemanly Deportment may linger in this weaving and spinning age"' (*BH*, ch. 23). Or the poetical Julia Mills, who keeps a journal for David Copperfield's benefit while his beloved Dora is secluded in mourning. Her entries include arch references to Viola's speech about hopeless love in *Twelfth Night*, to 'Patience on Monument. (Qy. Why on monument? J.M.)', and again: 'Thursday. D. certainly improved. Better night. Slight tinge of damask revisiting cheek' (*DC*, ch. 38). This is clever, and she knows it. So too does Steerforth:

> 'So much for that!' he said, making as if he tossed something light into the air with his hand.
>
> '"Why, being gone, I am a man again",
>
> like Macbeth. And now for dinner! If I have not (Macbeth-like) broken up the feast with most admired disorder, Daisy.' (*DC*, ch. 22)

Is it to Steerforth's credit that he can turn this on and toss it off so lightly? It is not always easy to tell how far a man or a woman may be in love with their own performance, or unable to let it go. Micawber is the great example, the performer who must surely know that he is performing – like Dickens himself.

The relations between Dickensian characters and their Shakespearean sources discussed so far are based on difference. Their main effect is of parody, burlesque, deflation, bathos, the standard idiom of the mock-heroic. In the hands of the narrator and some resourceful characters, Shakespearean allusion is a means of punishing pretension in others and of claiming the authority to do so. It is also a sign of performance – that someone is putting on a show, whether they know it or not. There is a particular role model in Shakespeare for this keen perception that no one is ever quite what he or she seems to be, including yourself: Hamlet. And in this sense Hamlet is the presiding spirit of all Dickens's mockery, as he had been for his eighteenth-century predecessors. But Hamlet is important to Dickens for more reasons than this, as he is to the nineteenth-century novel at large, not only for anglophone writers. He is not just the voice of the jester, the ironist, sceptic and satirist, intent on exposing the folly of others. He also turns his gaze on himself to reflect on who he might be and what he must do, caught as he is in a plot with a mother and more than one father, a crime and all sorts of guilt.

Hamlet and *Hamlet* are essential to the nineteenth-century novel (and beyond), at least from Goethe's *Wilhelm Meister* to Joyce's *Ulysses*.[6]

They provide a supreme model for what it might mean to be a character or to have a character of your own. This is a dream of autonomous selfhood such as the fictional Hamlet seems to achieve by his mythic independence from the play that gives him life. This is not a common feat. The only other Shakespearean character to reach this dizzy height is Falstaff (see pp. 82–9 above), though others such as Romeo and Juliet, Lady Macbeth and Richard of Gloucester may float at lower altitudes. One of the ways in which Dickens challenged comparison with Shakespeare was precisely his creation of characters capable of transcending the stories from which they take their being, especially Pickwick, Micawber, Mrs Gamp, Fagin and Scrooge. In more general terms Dickens was credited with the magical power to dream up a whole 'world' of characters, for which the only term of comparison was Shakespeare (as Figure 16 (p. 76) suggests). But here's the rub, for the storyteller. The incitement of *Hamlet* is that its protagonist's dream of infinite freedom jars endlessly against the circumstances that cabin, crib and confine it. And here it links up with another Shakespearean tragedy directly addressed through its central characters to the dream of transcending time: *Macbeth*. *Hamlet* and *Macbeth* are the two great Shakespearean plays about the murder of kings, about being haunted, about great expectations. They are the two plays of Shakespeare's that run most vividly in Dickens's memory and imagination.

This is often for comical purposes. Dickens is attracted to *Hamlet* and *Macbeth* because they both have ghosts (as *Othello* and *King Lear* do not), and because they both take particular interest in fear, superstition, haunting and cowardice. Dickens is intrigued by the relations between laughter and terror. He likes to make people's hair stand on end, his readers' to be sure, but often 'good' characters' of his own like Traddles or Pancks. The latter sticks his hair up to look 'like a journeyman Hamlet in conversation with his father's spirit' (*LD*, bk 2, ch. 13).

It is possible to think and laugh at the same time, as George Bernard Shaw insisted. There is a wonderful passage in *Nicholas Nickleby* in which Dickens thinks about his dealings with Shakespeare. Mrs Nickleby is recalling a visit to Stratford-upon-Avon, the tomb and the birthplace:

'we went back to the inn there, where we slept that night, and I
recollect that all night long I dreamt of nothing but a black
gentleman, at full length, in plaster-of-Paris, with a lay down
collar tied with two tassels, leaning against a post and thinking;
and when I woke in the morning and described him to
Mr Nickleby, he said it was Shakespeare just as he had been
when he was alive, which was very curious indeed. Stratford –
Stratford, ... I recollect I was in the family way with my son
Nicholas at the time, and I had been very much frightened by an
Italian image boy that very morning. In fact, it was quite a
mercy, ma'am, ... that my son didn't turn out to be a
Shakespeare, and what a dreadful thing that would have been!'
(*NN*, ch. 27)

Mrs Nickleby entertains a comic superstition about causes and
consequences under which a lot of Dickensian characters labour,
namely the belief that juxtaposition must mean connexion. Real people
in their habits as they live have been known to suffer from it. If you just
put one thing after another – one word, one sentence, one incident –
then surely they *must* be connected by an idea, a conception, a plot.
Just keep talking, just keep writing! This can often seem like the
desperate ambition of a Dickens novel itself, and indeed the charge he
incurred from censorious readers was that he merely piled one thing on
top of another and hoped they would add up. Think of those far-fetched
plots of which no one can recall all the details. Dickens is not the only
Victorian writer to incur such a charge – Henry James famously called
Middlemarch 'a treasure-house of details, but ... an indifferent whole'[7] –
and we shall return to this issue in chapter six. The anxiety about
Dickens's multitudinous detail is the corollary to the admiration he
arouses for the 'whole world' he creates, so full, so fertile, so peopled,
so Shakespeare. But *is* Dickens's world like Shakespeare's, where there
turn out to be deep connexions at once ethical and aesthetic? Or is it,
as Stephen Blackpool fears in *Hard Times* ''aw a muddle'? There are
certainly times at which the reader is tempted to exclaim, with Mr Toodle
the train-driver in *Dombey and Son*, 'What a Junction a man's thoughts

is ... to be sure!' (*DS*, ch. 38). But perhaps Dickens is no less alert than his readers to the nature of conjunctions. Dickens might turn out to be like Shakespeare after all, by virtue of creating characters like Mrs Nickleby, who reflects so shrewdly if inadvertently on the artistic problems her creator is facing.

Nicholas is one of several main characters in Dickens whose situation bears a resemblance to Hamlet's. He has a villainous uncle, he is deprived of his inheritance, he must somehow avenge his dead father, he spends time with a troupe of travelling players. He listens to the absurd Mr and Mrs Curdle lament the decline of the theatre, whose mark is the absence of anyone to present 'all those changing and prismatic colours with which the character of Hamlet is invested'; they agree that 'Hamlet is gone, perfectly gone' (*NN*, ch. 24). Nicholas does not challenge their verdict, and instead plays Romeo. There are other sons later in Dickens's career more heavily laden with allusions to Hamlet, notably the first-person narrators of the novels that most obviously qualify as *Bildungsromane* or 'education novels', *David Copperfield* and *Great Expectations*. Here there are particular verbal allusions, to the bourne from which no traveller returns, to conscience making cowards of us all, to a special providence. In the later novel Mr Wopsle gives a memorable performance of Hamlet which Pip and Herbert Pocket are kind enough to acclaim as 'massive and concrete' (*GE*, ch. 31). Prominent features of the shadowy continuing parallels with Shakespeare's play include graveyards, ghosts and guilt. But the case for hearing the resemblances to *Hamlet* as a paradigm against which these fictions are to be measured is concentrated in the novels' emphasis on a son who has been bereaved of his father and must in some way avenge that loss and make reparation for it.

Hamlet lies behind many of the sons in nineteenth-century novels who seek to claim their inheritance, a character they can call their own and a place in the world in which they can house it. But if they are not to end up like Hamlet, they will need someone with whom to share it. This is the story so violently thwarted in Shakespeare's play, to which Gertrude's sad little lament for Ophelia points: 'I hop'd thou shouldst have been my Hamlet's wife: / I thought thy bride-bed to have deck'd,

sweet maid, / And not have strew'd thy grave' (Ham, 5.1.242–4). What
of the daughter's role in the novel, if she is not to be an Ophelia or a
Juliet, destroyed by the men in her life? Their stories can be rewritten,
as Hamlet's can be. They can defy their parents and the world, and
survive, and their sisters in comedy can eagerly support them. But for
Dickens and his readers, there is another strong model in Shakespeare
for the relations between fathers and daughters which complements
Hamlet's for fathers and sons: King Lear.[8]

Readers of Dickens have often been put in mind of Lear and his
favourite daughter. Dickens boasted to Forster that Francis Lord Jeffrey
was reported to be driving round Edinburgh telling people there had
been 'nothing so good as Nell since Cordelia' (DPL, II, 238). The Old
Curiosity Shop (1840–1) was only one of a number of novels featuring
daughters devoted to their fathers (or in Nell's case, grandfather),
including Madeline Bray in Nicholas Nickleby, Florence Dombey in
Dombey and Son, Agnes Wickfield in David Copperfield, the eponymous
Little Dorrit, and Lucy Manette in A Tale of Two Cities. A number of
critics have made large claims for the significance of King Lear to
Dickens's imagination, and indeed to the earlier Victorians at large.[9]
Valerie Gager points out that the number of verbal allusions to the play
in Dickens's work does not seem to support these claims. She also
suggests the significance to Dickens of other plays in which the
relations between fathers and daughters are prominent, including
Sheridan Knowles's popular Virginius and the dramatic adaptation of
Mrs Opie's novel Father and Daughter (1801), known as The Lear of
Private Life (1820), as well as Shakespeare's own late plays, especially
The Winter's Tale (Gager, pp. 11–16).[10] But influence need not be
measured solely in verbal terms. Theatre and the visual arts were no
less potent means for impressing Shakespearean figures, scenes and
relationships, amongst which the images of Lear and Cordelia ranked
high, from James Barry's exhibition of King Lear Weeping over the Body of
Cordelia at the Boydell Gallery in 1789 to the widely disseminated
illustrations of Henry Irving's Lyceum production just over a century
later. John Harvey writes of the development of a cult and a myth,
centred on Cordelia, about the power of a woman's love to save a

man.[11] This is a story none the less powerful for its climactic embodiment in the image of the daughter dead in her father's arms, an ultimate sacrifice and redemption, though one not undisturbed by sexual overtones.

Modern readers are not the only ones who may be troubled by the Little Nells and Dorrits. Thackeray was thinking of more than this cult of female devotion when he told a correspondent in 1847 that Dickens did not like him: 'He knows that my books are a protest against his – that if one set are true, the other must be false.'[12] But the protest included a hostility to his ideal women. Nevertheless, there are several points to make in justification of the uses to which Dickens puts his Cordelia figures. One is that in *Little Dorrit* the narrative models derived from *Hamlet* and from *King Lear* are juxtaposed to very purposive effect. The *Lear* model sponsors the story of the patriarch and his selfless daughter, save that it reverses their story by beginning in prison and then liberating them to wander the world at leisure, in luxury. Meanwhile Arthur Clennam labours under the sign of *Hamlet*, save that he is oppressed not by a villainous pseudo-father like Ralph Nickleby or Murdstone, but by the false mother. It is this turn of the *Hamlet* plot towards the mother that provides the link with Cordelia, the daughter who has to mother her father. When each is freed from their particular parental tyranny, Clennam from his mother, Amy from her father, they may as it were be ready for each other.

Another point to make is that not all the daughters in Dickens are as endlessly compliant as Little Dorrit. In this they begin to mirror more closely the full version of Cordelia represented by Shakespeare's play, that is to say, the image of a daughter who defies her father and leaves him for another man, before returning to give and receive forgiveness. There are plenty of angry young women in Dickens, including the Jenny Wren who tries to mother her hopeless father Mr Dolls in *Our Mutual Friend*. Louisa Gradgrind is particularly important in that she is a Cordelia who comes very close to turning into one of her bad sisters. She is on the brink of running off with Harthouse, but instead comes back to confront her father and curse the hour in which she was born, before collapsing at his feet. By the end of *Hard Times* he is a broken man to whom she can play the forgiving Cordelia, thus bringing together the two aspects of the role – the rebellion and the reparation – which in Dickens are more usually divided between different characters.

There is another figure in *King Lear* no less important to Dickens's imagination than Lear and Cordelia and the dream of their reunion. Poor Tom is a figure for the 'houseless poverty' to which the disintegrating King becomes alive for the first time, and he represented for Dickens a powerful image of destitution, exposure and abandonment. Dickens was deeply attracted to the word 'houseless', and it helped to inspire one of his most memorable pieces of non-fiction, the essay entitled 'Night Walks' (1860).[13] The word recurs at moments when Dickens is contemplating the darkest side of the modern world, the one into which he might himself have fallen as a youth, as Oliver Twist and Little Nell do and Florence Dombey and David Copperfield could; the one out of which Jo and the inhabitants of Tom-All-Alone's in *Bleak House* will never manage to struggle. It is the abyss out of which loom the maimed and murderous doubles who haunt so many of the novels' primary characters, as Smike haunts Nicholas Nickleby, as Jo haunts Esther Summerson, as Orlick haunts Pip. They are the Poor Toms who never manage to recover or find the Edgar they might have been, nor the Cordelia with whom they might, in the blithest of endings, have been united.

Listen to this. A spectral man whose name we do not know wanders through the city streets by night 'with no more fixedness of purpose than to lose himself among their windings'. The narrator takes up the theme:

> To be shelterless and alone in the open country, hearing the wind moan and watching for day through the whole long weary night; to listen to the falling rain, and crouch for warmth beneath the lee of some old barn or rick, or in the hollow of a tree; are dismal things – but not so dismal as the wandering up and down where shelter is, and beds and sleepers are by thousands; a houseless rejected creature. To pace the echoing stones from hour to hour, counting the dull chimes of the clocks;

to watch the lights twinkling in chamber windows, to think what happy forgetfulness each house shuts in; that here are children coiled together in their beds, here youth, here age, here poverty, here wealth, all equal in their sleep, and all at rest; to have nothing in common with the slumbering world around, not even sleep, Heaven's gift to all its creatures, and be akin to nothing but despair; to feel, by the wretched contrast with everything on every hand, more utterly alone and cast away than in a trackless desert; this is a kind of suffering, on which the rivers of great cities close full many a time, and which the solitude in crowds alone awakens. (*BR*, ch. 18)

We can hear little verbal echoes of *King Lear* in this: the 'houseless rejected creature', the 'hollow of a tree' such as Edgar hides in. But the deep affinity is with the contrast between the housed and the houseless, and the obliviousness of the former to the latter. As we take the force of this further contrast between sweet forgetful sleep and waking nightmare, we may think of other Shakespearean kings who meditate in the dark, such as Henry IV and his son Henry V. Above all of Macbeth, who has murdered sleep.

Hamlet is certainly of huge and diffuse importance to Dickens, as to many other Victorian novelists, most notably as a prototype for the young person looking before and after to find a place in the world. For Dickens there was part of *King Lear* that could seem to complement this story, the part that sang of a woman's redemptive love. But there was always a shadow side to the good story and its happy ending, which the bleakest aspect of *King Lear* haunted and the horrors of *Macbeth* reinforced, a vision for which, as the novels darken from *Dombey and Son* onwards to the unfinished *Edwin Drood*, the word damnation seems increasingly appropriate.

GEORGE ELIOT

In the Forest of Arden the climate is not as lethal as it is on Lear's heath or in Dickens's London. There is winter and rough weather, but there is also the greenwood tree for shelter, there are friends, strangers and animals for company, distraction and food. And there is the leisure to moralize, as Duke Senior does, thus.

> Sweet are the uses of adversity
> Which like the toad, ugly and venomous,
> Wears yet a precious jewel in his head;
> And this our life, exempt from public haunt,
> Finds tongues in trees, books in the running brooks,
> Sermons in stones, and good in everything.
>
> (*AYL*, 2.1.12–17)

Reflecting on the courtiers' fall from grace, the Duke sounds less like King Lear confronting the image of unaccommodated man than like Edgar trying to make the best of things.

Dickens was fond of Duke Senior's lines. He was especially attracted to their closing admonition to find tongues in trees, books in brooks, sermons in stones and – a thought only slightly relieved of its banality by the relief from alliteration – good in everything (Gager, pp. 267–8). He used them to praise David Wilkie on the painter's death in 1841, and to inaugurate *Household Words* in 1850. The only occasion on which he specifically refers to the 'uses of adversity' is in *Little Dorrit*, when 'the whirling wheel of life' sees Arthur Clennam imprisoned in the Marshalsea and brought to the marked stop which brings 'the right perception with it': 'It comes with sickness, it comes with sorrow, it comes with the loss of the dearly beloved, it is one of the most frequent uses of adversity' (bk 2, ch. 27). But the idea of 'adversity' is of immense importance to Dickens, especially in this novel, as it is to Victorian ethical thinking in general. In *The Tempest* Trinculo expresses the down-and-out Beckettian thought, always good for a laugh, that 'misery acquaints a man with strange bed-fellows' (2.2.38–9). One of the chapter headings of *The Pickwick Papers* revises this to the less abject thought that it is 'adversity brings a man acquainted with strange bed-fellows' (ch. 41).

As You Like It is a play in the forefront of George Eliot's dealings with Shakespeare. Quotations from it feature more frequently in her letters

than from any other, particularly in the decade or so from 1839 to
1850. In the earliest example, the evangelical Marian Evans comforts a
sick friend with thoughts of the special blessings to be derived from the
endurance of suffering: 'I set so high a value on "the sweet uses of
adversity" that I am in danger of failing in sympathy for those who are
experiencing it' (GEL, I, pp. 15–16). In lighter vein she thanks friends
for making her laugh like Jaques so that 'my lungs did crow like
Chanticleer' (GEL, I, p. 266), compares her feelings about life at Geneva
with Touchstone's about the country (GEL, I, p. 324), and shares
holidays with G.H. Lewes that seemed to him, and one hopes her too,
to help 'fleet the time carelessly as in the golden age' (GEL, II, p. 331).
Most importantly for her own fiction, she invokes Rosalind as one of
Shakespeare's great examples of passionate women who can take the
initiative, along with Juliet, Desdemona and Portia.[14]

Another suggestive reference to the play comes in a letter of 1840.
Here she is complaining about the claustrophobia of family life: it seems
to her 'a *walled-in* world'. She yearns to have 'the wind of heaven blow
on one ..., to feel one's "heart leap up" after the pressure that
Shakspeare so admirably describes, "When a man's wit is not seconded
by the forward child understanding it strikes a man as dead as a large
reckoning in a small room"'.[15] A quarter of a century later she wrote a
grim poem about the view from a London drawing-room, of the cabs
and carriages hurrying by, 'All closed, in multiplied identity. / The world
seems one huge prison-house.'[16]

Some interesting contradictions in Marian Evans peep out of the
early informal references to Shakespeare's romantic comedy, and they
point to important issues in her subsequent writings. She identifies with
the Duke's advice about patience and the uses of adversity, but she also
seizes on the resourcefulness of the forward Rosalind and the witty
Touchstone to express her impatience with walls and small unpoetical
rooms. The single expression that means most to her from *As You Like It*
comes from Rosalind's exclamation 'O how full of briers is this working-
day world!' (1.3.11–12). When it comes to her own fiction she will
speak up for the virtues of the working-day world, as for the uses of
adversity, but its pains can prove far sharper than 'briers'. In *Adam Bede*

we hear the phrase 'no holiday-time in the working-day world', which out of context might be a rebuke to the world of leisure and its occupants, like the spoilt young country squire, Arthur Donnithorne, who seduces Hetty Sorrel. But in fact it is a sad reflection on the limits to which Adam's world has shrunk in his grief for Hetty and their paradise lost: 'now there was no margin of dreams for him beyond this daylight reality, no holiday-time in the working-day world' (*AB*, ch. 50). Duke Senior shows how easy it is to make 'adversity' sound more poetical than it really is, just as the Forest of Arden seems quite romantic to be begin with: most holiday venues do. But supposing adversity were a permanent condition with no margin of dreams, and the working-day world were a walled-in world you could not escape from? Then a poetical name like the Forest of Arden will not save you from ruin and despair, any more than the 'fine old woods' in the Introduction to *Felix Holt* really protect 'the park and mansion which they shut in from the working-day world'.

This points to George Eliot's double-edged feelings about Shakespeare, and indeed all authority, literary and otherwise.[17] Like Hazlitt before her, she is divided between admiration and suspicion. She admires and seeks to emulate Shakespeare's capacity for strong imaginative sympathy with the good, the bad and the indifferent up and down the social scale. Marianne Novy has written well about the political significance of 'sympathy' to the nineteenth century's understanding of Shakespeare, especially in its relation to George Eliot and other women writers.[18] But Eliot rejects any idea that Shakespeare's plays and poems are impartial in their representation of history and romantic love. They are tendentious (as all writing is bound to be), or more accurately, they are fissured by contrary tendencies (as only the best imaginative writing can be). They flatter the forms taken by power at the time when they were first written, in courts and families, on battlefields, in woods and in bedrooms. At the same time, in variable measure they test and contest them, questioning, deriding, imagining otherwise. It is precisely the unresolved conflict between these voices and visions in Shakespeare that invites subsequent writers to perpetuate them, with a difference: that is, to rewrite them. Borrowing from George Eliot, we can call it

Shakespeare's 'iridescence'. This is the fine word she applies to Gwendolen Harleth to describe in her 'the play of various, nay, contrary tendencies' (*DD*, ch. 4). In the next sentence she thinks of Macbeth.

George Eliot argues with Shakespeare – which is to say both 'by means of' and 'in opposition to'. She calls attention to the points at which her own plot-lines, story patterns, dramatic figures and predicaments converge with his, then asks the reader to reflect on the likeness and difference between them. She makes pointed use of *Coriolanus* in *Felix Holt*, and widespread reference to *Hamlet*, most generously in her representation of Daniel Deronda's sympathetic and hesitating nature.[19] She is, however, particularly concerned with the possible resemblances between her women and Shakespeare's, and in this sense she aligns herself with the tradition of women's rewriting of Shakespeare associated with Mary Lamb, Anna Jameson and Mary Cowden Clarke.[20] In 'Mr Gilfil's Love Story' the narrator compares the passionate heroine Caterina to 'Helen, and Dido, and Desdemona, and Juliet' (*SCL*, ch. 4). The tone here is nervous and uncertain, as it is when she tries to deal with poor Hetty Sorrel in *Adam Bede*, the tragic castaway whose 'rounded, pouting, childish prettiness' is impossibly associated with 'that wondrous Medusa-face, with the passionate, passionless lips' (ch. 37; the reference is to a sculpture known as the Rondanini Medusa, in Munich). The suicidal Ophelia is one of the models hovering round Hetty as she trudges towards Stratford-upon-Avon, but in *The Mill on the Floss* Maggie Tulliver's whole story can be understood as a rewriting of Ophelia's. Before she comes to her watery end, Maggie triumphantly wrests attention away from all the men in whose shade she is cast by Shakespeare's play. The title-character of *Romola* can also be thought of as a daughter who escapes the Shakespearean plot in which she might have been trapped. She refuses to play Cordelia to her father's King Lear or Miranda to his Prospero. In *Felix Holt* the portrayal of Mrs Transome draws deeply on the women of Shakespeare's history plays who stand forlornly on the sidelines waiting for bad news.

Eliot's novels give increasingly purposive attention to the figures subordinated by the Shakespearean history plays, and unnoticed in the tales told by official history. The stories she tells of Dorothea Brooke and Gwendolen Harleth bring this interest to a climax. In Dorothea's case there is a subdued association with the heroine of *Measure for Measure*, the Isabella whom Anna Jameson had compared to Saint Theresa.[21] Eliot treasured the Duke's exhortation to Angelo, that 'Spirits are not finely touch'd / But to fine issues' (*MM*, 1.1.35–6). She allows Felix Holt to adopt it for a speech he makes to Esther Lyon about the power for good that her beauty might do if it endured 'a good strong terrible vision' – 'such fine issues ... may come where a woman's spirit is finely touched' (*FH*, ch. 27). After Casaubon's death, she describes Dorothea's desire for Will Ladislaw, and reflects that 'Life would be no better than candle-light tinsel and daylight rubbish if our spirits were not touched by what has been, to issues of longing and constancy' (*M*, ch. 54). But it is the novel's sobering final paragraph that makes explicit Dorothea's identification with the heroine of Shakespeare's most generically disturbed comedy: 'Her finely-touched spirit had still its fine issues, though they were not widely visible' ('Finale').

 Daniel Deronda calls up a great range of Shakespearean models and allusions, to which in some cases the characters themselves are party, most obviously in the *tableau vivant* scene from *The Winter's Tale* and the roving archery outing which the guests think of as 'an extemporised "As you like it"' (ch. 14). Gwendolen Harleth here plays Rosalind as she has previously played Hermione. The particular role does not much matter to Gwendolen as long as she is the star. In both cases she promptly gets a shock, as if she were being punished for her role-playing. In the *tableau vivant* scene a mysterious panel in the wall flies open, petrifying her at just the moment when the statue she is playing is supposed to come to life. In the Arden pastiche she is suddenly confronted at the Whispering Stones by the woman with a prior claim to the man she is going to marry: 'it was as if some ghastly vision had come to her in a dream and said, "I am a woman's life"' (ch. 14). These are both versions of the good strong terrible vision that Felix imagined young Esther needed, but they do not save Gwendolen, or not yet. The epigraph to chapter thirty-one heralds her fatal marriage to Grandcourt with Camillo's lines from *The Winter's Tale*, predicting for her a more terrible voyage into the unknown than they did for the young lovers, Perdita and Florizel: 'a wild dedication of yourselves / To unpath'd waters, undream'd shores' (*WT*, 4.5.568–9).

In this her last novel Shakespearean romance has a very different role from the one it had played earlier in Eliot's writing. The most clear-cut instance of her deployment of a Shakespearean model is *Silas Marner*. This effectively takes over the core narrative of *The Winter's Tale* and rewrites it to balance the nurturing foster-father (Silas Marner, the shepherd) against the guilty natural father (Godfrey Cass, Leontes). It sets against each other the child and the gold which in Shakespeare the shepherd (and clown) find together. Silas loses the gold and finds the child; Godfrey is a Leontes who repents too late and fails to recover his daughter. As for the play's debate about the relative power of nature and nurture, the sixteen years that pass at the centre of the tale go to prove the power of nurture, so that when Godfrey asserts the claims of blood, his daughter Eppie stays loyal to the humble life she knows and the persons she has grown to love. The climax inverts not only its Shakespearean model but also the Judgment of Solomon, in that it is the child herself who chooses between the two parents.[22] There is none of that nonsense in Shakespearean romance about privileged genes, and no royal lover to tempt the abandoned child. Several of Eliot's letters refer approvingly to the 'art which does mend nature', most notably when she clarifies her views on women's place in 'zoological' and 'moral' evolution (*GEL*, IV, p. 364, text amended in VIII, p. 402).

Silas Marner expects the reader to recognize its ironic relation to *The Winter's Tale* even though it makes no single explicit allusion to it. It is a different matter with the two hundred and twenty-five chapter epigraphs, or mottoes as Eliot preferred to call them, with which her last three novels are supplied.[23] Of these, ninety-six appear to have been composed by the author herself; the remainder are from named authors, of whom Shakespeare provides by far the most (thirty-one). His nearest rival is Wordsworth (nine), whose consolation it is to have supplied the title mottoes to *Adam Bede* and *Silas Marner*. It is important that they are not in the main famous, high-profile lines or passages, but quirky, out-of-the way observations – as befits the kind of lives and their 'unhistoric acts' in which Eliot is interested.

These chapter mottoes occupy a privileged position. They are distinguished from the main body of the text by being inset and in smaller type. They can seem to carry oracular force (especially when they are anonymous), predicting the moral, emotional or psychological import of the chapter they herald. Or they can be thought of as speaking with a kind of 'choric' voice analogous to the choral songs that punctuate the dramatic action in Greek tragedy. As those once sought to provide explanations drawn from myth, traditional wisdom and folk memory, so the modern storyteller dips into the whole vast treasure-house of Western thought and writing (including Greek tragedy). The fragments that Eliot comes up with seem often enough clear in their application. When the narrator alters the pronouns in Canterbury's speech about the transformation in the young King Henry V (*H5*, 1.1.28–31), we have little difficulty in recognizing its application to Esther Lyon and her development: 'Consideration like an angel came / And whipped the offending Adam out of her' (*FH*, ch. 26; *H5*, 1.1.28–9). Two lines from sonnet 34 (11–12) herald the scene in which young Fred Vincy comes face to face with the real effects of his reckless actions on the Garth family who must bear his debts: 'The offender's sorrow brings but small relief / To him who wears the strong offence's cross' (*M*, ch. 24). Hero's acerbic comments about the pleasure Beatrice takes in her own wit reflect directly on Gwendolen Harleth (*DD*, ch. 5; *MA*, 3.1.52–4), whereas Cleopatra's confession that 'My desolation does begin to make / A better life' predicts her later chastening (ch. 53; *AC*, 5.2.1–2).

Yet if we think of these mottoes as a way for the author to give directions to the reader over the heads of her characters, then they often seem oblique, masked and mysterious. It is not at all clear why this passage from *Troilus and Cressida* is used to head a chapter in *Middlemarch*: 'He beats me and I rail at him: O worthy satisfaction! Would it were otherwise – that I could beat him while he railed at me' (*M*, ch. 26). What happens in the following chapter is that the Vincys call in Lydgate to treat their son Fred's typhoid fever, thus arousing the enmity of the ousted local doctor, Mr Wrench. Is the thought from Shakespeare that beneath the skin of civility the Wrenches and Vincys of provincial life swiftly revert to the bullying brutality of which Thersites speaks? To take another instance: how exactly do the two quotations which head a crucial passage between Esther Lyon and Felix Holt shed light on their developing relationship (*FH*, ch. 27)? We are offered the closing line from sonnet 23 ('To hear with eyes is part of love's rare wit'), and part of the speech in which Coriolanus protests against the power of 'custom' to heap up 'mountainous error' (*Cor*, 2.3.116–20). Does the one about love apply to Esther and the one about politics to Felix? Or is it the other way round, that the man has something urgent to learn about loving and listening, and the woman something about asking more questions of herself and the world around her? Or again: why is a critical meeting in Genoa between Daniel Deronda and 'his oldest friend' Sir Hugo Mallinger (*DD*, ch. 59) prefaced by lines from *Richard II* in which Bolingbroke, who has returned from exile to claim his rightful inheritance and will go on to seize the crown, greets young Harry Percy (Hotspur): 'I count myself in nothing else so happy / As in a soul remembering my good friends' (*R2*, 2.3.46–7)? Is the point of the Shakespearean reference to show just how bad such good friends will prove to be when their alliance explodes into civil war (in *1 Henry IV*), and thereby to reflect ominously on the deep concealed rift in the novel between Daniel and Sir Hugo?

The effect of these mottoes can be distinctly elusive. A particularly good example can be found in some words of Cardinal Wolsey that are selected to introduce the chapter that lies at the very centre of *Middlemarch*, the last chapter of book 4. In the scene from *Henry VIII* from which they are taken, Wolsey, as his enemies, led by the Earl of Surrey, close in for the kill, says, 'How much methinks, I could despise this man, / But that I am bound in charity against it' (3.2.297–8). It is the kind of thought that made a deep appeal to George Eliot's moral imagination: the collision between the impulse to 'despise' and the demands of 'charity'. Uprooted and replanted in *Middlemarch*, the Cardinal's words hold this powerful thought in suspense. To whom in the novel do they apply? As we read our way through the chapter, we think at first that they refer to Casaubon's hostility towards Ladislaw. But as we go on we come to Lydgate's amused contempt for Casaubon's futile scholarship, and finally to Dorothea's raging scorn for her husband's frigidity. The chapter puts various kinds of despite on show, and asks some questions about the charity that could or should restrain them. In Shakespeare it is hard to know how much weight there is to the Cardinal's reference to charity, but the novel takes it very seriously indeed. Transferred to Dorothea, it expresses the conflict in her between the impulse to unleash the violence she feels towards Casaubon and the impulse to restrain it. What is more, we may wonder if the Cardinal's words do not contain a challenge to the writer herself. For she too suffers from divided feelings, not only towards Casaubon. Many of Eliot's fictional creatures arouse in their author these double impulses to despite and to charity. So too do the writers and artists with whom she engages, including the Shakespeare who has furnished this motto. The novel delves deep into the moral and psychological complexity of the Cardinal's momentary spasm.

George Eliot was not above feeling despite for some aspects of Shakespeare's sonnets. They played a significant role in her thinking about *Middlemarch*. Entries in one of the notebooks she kept in preparation for the novel show her interest in both Shakespeare's and Drayton's sonnets,[24] and they were eventually to supply mottoes to chapters twenty-four, fifty-eight and eighty-two. Eliot takes a particularly quizzical interest in the poet's fluctuating sense of his own powers; she lists several sonnets under 'Confidence in his poetic immortality' and notes the way it ebbs and returns. She is repelled by the poet's capacity for self-abasement, finding some of the sonnets 'painfully abject ... language which might be taken to describe the miserable slavery of oppressed wives'. The early sequence urging the young man to leave posterity she finds simply 'wearisome'. The weariness emerges in a passage in *Middlemarch* where Casaubon reflects on what he expects to get out of marriage with Dorothea, namely

[to] receive family pleasures and leave behind him that copy of himself which seemed so urgently required of a man – to the

sonneteers of the sixteenth century. Times had altered since then,
and no sonneteer had insisted on Mr. Casaubon's leaving a copy
of himself; moreover, he had not yet succeeded in issuing copies
of his mythological key. (*M*, ch. 29)

This is a double strike at the man's sterility, perfection neither of the life
nor the work, nor anything approaching it. George Eliot concluded
with some asperity that there are 'hardly thirty sonnets out of the 150
that can be called fine, with the utmost liberality'. Most of them were
artificial creations, no more distinguished than those of his contemporaries. Why should we think of Shakespeare as always exceptional?
But this was not her last word on them. Two years later, a more
merciful and musical impulse prompted the confession that she loved
the sonnets better and better, for their 'tunes'.

This hesitation is exemplary of the arguments Eliot has with
Shakespeare, and with herself about Shakespeare, especially where
love, marriage and tragedy are concerned. She is both attracted and
repelled by the power of romantic love. She knows its power to abase
and even debase, but she also knows how hard it can be to resist its
allure, even for a progressive spirit like Will Ladislaw who would agree
with the narrator that for modern lovers 'it is preferable to have fewer
sonnets and more conversation' (*M*, ch. 37). Shakespeare does in fact
write a sonnet that is a conversation. It is the one he gives to Romeo
and Juliet when they first meet, which they seem miraculously to make
up together (*RJ*, 1.5.93–106). Dorothea and Casaubon will never do
this.

There is the matter of tragedy in the marriage between Dorothea and
Casaubon (as there is in that between Gwendolen and Grandcourt).
The epigraphs that brood over the novel's action often have a double
effect on our sense of the characters' stature, at once aggrandizing and
stealthily undermining. But there are many different kinds of tempo at
work in Eliot's mature writing, and she can get an extraordinary effect
from the sheer speed of an allusion, its 'flash'. Here is a good example
from the scene in the library at Lowick when Casaubon makes a vicious
remark about a possible visit from Ladislaw. He speaks of 'guests whose

desultory vivacity makes their presence a fatigue'. Dorothea instantly ignites, startling him with 'the flash of her eyes'. Her fire prompts the narrator to reach for *Macbeth*, to indicate the pity this wife does *not* feel for her husband: 'Pity, that "new-born babe" which was by-and-by to rule many a storm within her, did not "stride the blast" on this occasion' (*M*, ch. 29). Dorothea comes out of this allusion rather well, getting double credit both for the storm with which it associates her – Casaubon is doing her (and Will) a mean injustice and he deserves to be blasted – and also for the pity we are assured will by-and-by master it. But *Macbeth* is a dangerous play to get mixed up in. The complex psychology of pity features largely in the narrator's thoughts about the marriage between Dorothea and Casaubon. The most pitiful thing about Casaubon is that he shrinks from pity as from a force striding the blast that would expose his nakedness. But there is also an undercurrent of thought about what children and childlessness mean to this couple. The effect of invoking Macbeth's 'new-born babe' is to flash a sudden light on the murderous intensity of Dorothea's reaction. Out of her union with this man, no good will come to birth. Half an hour later Casaubon has an attack and collapses.

Such allusions in the body of the narrative carry a living intensity that is quite different from the monumental force of the chapter epigraphs. On one hand the allusion itself can be precipitate, glancing, uninsistent, as it is in this case when it is here and gone. At the same time the human conditions which these flashes illuminate can be interminably protracted. So many people never escape from their walled-in worlds. Narrative can do justice to the intensity *and* the protractedness as drama cannot. Here one should think in George Eliot's fiction not only of Maggie Tulliver, Dorothea Brooke and Gwendolen Harleth, but also of the great tragic figure in *Felix Holt* who endures in endless misery, Mrs Transome.

Shortly after Eliot's death in 1880 there appeared a long unsigned article by Peter Bayne in the magazine with which the novelist had been so closely associated, *Blackwood's*.[25] Bayne takes the comparison between Shakespeare and George Eliot very seriously. He accepts the widespread notion that if Shakespeare had lived in the Victorian age he would have written novels. 'The dramatist must put into an hour what the novelist spreads out into a volume' (p. 524), but Shakespeare's plays are uniquely concentrated with novelistic suggestion, such as tempts one sometimes 'to wish that he *had* written them out as novels' (p. 525). We can be grateful instead for the novelist best equipped to do so. We can imagine her 'tracking' and 'tracing' the spiritual history behind the words of Macbeth and Claudius, as she has behind her own Bulstrode and Tito Melema. Better still, we can imagine her exploring the inner life of the Helena in *All's Well* who loves with passion a man who does not deserve her. But Bayne's thoughts also turn to the great points of contrast between the Elizabethan dramatists and the Victorian novelist, above all the difference between the 'age of faith' that produced one and 'the age of scepticism' that has produced the other (p. 529). 'Reading George Eliot exclusively, we are apt to think too meanly of our kind, to figure man as a mere drift-log of circumstance', he concludes, whereas Shakespeare restores our faith in ourselves, the conviction 'that it is not in our stars, but in ourselves, if we are underlings' (p. 537). This is a bit risky, to invoke the authority of the conspiring and murderous Cassius in support of 'faith', and Bayne swiftly moves to safer ground with 'Shakespeare's worthy characters, from Henry V. to Fluellen', who all have 'an ingrained impression of religion' (p. 537). This is safer, but feebler.

Bayne has difficulty in controlling the comparison between the two writers because he wants to believe that Shakespeare represents with impartiality universal truths about human nature, whereas he sees even the finest writer of her age as bound by her volatile times. Eliot puts too much faith in science, he contends, and she is prejudiced in favour of women: 'The mystery of feminine malignity is barely touched upon' (p. 533). George Eliot would not have accepted this judgment. Much as she admired Shakespeare, she did not believe that he and his works stood outside history. For her there were other great dramatists in fifth-century Athens and other great visionary writers such as Dante; there were other faiths; and there were always more truths to experience than any art could capture, however 'great'. On this bank and shoal of time Shakespeare was not the be-all and end-all.

THOMAS HARDY

Hardy read Bayne's article and copied some extracts into a notebook, including the following:

> Spiritual Belief.
> 'There is no reason to believe that the state of half-belief in which we now exist will be permanent. Men will again, as in former ages, believe more than we, or they will push on to something like finality, & believe still less than we.'

Hardy's comment was 'bosh'.[26]

Some ten years before, his fourth published novel had reminded reviewers of George Eliot. But the author of *Middlemarch* had not gone on to write *Far from the Madding Crowd*, and Hardy was always quick to play down the connexions between them. This was partly a question of territorial rights. Hardy later claimed that Eliot had never touched 'the life of the fields', but their writing clearly did touch each other's on the margins where the life of the fields was being transformed by new roads, railways, telegraph wires, suburban development, money and education. There were some old stories they both retold, such as the one about the seduced country girl: Fanny Robin (*FMC*) and Tess Durbeyfield (*TD*) are aggressive rewritings of Hetty Sorrel, amongst others. They were both deeply engaged with 'the state of half-belief', not only in religious and spiritual matters. In some aspects Hardy can seem like the sympathetic younger brother George Eliot never had, angrier about the ways things are and gloomier about the way they are going.

But there were other women novelists to whom Hardy was affiliated. So at least it seemed to Havelock Ellis in a long essay on Hardy's novels to date published in the same month as Bayne's (*HCH*, pp. 103–32). Hardy belonged with the great modern novelists in English, Ellis claimed, and they were the women – Austen, the Brontës, Eliot. Why? Because they shared 'the conception of love as the one business of life' (*HCH*, p. 104). For Hardy's representation of passion it was the Brontës to whom one had to look for appropriate comparison. True, Charlotte's stern ethics and religious belief seemed to make her his polar opposite, and in this respect he was closer to the George Eliot who caused such dismay when she failed to make Dorothea Brooke, in her darkest hour, so much as pause to think of God. But when it came to portraying the darkest hour itself, Hardy's imagination drew closer to the Brontës – and to Shakespeare. Behind the heaths and moors in *Jane Eyre* and *Wuthering Heights* and *The Return of the Native* there lie the great landscapes of *King Lear* and *Macbeth*, with their visions of what it means to be abandoned, houseless, beyond the pale.

The Brontës and Hardy give these visions new features of their own. For the outcast Jane Eyre the heath is an ordeal she survives with the help of her religious faith and the rich welcome she receives from the Rivers family. Heathcliff's very name is composed of the two most salient aspects of *Lear*'s landscape, and for Cathy the heath is where the two of them belong together. Jane Eyre recalls Cordelia on her exhausted arrival at Moor House. When St John asks what she expects him to do for her she bluntly answers 'Nothing', then yields to the gentler Diana's appeal with words that are close to Cordelia's angry reflection on what the bad sisters have done to their father: 'If I were a masterless and stray dog, I know that you would not turn me from your hearth tonight' (ch. 28). (Cordelia says: 'Mine enemy's dog / Though he had bit me should have stood that night / Against my fire' (*KL*, 4.7.36–8).) If Jane is a daughter-wife who suffers and survives the Shakespearean ordeal of the father, then *The Return of the Native* gives a different turn to the Lear model when it stages the fate of a mother rejected by her son. Turning away in despair from 'The Closed Door' of the cottage on the heath, Mrs Yeobright works her own variation on the Shakespearean lines: 'I would not have done it against a neighbour's cat ... like an animal kicked out' (*RN*, bk 4, ch. 6).

Wuthering Heights drew frequent comparison with Greek and Shakespearean tragedy, not always comfortably ('written in a morbid phase of the mind' (*BCH*, p. 241), 'a picture so destitute of moral beauty and human worth' (*BCH*, p. 281)). But as time passed critics felt able to claim, as Angus Mackay did in 1898, that 'The whole story has something of the pathos of *King Lear* and much of the tragic force of *Macbeth*' (*BCH*, p. 447). The poet Swinburne freely acclaimed both

Charlotte and Emily with the epithet Shakespearean, and judged
Wuthering Heights a rare modern example of 'high and pure tragedy',
comparable with *King Lear* (*BCH*, p. 439). But the contemporary
response to the novel that clinches the kinship with Hardy comes again
from Peter Bayne. In 1881 he wrote of the cruelty at the heart of
Wuthering Heights. The vision of life that it presented was not in the end
like that of Greek and Shakespearean tragedy, where the roots of
suffering can be traced back to some act of wrong doing, of sin or folly
or lawless passion. In the novel people try to do good – old Earnshaw
brings Heathcliff home as an act of kindness – and the result is evil: 'in
Wuthering Heights the root of pain and misery is goodness, and the
world in which we move seems God-forsaken' (*BCH*, p. 427). It was this
vision of God-forsakenness that Hardy shared with Emily Brontë.

From the outset there was a sharper edge to Hardy's dealings with
Shakespeare than George Eliot's; there is also a certain edginess.[27] How
far is *Under the Greenwood Tree* designed to recall *As You Like It*? The
birdsong that Fancy Day and Dick Dewey hear as they drive away from
their wedding seems to hark back to Amiens's song (in 2.5): 'Tippiwit!
swe-e-et! ki-ki-ki! Come hither, come hither, come hither!' Doubtless
Fancy is correct when she says, 'O, 'tis the nightingale', as Juliet is
obviously not when she vainly tries to stop Romeo leaving at dawn by
saying 'It was the nightingale and not the lark' (*RJ*, 3.5.2). The
comparison scarcely works in favour of the respectably married but not
quite reliable woman, who in the final words of the tale 'thought of a
secret she would never tell' (*UGT*, Part Fifth, ch. 2). We can half believe
that Fancy will never stray again (Dick certainly will not), just as we
can half believe in the golden world imagined by Shakespearean
romantic comedy as a happy-ever-after. Like Shakespeare, Hardy
reminds us of the winter wind, the unpoetical Audreys and unsociable
Jaqueses. But the odds are more heavily on the golden world's
deterioration than they are in Shakespeare, even in *Under the
Greenwood Tree*, where the ironies are comparatively – indeed for
Hardy, uniquely – good-humoured.

The vision of an idealized pastoral world is of immense importance to
Hardy's writing. But from *Far from the Madding Crowd* onwards this

vision is increasingly attributed to expectations about 'the life of the
fields' entertained by educated, metropolitan readers whose knowledge
of it is restricted to writing – including Shakespeare's. These readers are
presumed to share their literary and cultural knowledge with the
narrator and some of his leading characters, including Parson Maybold
(*UGT*), Henry Knight (*PBE*), Clym Yeobright (*RN*), Lady Constantine
(*TT*), Fitzpiers (*W*) and Angel Clare (*TD*). The list is mainly but not
exclusively male. When Elizabeth-Jane observes Lucetta's devotion to
her husband Farfrae, we are told that she 'did not say to herself that
Farfrae should be thankful for such devotion, but, full of her reading,
she cited Rosalind's exclamation: "Mistress, know yourself; down on
your knees and thank Heaven fasting for a good man's love"' (*MoC*,
ch. 33). Elizabeth-Jane's ability to cite Shakespeare helps to ensure that
by the end of the tale she has won this fairly good man's love for herself.
It also contributes to her separation from the more passionate man who
has thought of himself as her father – Henchard. Of the several bitter
ironies in the novel's close one is our sense that, full of her reading, she
would recognize, as the man himself could not, the narrator's allusion
to Othello's last speech when he says of Henchard that 'it was a part of
his nature to extenuate nothing' (*MoC*, ch. 45). Indeed the sentence is
so angled that the thought if not the words may well be her own.

    The question of recognition is always essential to allusion, but where
Shakespeare and literary allusion in general are concerned, it draws in
Hardy's writing on a particular edge, separating those in the know
from those without. It is not always comfortable for readers to find
themselves with the former. Characters within Hardy's fiction who
consciously cite Shakespeare are rarely if ever to be trusted. Elfride
Swancourt's father in *A Pair of Blue Eyes*, for example, who takes a lofty
line on the humble origins of the man she (first) loves, Stephen Smith –
'Let a beast be lord of beasts, and his crib shall stand at the king's mess'
(*PBE*, ch. 9; this is Hamlet being rude about Osric (*Ham*, 5.2.87–9)).
When Lady Constantine disagrees with Swithin St Cleeve about the
weather forecast, she cites Hamlet's 'There is nothing either good or
bad, but thinking makes it so' (*TT*, ch. 16; *Ham*, 2.2.250–1). This is
instantly contradicted by a hurricane which rips the dome off the tower

they are on. So much for 'thinking', and for quotations. Outright
villains are always quick on the draw. When all the plots of the devilish
Dare have come to nothing in *A Laodicean*, he shrugs his shoulders and
borrows from Touchstone (*AYL*, 3.2.100): 'As for my conduct, cat will
after kind, you know' (*L*, bk 6, ch. 4). Alec D'Urberville has been to the
same school, where he has learnt to address girls as 'my pretty Coz' and
flirt with lines from Shakespearan comedy. Angel Clare is also too
comfortable with Shakespeare, telling his father that some of the wisest
members of old families '"exclaim against their own succession", as
Hamlet puts it' (*TD*, ch. 26; *Ham*, 2.2.350–1).

Nor is it any more auspicious for characters to bandy Shakespeare
between them. At the end of *The Woodlanders* Fitzpiers declares his
renewed love to Grace Melbury. It is a different kind of love, he says:
'"Less passionate; more profound. . . . 'Love talks with better knowledge,
and knowledge with dearer love.'"' But Grace can hear the quotation
marks. '"That's out of *Measure for Measure*," said she slily. "O yes –
I meant it as a citation," blandly replied Fitzpiers' (*W*, ch. 45). He is
lying. He has tried to pervert the Duke's words to mean 'better than in
the past', but in the play they are a rebuff to Lucio for slandering the
Duke in his supposed absence: they mean 'better and dearer than you
are displaying or than you are capable of'. But 'slily' robs Grace's
response of rebuff and turns it towards conniving carnality. Connivance
and carnality are prominent in the performance of *Love's Labour's Lost*
in *A Laodicean* at Stancy Castle. (The scene is a reprise of the amateur
theatricals in *Mansfield Park*.) George Somerset seethes with jealousy as
he watches his rival play the King of Navarre to Paula Power's Princess
of France. This is bad enough, but to spice things up his rival on stage
breaks into the sonnet from *Romeo and Juliet*, and 'the sound of a very
sweet and long-drawn osculation spread through the room, followed by
applause from the people in the cheap seats'(*L*, bk 3, ch. 8). George is
outraged. He remonstrates with Paula, who says it took her by surprise
and in any case it was not a real kiss. When George presses her further,
she responds with yet more Shakespeare: 'Perhaps I like you a little
more than a little, which is much too much! Yes, – Shakespeare says so,
and he is always right' (*L*, bk 3, ch. 9). But like the cloying honey which

gives rise to Henry IV's image of sudden excess (*1H4*, 3.2.71–3), a little more than a little Shakespeare between lovers may be much too much.

Quoting Shakespeare to oneself is a different matter. In the Luxellian tomb Elfride Swancourt finds herself silently convicted of treachery to her first love, Stephen Smith. She is on the arm of her new man, Knight, who knows nothing of their past liaison. Caught in two minds, Elfride loosens her grip from a sense of shame but she cannot let go of Knight completely: '"Can one be pardoned, and retain the offence?"' quoted Elfride's heart then' (*PBE*, ch. 27). Perhaps only poets know quite how hearts can quote, but it is certainly to Elfride's credit, her inwardness with Claudius's guilty question (*Ham*, 3.3.56). The narrator extends the same generosity to Tess when he says, after the wedding with Angel: 'She was conscious of the notion expressed by Friar Laurence: "These violent delights have violent ends"' (*TD*, ch. 33; *RJ*, 2.6.9). Angel himself judges his failure to live up to the standard of sonnet 116: 'His had been a love "which alters when it alteration finds"' (*TD*, ch. 53). These cases involve a degree of sexual and emotional guilt experienced by the character, towards whom the Shakespearean allusion helps to express and solicit a sense of fellow-feeling from narrator and reader.

It is a thorny issue in Hardy, this question of being in or out of the know. It is possible to invoke a Shakespearean model on behalf of those whom we know will not recognize it. There is no mistaking the polemical intent of the passage near the end of Hardy's important essay on 'The Dorsetshire Labourer' (1883), where he laments the disappearance of the 'half-independent villagers', ousted from their cottages as their life-hold falls in by the landowners only concerned with their own employees. He imagines the dispossessed expostulating in the words addressed to Henry IV:

> Our house, my sovereign liege, little deserves
> The scourge of greatness to be used on it;
> And that same greatness, too, which our own hands
> Have holp to make so portly.[28]

(*1H4*, 1.3.10–13)

These words might seem distinctly menacing to readers who recall that they are spoken by one of the Percys ('saucy Worcester') and that they herald the explosion of full-scale rebellion.

This is effective and uncomplicated because the reader pauses only briefly, if at all, to worry about whether the Dorsetshire labourer would recognize the quotation, or to care that he or she did not. But as soon as we move to more avowedly literary contexts, the association of high cultural éclat and low social status is likely to create interesting frictions, from the pleasantly humorous to the painfully ironic. Here is an instance of good humour from a scene in *Two on a Tower*. The main male character, Swithin St Cleeve, has gone to church to be confirmed.

> From the north side of the nave smiled a host of girls, gaily uniform in dress, age, and a temporary repression of their natural tendency to 'skip like a hare over the meshes of good counsel'. (*TT*, ch. 24)

This is from *The Merchant of Venice* (1.2.19–20), some words of Portia's from her opening scene with Nerissa when she is at her most unbuttoned in prose, most Rosalind. It would take a grim reader to object on behalf of the girls in Hardy's church that they cannot be expected to recognize a fancy allusion like this. Our sense of the chasm separating these local girls from the grand lady of Belmont is suspended by the gossipy mirth of the Shakespearean context and the loose mischievous proverbs about hot tempers leaping o'er cold decrees. It helps Shakespeare's high-spirited phrase leap o'er the cold differences that would otherwise separate Portia and Nerissa from these lowly rustics, such that you feel Nerissa at least would be quite welcome among them and probably her mistress too, for a bit.

The following is a more characteristically uneasy instance. In *Far from the Madding Crowd* Bathsheba finds she must appeal to Gabriel Oak for emergency help with her expiring sheep (ch. 21). Unfortunately she has just dismissed him in fury, so it is unsurprising that he gives her first imperious message short shrift. However, her messenger gets rather grander shrift from the narrator than we might expect. On his return with the bad news Laban Tall dismounts, 'his face tragic as

Morton's after the battle of Shrewsbury'. This refers to the opening scene of *2 Henry IV*, where Morton brings Northumberland and his wife the news of their son Harry Percy's death, and the end of the rebels' hopes. In Hardy's hands here the technique is classically mock-heroic in that the analogy falsely inflates the seriousness of the situation. These are, after all, only sheep at risk – sheep, as it happens, who are dying from wind and need to be deflated. But for farmers and their dependents sheep are no joke. They are serious business, as Gabriel has already learnt to his cost, and the reader with him. The fact that Gabriel now manages to save forty-nine of the precious creatures is no mean feat, the work of a local hero. No one inside the scene on the ground thinks all this is funny, so one may wonder on whom the mockery intended by this absurd Shakespearean reference falls.

Gabriel has been associated early on with a healthy ignorance of literary allusion. He has fallen for Bathsheba and keeps watching through the hedge for her regular coming, but he has not got anything to say to her,

> and not being able to frame love phrases which end where they begin; passionate tales –
>
> > – Full of sound and fury
> > – Signifying nothing –
>
> he said no word at all. (*FMC*, ch. 4)

The misapplication of Macbeth's famous words (*Mac*, 5.5.27–8) to 'love phrases' has the effect of cancelling any dishonour to Gabriel for failing to frame them. If this is what book-learning means, he is better off without it. The same seems to be true of the Durbeyfields. Hardy has been explaining how the new branch of their family – the so-called 'Stoke-d'Urbervilles' – have acquired their pedigree by inventing a family tree after an hour's research in the British Museum. Tess and her family are quite ignorant of this work of imagination: 'indeed the very possibility of such annexations was unknown to them; who supposed that, though to be well-favoured might be the gift of fortune, a family name came by nature' (*TD*, ch. 5). This may be innocent of them, but it is not the absurdity of Dogberry, who in his efforts to appoint a constable of the watch treats us to this: 'To be a well-favor'd man is the gift of fortune, but to read and write comes by nature' (*MA*, 3.3.14–16). This is a good instance of Hardy's way of recovering some dignity for the lower orders. In case we need it, there is evidence from his notebooks of the interest he took in American expressions of impatience with what would now be called Shakespeare's 'elitism', by Walt Whitman in particular (via John Addington Symonds).[29]

But Tess's innocence of literary allusion does leave her open to more educated predators. At the Slopes she is required to whistle tunes to the hens, but she cannot manage it. Alec swoops down on her: '"I have been watching you from over the wall – sitting like *Im*-patience on a monument, and pouting up that pretty red mouth"' (*TD*, ch. 9), and so on. The allusion to Viola's 'Patience' (*TN*, 2.4.115) is way beyond Tess. He shows her what to do with her mouth, like so: 'He suited the action to the word, and whistled a line of "Take, O take those lips away". But the allusion was lost upon Tess' (ch. 9). From Hamlet's suiting the action to the word (*Ham*, 3.2.17) to the song the boy sings for Mariana (*MM*, 4.1.1–7), Alec enjoys his own dazzling performance. Unlike Grace Melbury, Tess does not know her Shakespeare, so she cannot answer back, whether slyly or not. This is awkward for readers on whom Alec's allusions are not lost, in so far as it makes us complicit with him. And the same is true, more painfully so, when it comes to Tess's rupture with Angel after the wedding. In quick succession he admits that she was 'more sinned against than sinning' (ch. 35; *KL*, 3.2.60), is said to wear 'the face of a man who was no longer passion's slave' (ch. 35; *Ham*, 3.2.72–3), and asks her 'Don't you think we had better endure the ills we have than fly to others?' (ch. 36; *Ham*, 3.1.81–2). But as we must know, and he should know, these are between the two of them just so many lost allusions.

We have seen that when it came to expressing some of the bleakest and most painful aspects of the world around them, both Dickens and George Eliot were in their different ways drawn to Shakespearean tragedy. This was true for Hardy too in ways that it is worth, in conclusion, trying to distinguish. We can take a cue from an entry in one of his notebooks. In eighteenth-century France Voltaire had been bewildered by the mixture of crudity and beauty in Shakespeare, and thought that his success had ruined English drama: 'There are such beautiful scenes, there are passages so grand & so terrible in these monstrous farces which they call tragedies, that his pieces have always been played with great success.' Hardy copied down this passage from a *Life of Voltaire* published in 1881.[30] 'Monstrous farce' is close to what T.S. Eliot saw in Marlowe's *The Jew of Malta*; it is also close to the 'Gothic' perspective that A.P. Rossiter saw in Shakespearean tragedy in his chapter on 'Comic Relief' in *Angel with Horns* (1961). The raucous, ribald, scurrilous element that runs through Hardy's writing finds support in the 'primitive' aspects of Shakespeare, his contemporaries and their medieval predecessors. This is not the whole truth about the kind of tragedy Hardy writes, any more than it is about Shakespeare's own. But the black laughter that astonished Voltaire is one of the notes on which he and Shakespeare croak the same tune.

There are several leading voices that Hardy draws from Shakespeare for the distinctive form taken by tragedy in his work. There are of course others derived from the Greeks and the Old Testament, though they blend with those from Shakespeare. One is a voice we recognize as that of Hamlet in the graveyard and Macbeth in his last monologue, 'To-morrow, and to-morrow, and to-morrow' (5.5.19). At the moments when Hardy makes a prominent character speak or think with this voice, it becomes hard to distinguish from his own. Angel Clare is the character in his fiction most frequently associated with Hamlet, and there are points at which his relations with Tess are darkly shadowed by Hamlet's with Ophelia, especially in the extraordinary scene in which Angel carries her in his sleep down to the stream, as if to drown her (*TD*, ch. 37).[31] Here he is at Talbothays aged twenty-six, at the start of their relationship, taking Whitmanesque delight in the company of farm folk. All his conventional ideas about rural stereotypes are splintering into particularity.

> The typical and unvarying Hodge ceased to exist. He had been disintegrated into a number of varied fellow-creatures –

beings of many minds, beings infinite in difference; some happy, many serene, a few depressed, one here and there bright even to genius, some stupid, others wanton, others austere; some mutely Miltonic, some potentially Cromwellian; into men who had private views of each other, as he had of his friends; who could applaud or condemn each other, amuse or sadden themselves by the contemplation of each other's foibles or vices; men every one of whom walked in his own individual way the road to dusty death. (ch. 18)

'Infinite in difference' may carry a faint echo of Hamlet's 'infinite in faculties' in 'What a piece of work is a man' (*Ham*, 2.2.305–6), but walking the road to dusty death certainly recalls Macbeth's 'all our yesterdays have lighted fools / The way to dusty death. ... Life's but a walking shadow' (*Mac*, 5.5.22–4). How many characters in Hardy walk the dusty road, like the young man and woman and child on their way to Weydon-Priors at the start of *The Mayor of Casterbridge*. The reference to Gray's 'Elegy' (mute Miltons, potential Cromwells) reinforces this levelling view of life from the grave, far from the madding crowd. Yet there is also Tess's own particular voice to speak of what it means to *be* on the road with no hope, like Macbeth, when 'you seem to see numbers of to-morrows just all in a line, ...' (*TD*, ch. 19).

Another leading voice is also a levelling one. But it does not come burdened with the accents of high philosophic, religious or scientific learning. One of its positions is down to earth or even *in* it, like the gravediggers in *Hamlet* and Winnie in Samuel Beckett's *Happy Days*. We hear this voice in the wonderful scene in the Luxellian tomb in chapter twenty-six of *A Pair of Blue Eyes*, where Stephen's father and others sit around with their bread and cheese and ale, cheerfully gossiping about the dead and gone. It is a disengaged and even heartless voice that the narrator can wield with ease. We hear it slyly echoing Feste near the end of *Two on a Tower* when 'the whirligig of time' (*TN*, 5.1.369) again sets Viviette free for Swithin to marry her – only then promptly to kill her (*TT*, ch. 41). Another position from which it can speak is high up, from a great distance, looking down impassively on the insect life crawling across the face of the earth, like the aerial view down on Tess and Marian in the frozen fields at Flintcomb Ash.

But there is a third voice, characteristic of Hardy at his most moving. Less reflective than the previous two, it is simple, humble, gentle, resigned, and it depends for its force on the dramatic situation. In Shakespeare, kings and princes can speak with it no less than their servants and fools, though usually this is only when they come face to face with the limits of mortality: ''A was a man, take him for all in all'; 'the readiness is all'; 'Pray you now forget, and forgive'; 'No more but e'en a woman'; 'O mother, mother! / What have you done?' In Hardy this voice belongs typically not so much to his protagonists as to the loving kindly witnesses attendant on them, for whom Horatio, Emilia, Kent and the Fool, Enobarbus and Charmian are the Shakespearean equivalents. They are characters such as Able Whittle, who stays with Henchard because 'I see things be bad with 'ee, and ye wer kind-like to mother if ye were rough to me, and I would fain be kind-like to you' (*MoC*, ch. 45). Or Marty South, who will never forget Giles, 'for you was a good man, and did good things!' (*W*, ch. 48). Or the Widow Edlin who looks down at Jude in his coffin and simply says, 'How beautiful he is!' (*JO*, Part Sixth, ch. 11).

Chapter Five

POETRY

A WORTHIER STAGE

In this chapter I shall consider what the Victorians made of Shakespeare's non-dramatic poetry and what Shakespeare contributed to Victorian poetry. In this latter respect the most important texts are the sonnets, *Hamlet* and *Othello*.

Victorian poets sought inspiration from, alluded to and measured themselves against Shakespeare. The results were not always happy. In particular the attempts by Browning, Tennyson and others to write poetic drama of Shakespearean scope, resonance and vitality retain little interest for most modern readers (let alone actors and producers), save those already interested in Tennyson and Browning for other good reasons. James Sheridan Knowles is no longer a name to conjure with, yet there was a time when such plays as *Virginius* (1820) and *The Hunchback* (1832) made him thought of as a rival to Shakespeare.[1] He owed much of his success to Macready. There was a moment in the 1830s when it seemed as though the leading actor-manager of his generation might unite with another writer, a rising young poet of the next generation, to change the face of English drama. Macready boasted to his diary that Robert Browning had said 'that I had *bit* him by my performance of Othello, and I told him I hoped I should make the blood come'.[2] *Othello* would prove to be a major presence in Browning's imagination,[3] most obviously though not most effectively in *Luria*, one of the two closet dramas published just before his marriage to Elizabeth Barrett in 1846. In the 1852 'Essay on Shelley' Browning identifies

154

Shakespeare as 'the inventor of *Othello*' (*RBP*, I, p. 1001). The teeth-marks of *Othello* can also be detected in the murderous aspects of *Pippa Passes* (1841), *The Return of the Druses* and *A Blot in the 'Scutcheon* (both 1843), though there are other traces of Shakespeare as well, the plot of the last-named for instance being evidently based on *Romeo and Juliet*, assisted by a Beatrice and Benedick imported from *Much Ado*. In 1837 the immediately mordant effect of Macready's Shakespeare was the production of Browning's first play, *Strafford*, which had five reasonably promising performances at Covent Garden. Here it is the English and Roman history plays that are most obviously in evidence. This was followed six years later at Drury Lane, with less success, by *A Blot in the 'Scutcheon*, and several others that did not seek or find performance.

'Action in Character rather than Character in Action': this was Browning's motive, so the preface to the first edition of *Strafford* declared.[4] It was not, in the 1840s at least, a recipe for success in the theatre. Nor was Browning's benevolence conducive to the production of true tragic force. As Luria elicits the goodness and generosity out of those around him one by one, this Othello-figure exclaims: 'If we could wait! The only fault's with time; / All men become good creatures; but so slow!' (5.180–1).[5] And much too long for a play. Nevertheless, his theatrical experiments undoubtedly contributed to the verse form in which Browning was to achieve some of his greatest successes, the 'dramatic monologue'. Tennyson, by contrast, came to drama relatively late, with a series of historical romances including *Queen Mary* (1875) and *The Foresters* (1892) that owe something to Shakespeare. Of the latter Tennyson himself said that he had 'sketched the state of the people in another great transition period of the making of England' (*Memoir*, II, p. 173). A patriotic fantasia, it reworks elements from *As You Like It* and *A Midsummer Night's Dream* round the figures of Robin Hood and King Richard the Lion-Heart. In 1888 R.H. Hutton judged *Queen Mary* superior to *Henry VIII* in dramatic force and general power. But he conceded that it was as a lyric poet that 'the great poet of the nineteenth century' was great; he would 'certainly never be regarded as a great dramatist' (*TCH*, pp. 393–4).

It was not in the theatre or conventional dramatic form that Shakespeare's example and inspiration had the most positive effects on Victorian poetic writing. These are to be sought in poetry that finds new ways of being truly 'dramatic', whether its formal allegiances are to monologue, lyric or elegy. When Shakespeare helped the Victorians to distinctive poetic achievements it was by forcing them to think what they owed to their present no less than to their past. The best of them sought not directly to emulate but rather to gauge their distance from the old Shakespearean models of language and literary form. This meant asking themselves what made modern love *modern* – to borrow the title from a sequence of poems by George Meredith that measures itself against Shakespeare and his sonneteering contemporaries (see pp. 169–71). As for drama in the conventional sense of the term, Elizabeth Barrett Browning made her Aurora Leigh say that she would write no plays because the glories of ancient Greece and Shakespeare's England belonged irrecoverably to the past. We should leave the paraphernalia of theatre behind,

> And take for a worthier stage the soul itself,
> Its shifting fancies and celestial lights,
> With all its grand orchestral silences
> To keep the pauses of its rhythmic sounds.
>
> (Fifth Book, 340–3)[6]

Silence, pause, rhythm: the example of verse forms and techniques that could be redeployed to stage new kinds of inwardness, or even, ideally, 'the soul itself' – this was how Shakespeare could serve as inspiration.

Not that there is much inspiration evident in the numberless swansongs chanted by Victorian Ophelias such as Baron de Tabley's or Prosperos such as William Johnson Cory's and A.C. Benson's.[7] No grand orchestral silences punctuate the relentless languor of poems that begin 'Farewell, my airy pursuivants, farewell' (Cory's) and 'O close the book and let the pages lie' (Benson's). A better example of what a more gifted poet could do with Shakespearean incitement can be found in Christina Rossetti's fine ballad entitled '"Cannot sweeten"' (1866). This was not the first poem of hers to seize a cue from the sleepwalking scene in which Lady Macbeth laments that 'all the perfumes of Arabia will not sweeten this little hand' (*Mac*, 5.1.51–3). Twenty years earlier, in 'Will These Hands Ne'er Be Clean?', a relatively simple voice passed judgment on a guilty second person (the MS title is 'To a Murderer'), and predicted his eternal damnation: 'Ages may pass away, worlds rise and set – / But thou shalt not forget.' '"Cannot sweeten"', by contrast, begins with the ballad formula of question and answer, then lets the guilty respondent bloom into confession: 'I ate his life as a banquet, / I drank his life as new wine'. Her hands are black and her feet are red, but 'Blacker, redder my heart of guilt'. In the final stanza all colour drains away to leave a heart of stone that will never be softened by endless tears.

> Cold as a stone, as hard, as heavy;
> All my sighs ease it no whit,
> All my sighs make it no cleaner
> Dropping dropping dropping on it.

This is to find a new 'rhythmic sound' for 'the soul itself', or for this particular soul in torment, condemned to the monosyllabic immobility of the second line and the nerveless expiry of the last. This is what it might mean to take a cue from Shakespeare and make of it something new, your own, here and now.[8]

ANTHOLOGIES

A major strand in the story I am telling is the attempt to rescue Shakespeare the Poet from the theatre, from performance, from the flesh, from mortality. This meant various things. It meant, from the Romantics onwards, decrying the theatre as coarse, vulgar, impossible. Tennyson took a conventional view of *King Lear*, for example, when he said that it 'cannot possibly be acted, it is too titanic' (*Memoir*, II, p. 292). It meant privileging the act of reading over theatrical performance. It meant, from Bowdler onwards, various forms of editing, censorship and abridgment to make the Shakespearean texts acceptable for an expanding number of readers and spectators. And it meant, in a complementary way, extracting choice treasures from the Shakespearean texts and re-presenting them in new forms, especially that of the anthology, literally a 'selection of flowers'.

The importance of the anthology to understanding the way the Victorians encountered Shakespeare cannot be overestimated. The latter half of the eighteenth century had first seen the dispersal of Shakespeare's texts into bits and pieces. He was a predictably prime resource for the dominant selections, William Enfield's *The Speaker* (1774) and Vicesimus Knox's *Elegant Extracts* (1784), or to give the relevant volume its full subtitle, *Elegant Extracts: or Useful and Entertaining Pieces of Poetry, Selected for the Improvement of Youth in Speaking, Reading, Thinking, Composing; and in the Conduct of Life.*[9] The general reader was well served by William Dodd's astonishingly durable *The Beauties of Shakespeare*. First published in 1752, it retained its popularity throughout the nineteenth century and beyond, enjoying many new editions.[10] Dodd's original preface remained current too, in which he urged on readers the need for imaginative participation in the act of poetic creation. Shakespeare is full of fine passages that have been condemned as rant and bombast, but read them 'with the least glow of the same imagination that warmed the writer's bosom', he urges, and they will 'blaze in the robes of sublimity, and obtain the commendations of a Longinus' (p. vi). To read Shakespeare thus was to become poetical, inspired, sublime. It was to enjoy his pride and pomp freed from circumstance, for it meant losing or being saved from story and plot. These 'Beauties' no longer issue from a particular speaker's mouth, save when required by a passage of dialogue. One consequence is that they stand little chance of preserving a sense of humour, though the sense of wit is a different matter. Dodd notes that many passages in the plays are so closely tied to plot and character that it would be absurd to extract them. So the reader would find little of Falstaff in the *Beauties* and nothing at all from *The Merry Wives of Windsor*, 'one of Shakspeare's best and most justly admired comedies' (p. ix). Nor did the *Beauties* urge readers to be perpetually blazing with sublimity or burning with a gemlike flame. The existence of an index encouraged them to more sober edification, with entries such as 'Beauty, the virtuous power of' (Isabella), 'Continence before marriage' (Prospero),

'England, invincible if unanimous' (*King John*) and 'Insects, cruelty to' (*Titus Andronicus*, though there is a good candidate in *Coriolanus* too).

There were numerous variants on Dodd. In 1848, for example, Mary Cowden Clarke issued a little volume of *Shakespeare Proverbs* designed to fit into readers' pockets, especially those of 'the poor, who need these consolatory aids even more than the rich' (p. 7). The proverbial form was particularly congenial to Shakespeare, she said, 'with its mixture of ideality and matter-of-fact worldly wisdom'. It was Shakespeare's gift to have distilled 'quintessential drops of wisdom' that united the sublime and the everyday. Yet the effect of isolating these drops of wisdom is unnerving, especially when the principle of their organization is simply alphabetical. It makes a difference whether it is Hamlet speaking, or Polonius, or Iago. 'A man is never undone till he be hanged'; 'A woman sometimes scorns what best contents her'; and 'Love will not be spurr'd to what it loathes'. Without any ascription of speaker or play, it could be a scholarly game or an old-fashioned exam question, to name where they come from. (In fact they are all from *The Two Gentlemen of Verona*, the speakers being Launce, Valentine and Julia.)

As the century wore on Shakespeare was pressed into ever more commercialized service. By 1877 you could buy a *Cupid's Birthday Book: one thousand love-darts from Shakespeare*, 'gathered and arranged for every day in the year by Geo. Johnston'. Or, a few years later, Mary F.P. Dunbar's *Shakespeare Birthday Book* (1884), which selects two or three little passages for each month and day of the year. The month of August is hailed by lines beginning 'You sunburnt sickle-men', from the masque in *The Tempest*, and 'The year growing ancient', from Perdita's flower speech in *The Winter's Tale*; 13 November is marked by Hamlet's 'What a piece of work is a man!' and Iago's 'Men should be what they seem.' Quite how these extracts were supposed to illuminate your birthday or those of your nearest and dearest remains a mystery. More transparent in its aims and objectives was *The Sweet Silvery Sayings of Shakespeare on the Softer Sex, compiled by an Old Soldier* (1877). This is an almost entirely predictable concoction, 'a little sugar-sweet book' for young men and women that recycles praise of Shakespeare's exemplary women such as Imogen. Yet one cannot help wondering about the Old

Soldier. He has evidently served out in India and witnessed the horrors of war. When Blanche in *King John* has her one great outburst ('The sun's o'ercast with blood', 3.1.252), the Old Soldier is moved to exclaim: 'O! that some great and good lady of the land at the head of society would commence a crusade to obliterate war from the face of this beautiful world! ... It is time for women to interfere, men have made such a sad mess of things' (p. 322). He quotes Hamlet on the futility of dying for a fantasy and trick of fame, he cites the prologue to *Henry V*, and he rounds off his tirade with Isabella's 'O, but man, proud man, / Drest in a little brief authority' (*MM*, 2.2.118–19). The softer sex suddenly sounds less sweet and silvery as we glimpse the wounds made by a real world from which Shakespeare might provide a precious respite. In their different ways these examples suggest how 'Shakespeare' percolated into the nooks and crannies of the 'everyday life' to which Mary Cowden Clarke refers.

SONNETS

The effect of presenting and reading Shakespeare in this way is to purge the words of their origins, erasing the source of utterance in a particular character's voice and dramatic context. This has the effect not merely of masking the rather large differences between *Hamlet* and the sonnets, but of elevating the non-dramatic verse until it become the touchstone against which 'poetic' extracts from the plays are to be measured. This is particularly true of the sonnets. The narrative poems *Venus and Adonis* and *The Rape of Lucrece* could never quite compete at this level; after their immediate spell in the limelight at the end of the sixteenth and early seventeenth centuries they mainly drop out of sight for two hundred years or so, save for some memorable observations from Coleridge on *Venus and Adonis*.[11] It is, however, a sign of the 'decadent' times when near the end of the nineteenth century John Addington Symonds confesses to the effect the young Adonis had on him as a child: 'In some confused way I identified myself with Adonis; but at the same time I yearned after him as an adorable object of passionate love.'[12] Symonds was an important pioneer in exploring the 'identifications' and 'yearnings' that Wilde and others would pursue further through the beautiful youth of the sonnets. *The Phoenix and Turtle* was not widely noticed, though it sometimes featured in collections of the *Songs and Sonnets*, such as F.T. Palgrave's (1865).

The songs from the plays were a different matter. Printed together with the sonnets, as in Palgrave's volume and his highly successful *Golden Treasury* (first published 1861), they produce a distilled lyricism that repeats the claims made by some of the sonnets themselves to defy the insidious power of time. The difference is that Shakespeare's sonnets are themselves 'dramatic' in the contest they stage between the power of time and mortality and the desire to resist or transcend it. The speaking voice is always addressing someone or something. The 'I' knows who might answer back – a beloved young man, a dangerous mistress – and what will never do so, at least in words – devouring Time, sad mortality, black night, the hungry ocean. The voice of the sonnets knows what and whom it is up against, and this sense of its mute respondents provokes its own fluctuations, the ebb, flow and eddy of faith and hope and despair. But release the voice from the expectation of a reply or belief in its possibility, and one seems to have entered a world elsewhere.

It was the Romantic poets who rescued Shakespeare's sonnets from lengthy neglect, and the Victorians took them up with nervous relish. The subject-matter made them nervous, but they relished the prospect of finding a key to the understanding of Shakespeare Himself. Tennyson and Browning deplored readers' fascination with the writer's private life, the lust for anecdotes, gossip and autographs. It was like pigs being ripped open in public, said Tennyson. He thanked God Almighty that Shakespeare at least had escaped, that we knew nothing of him but his writings.[13] All the more reason, however, so it seemed to many, to peer intensely into those writings in which he seemed to speak in his own voice. Tennyson's predecessor as Poet Laureate provided influential authority for treating the sonnets in this way. 'Scorn not the sonnet', advised Wordsworth, for 'with this key / Shakspeare unlocked his heart' (*WP*, II, p. 635). Browning would have none of it. 'Did Shakespeare? If so, the less Shakespeare he!' he signed off his poem

'House' (1876) indignantly. 'At the "Mermaid"' (also 1876) similarly rebuffs the idea that we can read a poet's true self from his writing.

Keats's friend Charles Armitage Brown pointed a way to the future when in 1838 he published *Shakespeare's Autobiographical Poems: Being His Sonnets Clearly Developed; with His Character Drawn Chiefly from His Works*.[14] This set the tone for innumerable editions and commentaries up to the end of the century. The consensus that the sonnets reveal something or somebody is as adamant as the impossibility of agreeing what or who exactly it is: the usual glory of allegory. Typical examples from the end of our period include *Shakespeare Self-Revealed in his 'Sonnets' and 'Phoenix and Turtle'* with introduction and analyses by 'J.M.' (1904), *The Christ in Shakespeare: Dramas and Sonnets*, interpreted by Charles Ellis (3rd edn, 1902), and an edition of the *Sonnets* (1904) by H.C. Beeching in a series designed for schools, colleges and the general reader.

It is worth taking a closer look. For 'J.M.', the key to understanding the whole sequence is sonnet 144, where the 'better angel' is identified as the Love of Beauty (the man) and the 'worse' as the Love of Fame (the woman). 'J.M.' was by no means the only Victorian reader to deny any physical reality to the man and the woman addressees, and affirm instead the Platonic pursuit of Truth and Beauty. The Poet becomes a Christ-figure, betrayed and rejected by his contemporaries, particularly 'the people'. Alternatively, he is a Prospero rewarded by the Calibans with base ingratitude: 'Shakespeare, who loved Truth and Beauty as none other did, and who knew his works to be – what everyone now knows them to be – a lay bible, was then held suspect; his work considered moral leprosy; and he was deeply hurt' (p. 137). Not much like a prosperous Stratford burgher, this Poet lives at such an ethereal level that the only candidate imaginable for the Rival of the sonnets is – Edmund Spenser. As for *The Phoenix and Turtle*, it shares the same enigma: the Poet is the Turtle Dove who loved Beauty the Phoenix and died to posterity as Love's Martyr.

No less idealistic are the Christianizing interpretations by Charles Ellis which began with an edition of the sonnets alone in 1896, added the dramas the following year, and expanded further in a third edition of 1902. Ellis has no compunction about selecting and reordering the sonnets (a mere fifty in the first edition). He writes in the Preface: 'As they exist in their accepted order they are buried – lost to the general reader, and barred to the Christian life' (pp. 24–5). Ellis's task is to resurrect a purified and reorganized body, supported (by the time of the third edition) by prefatory, interpolated and suffixed material including quotations from Milton, Cowper, Wordsworth, Bulwer-Lytton and Archbishop Chevenix Trench's sermon for the 1864 Tercentenary. Passages are also freely lifted from Shakespeare's plays, beginning with a long sequence from *The Merchant of Venice* that takes us from the caskets to the trial scene (3.2 to 4.1), prefaced thus:

> The Poet meditates on the good and evil influences ever acting upon mankind to their happy freedom from strife, or to their unrest and confusion, and having himself learned that the grace of God alone can preserve the one or foil the other, either to Jew or Gentile, he proceeds to the display of both conditions by examples. (p. 49)

Such an account of the play is itself singularly free from unrest and confusion. So too by implication is a view of that restless and confusing play *Measure for Measure* that permits the extraction of memorable utterances by the Duke ('Spirits are not finely touch'd, / But to fine issues', 1.1.35–6) and Isabella ('Why, all the souls that were, were forfeit once', 2.2.73). Morally uplifting passages are similarly uplifted from the histories, *Macbeth* and *Hamlet*. As for the (selected) sonnets themselves, the 'Love' addressed and invoked is Christ, and the 'two loves of comfort and despair' in the inevitably crucial sonnet 144 simply those of Christ and the mortal fallible poet himself.

Beeching's edition is more closely aligned with the dominant trends in literary criticism at the turn of the century, as witness its dedication to his influential Balliol friends, the critic A.C. Bradley and biographer Sidney Lee. This is a recognizably 'professional' enterprise, doffing its cap to Malone and to other modern editors such as Dowden (1875), dissenting from critics and commentators such as George Wyndham (1898 – too much philosophy) and Samuel Butler (1899 – too

ingeniously paradoxical), and politely demurring at Lee's theory that
the poems are a fashionable exercise, brilliant but conventional,
unimbued with personal passion. As a key to the sonnets, the idea that
they are the product of heartless technique has its shallow attractions,
but they come at the price of imagining the poet as Iago. Or rather – for
there is indeed an Iago loose in some of the sonnets – at the price of
imagining Iago as the author of the entire sequence, such that no
profession of faith remains uncorrupted. (Think of Iago solemnly
intoning 'Let me not to the marriage of true minds / Admit
impediments' (sonnet 116).) Beeching's aim is to retain belief in the
sincerity of the emotions expressed while staving off the anxiety that
the passions involved might be dangerous or even positively
illegitimate. This was the Victorian readers' dilemma. It afflicted their
response to all of Shakespeare, but the sonnets were a particularly
painful case because it was as exciting to believe that here the Poet was
speaking in his own person as it was dismaying to encounter the
passions to which he was giving utterance. 'Too hot, too hot!',
murmurs Leontes (*WT*, 1.2.108). If you believed in the physical reality
of the man and the woman addressed by the sonnets, and the reality of
the desires they provoked, it was hard for a Victorian reader to resist the
feeling that something somewhere was distinctly too hot.

This anxiety was influentially expressed in 1839 by Henry Hallam,
father of Tennyson's great and much mourned friend Arthur, the
inspiration for *In Memoriam A.H.H.* (to which we shall come in due
course). Hallam Senior was worried by the extravagance of the
attachment to the friend. He concluded magisterially:

> Notwithstanding the frequent beauties of these sonnets, ...
> it is impossible not to wish that Shakespeare had never written
> them. There is a weakness and folly in all excessive and mis-placed
> affection, which is not redeemed by the touches of nobler
> sentiment that abound in this long series of sonnets. (quoted by
> Ricks, *TP*, II, p. 314)

No less magisterially, Tennyson bluntly replied that Hallam had made
'a great mistake about them: they are noble' (*Memoir*, II, p. 289).

But more active measures than this were required to protect their reputation, and Shakespeare's. Beeching's tactics are representative. 'Romantic friendship' between two men of different age has a respectable pedigree, he says, not only historically but also psychologically. As they grow older, the imaginative naturally experience 'a strong disposition to consort with young people, and a keen pleasure in their society, as though to atone for the slow sapping of youthful strength and ardour in themselves' (p. xiii). This seems innocent enough. At the same time Beeching demotes the 'Dark Lady' sonnets to the level of an appendix, the sequence from sonnet 127 to the end being 'largely concerned with an incident already handled in the earlier part of the first series, only from another point of view' (p. lxvi). (It was common to suppose that sonnets 127–52 properly 'belonged' to an earlier moment in the story, between sonnets 32 and 33.) Palgrave takes a different line. Poets are different from the rest of us. They must be allowed the 'excess' that Hallam deplores, the ecstasy or divine madness acknowledged by a greater authority than Hallam, the Plato of the *Phaedrus*. The sonnets are for Palgrave 'perhaps the most powerful and certainly the most singular, utterances of passion which Poetry has yet supplied'. But there is a vital codicil. The pleasure we take in them depends on the belief that 'this phase of feeling was transient' – we shall see Jowett taking a similar line on *In Memoriam* – and that the writer returned to 'the sanity which, not less than ecstasy, is an especial attribute of the great poet' (p. 243). This sounds reassuring, or complacent, like the tolerance of a Theseus for the madman, the lover and the poet.

It was possible to take a more troubled view of the mysterious relations between passion and transience explored by the sonnets. For some thirty years from 1865 onwards David Masson lectured on Shakespeare in Edinburgh, and in 1914 his thoughts were collected and published by his daughter in *Shakespeare Personally*. To Masson it seemed that the figure within the plays whom their author most resembled was that of the fantastical Duke of dark corners in *Measure for Measure*, 'always present and vigilant somehow, and knowing all that is going on, but masked and cowled' (p. 46). To the general rule of his personal elusiveness the sonnets seemed a massive exception, 'as if there after all did require to be some secret safety-valve for this heart of mighty habitual self-repression' (p. 66). Masson thinks of the poems as 'a kind of metrical diary' in which Shakespeare locked up his deepest moods and keenest self-confessions. These were to be shared with one or two intimate friends, not intended for general circulation, so that what has come down to us is 'like a barred antique jewel-chest which no key has been found to fit' (p. 67).

This is a particularly appropriate image in so far as it draws on the jewels and chests that feature in the sonnets themselves, in numbers 48 and 52, and most notably in 65:

> O fearful meditation! Where, alack,
> Shall time's best jewel from time's chest lie hid?

If time's chest represents the horror of having your best jewel locked up for eternity, a good way of saving it from this fate would be to hide it in *another* kind of chest, a stout little poem for instance, or something that rhymes with it like 'the gentle closure of my breast' (48.11). But is 'time's chest' really such a fearful prospect? It might be a good hiding place after all, as it seems to be in number 52, where time's chest and wardrobe permit the treasure to be brought out 'To make some special instant special blessed'. But Masson's ear is not so much taken with the power of rhyme to live with time and against it, to make some special instant special blest and hail 'The living record of your memory' (55.8). It is more taken by the sense of waste and ruin and ending. This draws him to the culminating figure of authority in Shakespeare's dramatic works, Prospero. The great speech beginning 'Our revels now are ended' (*Tem*, 4.1.148) seems to Masson 'the most characteristic passage ever written by Shakespeare, inasmuch as it expresses so wonderfully his deepest constitutional feeling, his sense of the merely phantasmagoric character and inevitable evanescence of all that now so bravely exists' (p. 187). So there is after all a 'key' to the jewel-chest of the sonnets. It is provided by Prospero's elegy for the transience of all mortal things, the whole 'phantasmagoria'. With this clue Masson turns back to the plays to find comparable moments of impassioned meditation on mortality, in *Richard II*, in Claudio's prison speech in *Measure for*

Measure, in *Cymbeline*'s dirge. This is all very congenial to the philosophic pessimism of the *fin de siècle*, the inverse of Ellis's upbeat Christian idealism.

There was another way of thinking about the sonnets in the last decades of the century. It was not one conducive to the allaying of anxieties such as Henry Hallam had voiced. In *The Picture of Dorian Gray* (1891) the painter Basil Hallward confesses to the beautiful youth of the title, 'I was dominated, soul, brain, and power by you. ... I worshipped you' (Wilde, p. 89). Cross-examining Oscar Wilde in the first of the three trials that brought his downfall in 1895, Edward Carson pressed him to admit that Basil was expressing his author's own feelings for young men. Not at all, answered Wilde: 'the whole idea was borrowed from Shakespeare, I regret to say – yes, from Shakespeare's *Sonnets*'.[15] This was a brave and risky move. Everyone likes to have the Bard on their side, and for all good Victorians it was a way of claiming to be above suspicion. But this is just what the sonnets were not. Editors could assure anxious readers that the love expressed for another man was pure, or that it meant something else, or that this was just the way men behaved way back then. But no matter how dull editors try to make it, readers are excited by what poetry means to them right here and now. The Poet Laureate could declare the sonnets 'noble', but so could Oscar Wilde. In his second trial Wilde was moved to an even more fulsome parade of cultural authority on behalf of 'the love that dare not speak its name'. Think of David and Jonathan, of Plato, of the sonnets of Michelangelo and Shakespeare, he said: all witnesses to 'the noblest form of affection', 'that deep, spiritual affection that is as pure as it is perfect'.[16] The law declared otherwise. And the role Wilde had claimed for Shakespeare as witness for the defence meant that when he was convicted the sonnets were in some sense guilty of perjury.

Wilde had made his most arresting contribution to Victorian debates about the sonnets a few years earlier with his teasing little tale 'The Portrait of Mr. W.H.' (1889).[17] One of the three male figures in the story believes he has discovered 'the true secret of Shakespeare's Sonnets' (Wilde, p. 305), that they were inspired by a young boy actor named Willie Hughes. The theory is not itself an invention of Wilde's. It was proposed by Thomas Tyrwhitt in 1766 and endorsed by Edmond Malone in his 1790 edition of the sonnets. But Wilde puts it to flamboyant new use in challenging a nexus of notions about sincerity, selfhood, reading and performance. The most important thing about Willie Hughes is not that he is a beautiful boy but that he is an actor, 'the very source of Shakespeare's inspiration; the very incarnation of Shakespeare's dreams', *the* actor for whom the dramatist created 'Viola and Imogen, Juliet and Rosalind, Portia and Desdemona, and Cleopatra herself' (pp. 307–8). It is true that the crucial portrait turns out to be forged, and that while all three men in the tale believe in the theory at some point, no two of them share it at any one time. It is as if the shade of Willie Hughes were doomed to separate rather than to unite them. This insidious sense of treachery is the dark side of the fable's liberating claim both through and on behalf of Shakespeare, that the dominant critical assumptions of the age are all wrong. The tale argues that the sonnets do not unlock the key of Shakespeare's heart; that writing does not give us access to higher or deeper or truer truths than performance; that there is no single real self to be found behind or within, but only a multitude of selves to be performed; that all writing is dramatic and so is all reading, a performance in service of the truth of masks.

'Your sonnet is quite lovely': thus begins a love letter Wilde had written to Lord Alfred Douglas. It featured significantly in the evidence brought against him in court.[18] There is reason to believe that after 1870 the sonnet cycle became associated with 'illicit love', as for example in John Addington Symonds's *Stella Maris*, privately printed in 1884.[19] Douglas himself was obsessed with lovely sonnets and sonnet sequences, composing an early one 'To Shakespeare', a 'Sonnet on the Sonnet' and, in 1934, in conscious homage to Shakespeare's sonnet 12 ('When I do count the clock that tells the time'), what may well be his own best poem, 'The Wastes of Time'.[20] The previous year Douglas had published, with a depressing absence of irony, as if he had learnt nothing from Wilde after all, *The True History of Shakespeare's Sonnets*.

Shakespeare has never been the sole model for sonnet writers, who can look back not only to Petrarch but also to other major exponents in English from Wyatt, Surrey, Sidney, Daniel and Spenser to Milton,

Wordsworth and Keats. It is not obvious that two of the major sonnet sequences produced by Victorian poets owe much if anything to Shakespeare's example: Elizabeth Barrett Browning's *Sonnets from the Portuguese* (1850) and Dante Gabriel Rossetti's 'The House of Life' (*Poems*, 1870, and *Ballads and Sonnets*, 1881). This did not stop readers making the comparison, especially where Barrett Browning was concerned. For many it was exactly as an antidote to Shakespeare that her *Sonnets* were to be celebrated. In 1873 E.C. Stedman claimed that their 'music is showered from a higher and purer atmosphere than that of the Swan of Avon', and some twenty years later Edmund Gosse thought them 'more wholesome and more intelligible'.[21] George Barnett Smith wondered whether she was better described as 'Tennyson's sister' or 'Shakspere's daughter'. Henry James unkindly suggested the alternative options of 'Wordsworth's niece' or 'Swinburne's aunt': he thought that she possessed 'the real poetic heat in a high degree' but that 'her sense of the poetic form was an absolute muddle'.[22] More generously, in a letter to the poet's husband Ruskin hailed *Aurora Leigh* (1857) as 'the greatest *poem* in the English language, unsurpassed by anything but Shakespeare – *not* surpassed by Shakespeare's *sonnets*, and therefore the greatest poem in the language' (Ruskin, XXXVI, p. 247).

George Meredith's *Modern Love* (1862) was in part a response to the idealism of Elizabeth Barrett Browning's *Sonnets from the Portuguese*. Meredith's sequence of fifty short poems tells the story of a failed marriage. It was not popular. It had a strong autobiographical basis in its author's experience with Mary Nicholls, daughter of Thomas Love Peacock, who died the year before their publication.[23] Both in form and content, Meredith's poems take an acerbically quizzical stance towards the conventions of the sonnet sequence. They are each composed of sixteen lines rather than the usual fourteen, yet so far from extending the imaginative space this has the curious effect of diminishing it. The couplet that closes the Shakespearean sonnet offers the promise at once of resolution and of escape. By contrast, Meredith's is a claustrophobically four-square structure – four rhyming quatrains of four lines each – that offers little hope of release from the writhing drama it contains. This effect of turbulent matter violently confined is heightened by the vertiginous shifts of thought and tone, by ellipses, by bewildering dislocations of syntax, by the shifts of personal pronoun from 'He' to 'I'.[24] In so far as these poems draw or reflect on Shakespearean sources, they do so by reference to the language of dissonance, treachery and violence at large in the sonnets and in the tragedies. Meredith's 'the honey of the Spring' (XI. 2) and 'the sweet wild rose' (XLV. 1) recall the 'summer's honey breath' of Shakespeare's sonnet 65 that will not hold out against 'the wreckful siege of batt'ring days', and the various roses that are prey to canker and armed with thorns. The 'ocean's moaning verge' (XLIX) and the 'midnight ocean's force' (L) recall 'the hungry ocean' of sonnet 64. The exclamation 'heaven and hell!' (XIX) repeats Hamlet's declaration that he is 'prompted to my revenge by heaven and hell' (2.2.584), and the plucking and smelling of the rose (XLV) incite memories of Othello's murder scene ('when I have plucked the rose / ... I'll smell thee on the tree', 5.2.13–15). Indeed, over the whole sequence there looms the shadow of *Othello*, which is unsurprising, given the topic of murderous marital passion. In the bedroom of XV an explicit allusion blossoms. As the man approaches his sleeping wife with written proof of her infidelity, he thinks of himself as 'The Poet's black stage-lion of wronged love' but then he disavows the identification. Or rather, with typically ironic speed, he disavows and then casts a glance of regret at the impossibility for a modern husband of wielding Othello's momentous violence. 'The Poet's black stage-lion ... / Frights not our modern dames: – well if he did!' There is a familiar nostalgia for the language of passion for which Shakespeare stands as the traditional model. In 1901 the *Saturday Review* thought of *Othello* when it spoke of the poems' 'acuteness of sensation carried to the point of agony' (*MCH*, p. 480); in 1948 C. Day Lewis said that Meredith had 'exposed his heart for daws to peck at', which was just what Iago had said he would not do (1.1.63–4).[25] For his acrid portrayal of sexual and emotional treachery Meredith also took heart from the darkest aspects of Shakespeare's own sonnets, from the challenge they mount to the conventional idealism that dominates the whole sonnet tradition up to Shakespeare himself.[26]

No wonder the first reviewers spoke of Meredith's anatomy of marriage as 'loathsome', 'a grave moral mistake', of its 'flippancy' and 'cynicism'.[27]

ROBERT BROWNING

Other poets, however, admired it, including Swinburne, Dante Gabriel Rossetti and Robert Browning. A year after the publication of *Modern Love*, one of Browning's readers praised his poetry in terms that suggest an affinity with Meredith – and a partial affinity with Shakespeare. 'How he delights to work and worm and wind his way to the subtlest places of the soul, and to the mazy problems which the soul is perpetually seeking to solve!' exclaimed E.P. Hood (*RBCH*, p. 211). Less approvingly, the *Saturday Review* compared Browning in 1865 to both Shakespeare and Shelley as writers who are 'apt to entangle the reader in labyrinthine thoughts and verbal perplexities' (*RBCH*, p. 263). For Browning himself Shakespeare and Shelley represented opposite poles. In his 1852 'Essay on Shelley' Browning had identified them respectively as types of the 'objective' and 'subjective' poet. Shakespeare was the model of the maker, the fashioner, 'and the thing fashioned, his poetry, will of necessity be substantive, projected from himself and distinct' (*RBP*, I, 1001). Shelley, by contrast, was more of a 'seer', his poetry 'less a work than an effluence' (*RBP*, I, p. 1002). The former looked down on 'the many' below, the latter up to 'the one' above. This was a way for Browning to describe the surging contrarieties in his own creativity, out (and down) to 'the inexhaustible variety of existence', up (and in) to 'the *Ideas* of Plato, seeds of creation lying burningly on the Divine Hand' (*RBP*, I, p. 1002).

There is a well-established story about Shakespeare's redemptive role in Browning's development, according to which Shakespeare was the Ariadne who escorted him out of the labyrinth of Shelleyan subjectivity. At the end of *Pauline* (1833) Browning appended an odd little note of a place and a date: Richmond, 22 October 1832. This is odd because without inside information the ordinary reader has no means of knowing what this meant to the writer: that it marked the evening he saw the great failing Edmund Kean as Richard III. (The character and play remained a favourite with Browning throughout his life.) The constellation of Kean, Richard and Shakespeare seems to have inspired the young poet with the sense of 'a way out of the big professions, concomitant despair, and endless labyrinth of confessional vacillation in *Pauline*'.[28] It was as if the three figures conspired together – dramatist, fictional king and performer – to produce a vision of rampant spirit, of courage and even triumph in the teeth of failure. These lines from *Pauline* were Browning's tribute to Kean:

> and there shall come
> A time requiring youth's best energies;
> And lo, I fling age, sorrow, sickness off,
> And rise triumphant, triumph through decay.
>
> (672–5)[29]

Some six months after Browning saw him at Richmond, Kean was dead.

Shakespeare was for Browning a force for flinging off and rising, an active means of resisting the threat of gravity, incarceration, paralysis. But there was another and more important way in which Shakespeare figured for Browning. Consider this astonishing passage in the 'Essay on Shelley', where Browning is thinking about Shakespeare's personality, the impossibility of our knowing it and the inevitability of our speculating about it:

> Did the personality of such an one stand like an open watch-tower in the midst of the territory it is erected to gaze on, and were the storms and calms, the stars and meteors, its watchman was wont to report of, the habitual variegation of his every-day life, as they glanced across its open roof or lay reflected on its four-square parapet? Or did some sunken and darkened chamber of imagery witness, in the artificial illumination of every storied compartment we are permitted to contemplate, how rare and precious were the outlooks through here and there an embrasure upon a world beyond, and how blankly would have pressed on

the artificer the boundary of his daily life, except for the amorous
diligence with which he had rendered permanent by art
whatever came to diversify the gloom? (*RBP*, I, p. 1002)

In so far as these questions require an answer, it is clearly 'both'. The
mystery is that the alternatives are not mutually exclusive: the watch-
tower exposed to the elements and the deep inward gloom punctured
by chinks of light, the loyalty of the watchman and the 'amorous
diligence' of the prisoner. This fastness comprises both watch-tower and
dark-room, and its impregnability guarantees the elusiveness of the self
it harbours. There are many towers in Browning's writing, most
famously the 'Dark Tower' to which Childe Roland comes in a poem
that takes off from a moment in Shakespeare. There is a sense in which
Shakespeare *is* the dark tower by which Browning's endless meditations
on the mysteries of the self are inspired, round which they circulate.

The comparison and contrast between Browning and Shakespeare
was frequent. The heroine of *The Ring and the Book* (1868–9) was
compared amongst others to Imogen, Cordelia and Juliet (*RBCH*,
p. 318). More thoughtfully, J.H. Stirling suggested that the comparison
between Tennyson and Browning might be illuminated by that between
Milton and Shakespeare. For sheer verbal music Milton may have been
as superior to Shakespeare as Tennyson was to Browning, yet we would
not for that reason alone place Milton higher than Shakespeare. If only
Browning could add 'action' to the brilliant psychological studies that
were already 'essentially dramatic', thought Stirling, he might become
a true second Shakespeare. He had already given us a younger brother
to Othello, in character at least (he means the title-character of *Luria*
(1846)). Was it beyond him to produce another *Cymbeline*, or *Taming of
the Shrew*, or *Lear* (*RBCH*, pp. 282–3)? (The choices are curious.)
Browning's genius was clearly 'dramatic' even or especially when it did
not take the conventional form of drama, for performance in public. Did
it matter? His readers puzzled over this. The first instalment of *The Ring
and the Book* prompted R.W. Buchanan to reflect on its differences from
'a Shakspearean exhibition'. He concluded that 'the drama is glorious,
we all know, but we want this thing as well; – we must have Browning

as well as Shakspeare' (*RBCH*, p. 294). There was no need for rivalry then, except for Browning partisans who wanted to go beyond the belief that their man was 'the greatest thinker in poetry since Shakespeare', and claim that he was 'necessarily superior to Shakespeare, as being the all-receptive child of the century of science and travel' (*RBCH*, pp. 492, 473).

It was the creatively oblique relation to Shakespearean drama that was the key issue. This was how Hood saw the comparison with Shakespeare. If Browning's poems were, to borrow the title of one of his own plays, 'soul tragedies', then they presented 'an order of tragedy differing from Shakespeare's – the agony, the strife, the internal stress are more internalised' (*RBCH*, p. 211). Hood's claim puts Browning on a par with George Eliot, as one of the two great Victorian writers, poet and novelist, who find new ways of making great drama 'internal' – and therefore, distinctively 'modern'. The figures of the maze and the labyrinth to which Hood has recourse are those to which Eliot herself would be increasingly drawn for her own 'soul tragedies'. In another sense, they become figures not just for the activity of Victorian writers in verse or in prose, but also for the experience of readers as they pass through the twists and turns of the text.

Yet there are likely to be major differences in this respect between the poet and the novelist, at least in the nineteenth century. Poets are less committed to narrative, though they may choose ways in which to commit themselves, just as novelists may choose to challenge their commitment and rewrite its terms. Elizabeth Barrett and Robert Browning produced two of their most astonishing works of verse, *Aurora Leigh* and *The Ring and the Book*, in narrative form. Nevertheless these are both inconceivable without their authors' prior experience with the first-person voice, and, especially in Robert's case, the development of a style of writing that seemed tortuous, elliptical, unpredictable. In its formation it owed a double debt to Shakespeare. For its 'obscurity' it found authority in the riddles of the sonnets. In 1863 one of Browning's readers, Sir F.T. Marzials, spoke of his poems as 'a deep and often a dark and difficult mine; but there is gold to be found at the bottom: they are a casket the lock of which is hard to pick, but which contains rich treasures' (*RBCH*, p. 213). Sure enough, when Marzials looks for precedents it is to Shakespeare's sonnets (and some of Coleridge's poems). But the 'I' or 'I's' who speak the sonnets are less clearly distinct from their author than the first persons who speak (in) Browning's greatest poems. This is because these latter are more immediately 'dramatic', in the sense that they are provided with more material circumstances than the 'I' of the sonnets, a more exigent sense of story, and above all the consciousness that other men and women are listening to them. The other aspect of the debt is provided by the great soliloquizers of the plays themselves, especially Hamlet and Iago.

E.P. Hood had remarked of the obstacles to Browning's popularity that the English reader feels unaddressed because the poet lives so much in other ages and countries. It was exactly to combat such parochialism that Browning *did* seek out subjects and stories from other countries, other ages. Hood finds a quietly unexpected word to describe Browning's activity (too quiet for the *OED* to have noticed it). He says that Browning 'unconditions himself from those circumstances which would attract English readers' (*RBCH*, p. 211). But if Browning does uncondition himself, it is with a view to exploring all sorts of new conditions, both for himself and for his fictional characters, all densely embodied and embedded in their little worlds of circumstance. Amongst these circumstances we need to include the other human beings to whom they are nearest if not always simply, given the vicissitudes of love, dearest. Othello assures Iago that it is only the force of his love for Desdemona that has made him surrender 'my unhoused free condition' (1.2.26). *Othello* is obsessed with the thought of what a 'free condition' might be, and the fear of everything that threatens its possibility. These are questions at the heart of Browning's most memorable poetry, so often focused on the ordeals of love and marriage, as for example in 'Any Wife to Any Husband', 'My Last Duchess' and 'Andrea del Sarto'.

The Ring and the Book draws some inspiration from Shakespeare.[30] There is a certain diffusion of Shakespearean diction, of words such as 'coil' and 'chop-fallen' (cf. *Ham*, 5.1.190). An advocate thinks, of his opposing counsel: '– Ha, my Bottini, have I thee on hip?' (8.165;

cf. *Oth*, 2.1.302), and rounds off his Book with the injunction, 'Sing "Tra-la-la, for lambkins, we must live!"' (8.1805). This is a memory of Pistol's line as he exits with his friends to condole with the dying Falstaff (*H5*, 2.1.126). Reflecting on the 'strange temptation' endured by 'Pompilia, wife, and Caponsacchi, priest', the Pope recalls Hamlet's 'Promptings from heaven and hell' (10.662; *Ham*, 2.2.586). But it is *Othello* that provides the most significant points of reference. The lawyer Bottini echoes Othello's 'balmy breath' (5.2.16) as he imagines the priest Caponsacchi leaning over the sleeping Pompilia and stealing 'a balmy breath perhaps / For more assurance sleep was not decease' (9.743–4). Caponsacchi speaks of a further killing, of a cousin poisoned because he knew too much: 'Does that much strike you as a sin? Not much, / After the present murder, – one mark more / On the Moor's skin, – what is black by blacker still?' (6.2033–5). Pompilia's husband Guido refers to himself as 'Sir Jealousy' (5.1147), and thinks of the effect of his jealousy on the wine he drinks, 'Weak once, now acrid with the toad's-head-squeeze' (5.1389). Shakespearean toads and birds run freely in his mind: looking back on his marriage to Pompilia, he reflects that he bought no pigeon, Venus' pet, but a hawk.

> 'I have paid my pound, await my penny's worth,
> So, hoodwink, starve and properly train my bird,
> And, should she prove a haggard, – twist her neck!'
>
> (5.708–10)

This echoes a cry of Othello's (3.3.264–7), though he spoke of whistling her off and letting her down the wind rather than twisting her neck. From 'Porphyria's Lover' (1836) onwards there is a lot of strangling in Browning, and an intimate familiarity with *Othello* seems common to many of his characters. It is also assumed in his readers. Amongst other things *The Ring and the Book* may be thought of as a rewriting of the play's central knot of relations. Pompilia is a true Desdemona, rescued from her repellent murderous husband by Caponsacchi, the loyal and loving Cassio with whom she is falsely suspected of having illicit relations. But the great creative turn that Browning gives to the Shakespearean model of marital murder comes from fusing the two roles that the dramatist divides. This produces the new nightmare figure of Guido, who is at once Othello and Iago.

Two of Browning's most remarkable poems explicitly acknowledge a Shakespearean source. 'Caliban upon Setebos; or, Natural Theology in the Island' (1864) is a brilliant variation on Browning's characteristic dramatic monologues. It is spoken by the single figure of Caliban, albeit he switches between speaking of himself in the third person, the first person and most weirdly, no person at all, as in his opening words, '['Will sprawl, ...]'. But Browning's other great monologues are distinguished by the speaker's palpable consciousness of a hearer or hearers who could, and sometimes implicitly do, speak back. The sense of potential dialogue is paramount. 'Caliban' is by contrast a study in terrible loneliness, the imagination of a being who can only talk to himself, yet who lives in terror of being overheard by the ferocious Setebos, his god. The 'upon' of the poem's title is ironic, given how comprehensively 'under' is its poor speaker. This is what it means to be a slave. For the slave, to speak is not to seek a response from another, whether human or divine; it is only to risk punishment from an infinitely stronger creature. And this is what Caliban is, and lives amongst: creatures. Browning draws to wonderful effect on the relish for his natural habitat with which Shakespeare endowed his Caliban – his lyrical zest for the crabs, pig-nuts, jay's nests, nimble marmosets, clustering filberts and young scamels (*Tem*, 2.2.165–70), or again for the 'Sounds and sweet airs, that give delight, and hurt not' (3.2.138). As the rank tongue of Browning's Caliban blossoms into speech (23), he hails 'Yon otter, sleek-wet, black, lithe as a leech; / Yon auk, one fire-eye in a ball of foam, / That floats and feeds' (46–8). This sounds like liberty, both for the otter, auk and speaker alike. But it is an illusion. There is no freedom in this world because there is no love between its creator and its creatures, and thus between the creatures themselves. Its principle is 'spite' and its prime activity 'to vex'. There is no love, no dialogue, no mating, just casual sadistic play. Everything is only made to be toyed with, tormented or spared or discarded at whim, whether by Setebos or his creature Caliban. The nearest thing Caliban gets to a mate is 'A four-legged serpent he makes cower and couch, / Now snarl, now hold its breath and mind his eye'. He calls this, grotesquely, 'Miranda and my wife' (158–60).

Yet there are a few intimations of Caliban's yearning for another kind of creation, one in which the icy fish would have succeeded in escaping from its rock-stream into the welcoming warmth of the sea. Instead, so he thinks, the fish recoiled: 'Flounced back from bliss she was not born to breathe, / And in her old bounds buried her despair' (41–2). The desire for escape from the old bounds into new life and the disappointment at its failure are captured in the extraordinary sexual image of 'A crystal spike 'twixt two warm walls of wave' (37). Another expression of Caliban's yearning is his imagination of 'the something over Setebos' (129), a prior or superior 'Quiet', into which perhaps one day Setebos may grow, 'As grubs grow butterflies: else, here are we, / And there is He, and nowhere help at all' (248–9). Shakespeare's Caliban inspired Browning to imagine the hell of a world without love, as perceived by a creature still yearning, without either hope or faith, for escape to something other and better, out of nature. At the end of 'Halbert and Hob' (1879) Browning suddenly introduces a question asked by King Lear at the height of his disenchantment with human nature – and answers it, thus:

'Is there any reason in nature for these hard hearts?' O Lear,
That a reason out of nature must turn them soft, seems clear!

In its extraordinary way 'Caliban upon Setebos' is a tragic meditation on *The Tempest*, as seen from the position of total abjection and exclusion from a world of love, friendship and sociability.

This is exactly the position represented in *King Lear* by the idea of Poor Tom, who stands for all the 'Poor naked wretches' (3.4.28) exposed to the wind and rain. The other great poem of Browning's inspired by Shakespeare, '"Childe Roland to the Dark Tower Came"' (1855) takes its title from the 'song' uttered by Edgar at the end of this scene, presumably in his role as Poor Tom, just before the King enters his hovel. He begins, 'Childe Rowland to the dark tower came', and continues, 'His word was still "Fie, foh, and fum, / I smell the blood of a British man"' (3.4.178–80). The opening line sounds magnificent, as if it were drawn from an old heroic ballad (which it may be); but it is swiftly punctured by the fairytale grotesque of the next two. It moves in a flash from 'Childe' to 'child', as it were, from the epic world of chivalric quest to the play-world of real youngsters. Why does Poor Tom recall these lines at precisely this moment? Presumably to mark the rite of passage from heath into hovel, from the grand rhetoric the King has believed he requires to the new language he will find, in more than one sense, 'inside'.

The speaker of Browning's poem tells the story of his progress across a kind of heath or 'ominous tract' towards 'the Dark Tower' that is the object of a lifelong quest. He succeeds in reaching it but he does not enter. Watched by 'all the lost adventurers my peers ... ranged along the hill-sides' (195–9), like an audience in a theatre, he raises his 'slug-horn' to his lips and blows, to wonderfully mysterious effect, the words of the poem's title, or the musical notes by which we suppose them to be identified: '*Childe Roland to the Dark Tower came*'. And here the poem ends. The speaker is anonymous. Yet the way he utters these sonorous inaudible words makes it seem as though he becomes at such a moment 'Childe Roland' himself. The poem closes with this statement of heroic defiance, of indomitable self-assertion, of triumph in ruin. For it has been made clear, as he crosses the desolate nightmare landscape – 'Bog, clay and rubble, sand and stark black dearth' (150) – that 'the safe road' is long gone and there is no way back. In so far as the poem reflects on the journeys undertaken by Shakespearean tragic protagonists, this culminating utterance bears comparison with such brave exclamations as 'This is I, / Hamlet the Dane' (*Ham*, 5.1.255–6) or 'I am / Antony yet' (*AC*, 3.13.97–8). Or more exactly with the moments in which a character stands on the brink of death and makes a mighty final assertion of self before giving up the ghost – Othello's last speech, for example. Several echoes from Shakespeare have flitted through the poem, including the 'Toads in a poisoned tank' (131) that recall Othello's 'cistern for foul toads / To knot and gender in' (4.2.62–3). The reader does not need to think too specifically of the witches' brew in *Macbeth* when the speaker asks 'Will the night send a howlet or a bat?' (106). Nor specifically of Ophelia at hearing of the

'Drenched willows ... a suicidal throng' (117–18), nor of Ariel at 'The tempest's mocking elf' (184), nor of Antony's 'sad captains' (*AC*, 3.13.189) at 'all the lost adventurers my peers' (195). But the sense of diffused allusion to Shakespeare is set in motion by a reference that it is harder to miss. This is when the speaker says: 'I shut my eyes and turned them on my heart. / As a man calls for wine before he fights' (85–6). Richard III is not the only man in fact or in fiction to call for wine before he fights (*R3*, 5.3.64, 73), but he must be the great Shakespearean instance. Instead of the ghosts that then appear to Shakespeare's Richard the night before Bosworth Field, Browning's speaker is attended by the memories of his comrades Cuthbert and Giles, by which he expects to be heartened. He is bitterly disappointed as he recalls their disgrace, so that he too, like Richard, goes to meet his final ordeal even more inwardly destitute. 'Childe Roland to the Dark Tower came.' 'A horse! A horse! My kingdom for a horse!' The speakers almost disappear into the bravura utterances by which they will be remembered.

Browning's is a dramatic narrative that chooses to conclude or simply break off at a point and in a manner impossible to Shakespearean drama. But mature Shakespeare plays such as *King Lear* are composed of several narratives, and Browning has here identified and extricated one in particular, an old heroic story of honour lost and regained. This is embodied in Gloucester's legitimate son and heir. It is Edgar who ensures that the trumpets will sound the summons to judgment; whose name is lost; who tries most urgently to hold the play's whole story together and bring it to a collective promised end, even as it shatters into particular final partings. Tragedy incites a desire for the 'real story'. We need it to explain all the mess and the pain and the waste and tell us what they are *for*. We need a story that will carry us through the years and across the ominous tract to the promised end. But what if there is no meaning or value or significance to the story? What if it is just a way of passing the time and crossing the space? 'I might go on; nought else remained to do' (54), says the speaker at the end of one stanza. 'So, on I went' (55), he begins the next, with proto-Beckettian glumness.

ALFRED LORD TENNYSON

Like his great contemporary, Tennyson was rich in memories of Shakespeare. These sometimes contribute to an artificial sheen. In 'Recollections of the Arabian Nights' the phrases 'golden prime' (10) and 'stilly sound' (103) need not excite conscious recollections of their sources in *Richard III* (1.2.252) and *Henry V* (4.0.5).[31] Nor will all readers pick up the Shakespearean provenance of such singletons, however striking, as 'tanling', 'vauntcourier', 'sober-suited', 'swinge-buckler', 'master-chord' and 'steep-up'. There were those of his contemporaries who found Tennyson's diction precious, over-cultivated, flowers of the garden and not of wild nature, as the belligerent Alfred Austin put it (*TCH*, p. 301). The young Gerard Manley Hopkins was prompted by Tennyson's example to identify a kind of verse he called 'Parnassian', that settles into predictability and runs 'in an intelligibly laid down path', such as makes you think you could write or walk it yourself.[32] Shakespeare is the antitype of the Parnassian poet because he always takes the reader by surprise. Reflecting famously on the challenge of translating Homer, Matthew Arnold brought a different charge against Tennyson for his lack of plainness, his fondness for 'an extreme subtlety and curious elaborateness of thought, an extreme subtlety and curious elaborateness of expression' (*TCH*, p. 267). These were characteristics he shared with the Elizabethans, including Shakespeare. They were to Arnold's mind dangerous role models for the modern poet – unlike Sophocles. Look at the damage Shakespeare had done to poor Keats, who was in key respects Tennyson's predecessor.

These are significant worries. Tennyson's critics express a set of anxieties about being indebted to great predecessors, about getting stuck in a rut, about being self-absorbed, introverted and excessively concerned with detail. However these are not merely symptoms of a malaise by which Tennyson's poetry is vitiated. They are also the subjects it addresses. ''Twere to consider too curiously, to consider so', says Horatio, mildly (*Ham*, 5.1.203–4). But Horatio will never be anyone's model for creative thought or expression. *Hamlet* was for Tennyson 'the greatest creation in literature that I know of' (*Memoir*, II,

p. 291), and its hero one of his most important patrons, not least because he considers everything so curiously, especially the experience of mourning.

Nevertheless a true sense of what Tennyson owes to Shakespeare and what he makes of him must take into account the ways in which they are quite unlike each other. Walter Bagehot pointed to some key issues in 1859, when he judged the *Idylls of the King* to be 'deficient in dramatic power'. He went on to contrast soliloquy with conversation: 'The glancing mind will tend to one sort of composition; the meditative, solitary, and heavy mind to the other.' Tennyson was the polar opposite of Shakespeare:

> His genius gives the notion of a slow depositing instinct; day by day, as the hours pass, the delicate sand falls into beautiful forms – in stillness, in peace, in brooding. You fancy Shakespeare writing quick, the hasty dialogue of the parties passing quickly through his brain: we have no such idea of our great contemporary poet. (*TCH*, pp. 230–1)

The contrast is partly explained by the difference between the lyric and the dramatic poet, but the question of tempo, momentum and direction is no less significant, of slow falling as against swift passage through.

'Mariana' (1830) was inspired by the character in *Measure for Measure*, or more exactly, by the Duke's reference to 'the moated grange' where the dejected woman resides, abandoned by her lover Angelo. David Masson linked it with Browning's 'Childe Roland' in the way it expanded on a slight Shakespearean hint (*RBCH*, p. 181), and there are evident parallels with the extrapolation of Shakespearean women by visual artists discussed in chapter two, and by some storytellers discussed in chapter three. Faint further reference to Shakespeare's play is made by the phrase 'Upon the middle of the night' (25). This numbly echoes Isabella's 'Upon the heavy middle of the night' (*MM*, 4.1.35) and yearningly recalls Keats's luscious transformation of 'heavy' into 'honeyed' in 'The Eve of St Agnes' (49).[33] The memory of other and better love stories is also dimly furthered by 'the gray-eyed morn' (31) from *Romeo and Juliet* (2.2.188). Tennyson beautifully wrote of his poem that 'The *moated grange* was no particular grange, but one which rose to the music of Shakespeare's words' (quoted in *TP*, I, 205). This has the ring of myth or fairy tale, of a 'dreamy house' (61) not only raised by the power of sound but also composed of it. Falling and rising: this vertical scale is often at the heart of Tennyson, a measure with theological, psychological, biological aspects. It is complemented by an opposition between the stillness, peace and brooding to which Bagehot points, and a vigorous sense of expedition and exercise, of vigorous forward movement. Downward and inward, upward and outward: the former tends to inertia, stagnation, paralysis, to metaphors of rotting and rusting, and the latter to dynamic currents, to the figures of water and wind in full flow. Though there is often no need to hear a specific connexion, Tennyson's attraction to images of water suggests at the least an affinity with Shakespeare's deployment of the waves that 'make towards the pebbled shore' (sonnet 60), or of the 'sea-change / Into something rich and strange' of which Ariel sings in *The Tempest* (1.2.403–4).

One of the charms in the word 'grange' is that it rhymes with 'strange' and 'change'. Compare this stanza from *In Memoriam*, XLI.

> But thou art turned to something strange,
>   And I have lost the links that bound
>   Thy changes; here upon the ground,
> No more partaker of thy change.

> (5–8)

This is not the watery element of *The Tempest*, but fire and air: Hallam's spirit is flying upwards while the poet is left behind on earth.

Unlike the magical metamorphoses enjoyed by Shakespearean characters in the comedies and romances, but like Browning's Caliban, Mariana endures a state that seems to be precisely 'without hope of change'. Like Tennyson's Tithonus she longs for conclusion, and at the end she edges slightly towards it when her refrain modulates into the certainty that 'He will not come', into tears, and the invocation of God. But is she right, that he will not come? Not if we recall the Shakespearean source, in which Mariana is reunited with a contrite

Angelo. Christopher Ricks finely describes it as 'one of Tennyson's masterpieces in the art of the penultimate', a poem 'in which the final ending is shrouded but magnetic'.[34]

Mariana is the most memorable of a bevy of desirable lonely women in Tennyson's early poetry. The *Blackwood's* reviewer of the 1832 *Poems* allowed himself to wax sentimental: 'We are in love – as an old man ought to be – as a father is with his ideal daughters – with them all – with Claribel, and Lilian, and Isabel, and Mariana, and Adeline, and Hero, and Almeida, and the Sleeping Beauty, and Oriana' (*TCH*, p. 60). But it is not a fatherly, let alone grandfatherly, interest the reader is asked to take in these women. The reviewer thinks of the young poet dreaming over the vision of Mariana, 'On this hint Alfred Tennyson speaks' – as Othello spoke to Desdemona (1.3.167). In the Shakespeare play from which Tennyson has extracted Mariana, it is of course her old lover Angelo for whom the dejected woman waits. Tennyson's Mariana seems to draw to her a force of erotic desire enveloping other Shakespearean women such as Desdemona and Juliet. (There is a feverish 1830 poem, not reprinted in Tennyson's lifetime, addressed to 'Sainted Juliet! Dearest name!') Mariana justifies Arthur Hallam's fine comment on these poems that 'They are like summaries of mighty dramas' (*TCH*, p. 48).

Take 'Rosalind' (1832) for example. If the title suggests the heroine of *As You Like It*, it is also close kin to Rosaline, the name of one of the leading women in *Love's Labour's Lost*, and of the icily Petrarchan lady Romeo thinks he is in love with until he meets the real thing. In fact *Romeo and Juliet* seems to be running powerfully in the poet's mind, or the voice of the male lover he is staging. This Rosalind is his 'bright-eyed, wild-eyed falcon' (6), his 'gay young hawk' (34). Her sexual independence is alluring and threatening, so 'we must hood your random eyes, / That care not whom they kill' (37–8).

> We'll bind you fast in silken cords,
> And kiss away the bitter words
> From off your rosy mouth.

> (49–51)

It is as if the speaker is grimly reclaiming the beautiful metaphors so gently wielded by Shakespeare's Juliet as she explores her new relationship with Romeo: 'O for a falconer's voice / To lure this tassel-gentle back again' (2.2.158–9). The 'silken cords' of which Tennyson's lover dreams recall the more delicate 'silken thread' that Juliet thinks of plucking Romeo back by, 'So loving-jealous of his liberty' (2.2.180–1). Cleopatra's barge boasts 'silken tackle' (*AC*, 2.2.219); she makes an ominous appearance in 'A Dream of Fair Women', and glancingly again in *Maud*, when the speaker speculates, as he begins to fall in love with Maud, that she may have meant 'To entangle me when we met, / To have her lion roll in a silken net' (I.217–18). This darker form of 'loving jealousy' is the subject of Tennyson's 'Rosalind'. It is a meditation on the psychology of mastery and submission explored by Shakespeare through the early comedies. The woman addressed here in Tennyson is more like Romeo's Rosaline than his Juliet, and the voice of the male lover a combination of Petruchio, Berowne, Benedick and an unreformed Romeo. There is a sense in which the early Tennyson, like other Victorian poets, is 'loving jealous' of Shakespeare himself, especially the creator of Romeo and Juliet.

Romeo and Juliet is important to a far more substantial poem, one of Tennyson's greatest: *Maud: A Monodrama* (1855). It is true that the poet's own thoughts in retrospect ran on *Hamlet*. Here are Hallam Tennyson's memories of his father reading the poem.

> You were at once put in sympathy with the hero. As he said himself, 'This poem is a little *Hamlet*', the history of a morbid poetic soul, under the blighting influence of a recklessly speculative age. He is the heir of madness, an egotist with the makings of a cynic, raised to sanity by a pure and holy love which elevates his whole nature, passing from the height of triumph to the lowest depths of misery, driven into madness by the loss of her whom he has loved, and, when he has at length passed through the fiery furnace, and has recovered his reason, giving himself up to work for the good of mankind through the unselfishness born of his great passion. (*Memoir*, II, p. 212)

He went on to say that 'The peculiarity of this poem ... is that different phases of passion in one person take the place of different characters' (*Memoir*, II, p. 213). As with Browning's dramatic monologues, *Maud* finds a rich way of assimilating and putting to new uses its Shakespearean models and sources. George Brimley defended the poem against myopic charges that the main character was morbid, hysterical, spasmodic: 'The fact is, that Mr Tennyson, without abandoning his lyric forms, has in *Maud* written a tragedy' (*TCH*, p. 196).

The anonymous speaker of *Maud* confesses to a 'morbid-hate' of the world, and to 'a morbid eating lichen fixt / On a heart half-turned to stone' (I.264, 266). Tennyson's poetry was often described at the time as 'morbid'. It is not a word that Shakespeare knew (the earliest *OED* citation is 1656), but when Charles Kingsley wrote of 'morbid melancholy' in 1842 (cited by *OED*), he coupled it with the state of being inextricably associated with Hamlet. To John Stuart Mill 'Mariana' expressed 'the dreariness which speaks not merely of being far from human converse and sympathy, but of being *deserted* by it' (*TCH*, p. 87). The *Maud*-speaker identifies himself with Mariana's abandonment by recalling the mouse that behind the mouldering wainscot shrieked ('And the shrieking rush of the wainscot mouse', I.260). James Spedding was moved by *Poems* (1842), especially by 'The Palace of Art', to think of Richard III, and 'the despair which the sense of being cut off from human sympathy ... inevitably brings' (*TCH*, p. 148). But Hamlet, above all in his soliloquies, is unequalled as a model for the expression and anatomy of morbid melancholy.

Shakespearean tragedy provided Tennyson with a certain rhetoric of 'heroism'. In the early poem 'The Old Chieftain' (1827), reference is made to the 'heaven-kissing towers' (15). The epithet is Hamlet's in the confrontation with his mother, reminding her of his god-like father, as he wishes to remember him (3.4.59). Another early piece 'To Poesy' (1828) seizes on Macbeth's 'trumpet-tongu'd' (1.7.19) and makes its angelic reverberations serve the good cause of 'Mind, / Whose trumpet-tongued, aerial melody / May blow alarum loud to every wind' (2–4). When the title-character of 'Ulysses' vows that he will 'drink / Life to the lees' (6–7), he is defying Macbeth's 'The wine of life is drawn, and the mere lees / Is left this vault to brag of' (2.3.93–4). The *Maud*-speaker mimics Macbeth's bravado when he exclaims 'Then let come what come may' (I.402). This follows hot on the heels of his most blatant appeal for 'a man with heart, head, hand, / Like some of the simple great ones gone/ For ever and ever by' (389–1). 'A was a man, take him for all in all. There is always a fair chance that *Hamlet* will be running in the mind of the writer and reader, in the nineteenth century and beyond, when a son grieves for his lost father and yearns 'for a man to arise in me' (I.396).

But *Hamlet* also provides, as no other tragedy does, the language of doubt, vacillation and estrangement. In 'Supposed Confessions of a Second-Rate Sensitive Mind' (but Hamlet's is *first*-rate), there is a strong sense of the graveyard grotesquerie – 'that sharp-headed worm begins / In the gross blackness underneath' (186–7) – in which Thomas Hardy will later revel (see for instance his 'Voices from Things Growing in a Churchyard'). 'The Two Voices' was first entitled 'Thoughts of a Suicide', and the voice of idealism protests, like Hamlet, against the prospect of 'rotting like a weed' (142).[35] The rhyme words 'seed' and 'deed' here point to the conflict at the heart of the poem. Ulysses remembers Hamlet's resolution (4.4.33–9) when he repudiates the 'savage race, / That hoard, and sleep, and feed, and know not me' (4–5).

Yet it is *Romeo and Juliet* that takes over from *Hamlet* in providing the main plot structure of *Maud*.[36] The lovers are radically estranged by the rivalry of their two houses, and the accidental death in a duel of Maud's brother has the same plot-function as the death of Tybalt in exposing their love and driving them apart. The 'mad' sequence which follows (Part II) seems to draw on *King Lear*; in the speaker's 'Arsenic, arsenic, sure, would do it' (300), there surfaces Lear's 'peace, peace; this piece of toasted cheese will do't' (4.6.89–90). The most problematic part of the poem, however, involves the speaker's recovery from derangement, which is not to the arms of a loving woman. Instead the speaker turns, as it were, into Fortinbras: there have been earlier hints of this possibility in his longing for martial action as a means to political and personal health. As with 'Ulysses', it is impossible to say how far the poet endorses the surge to commitment, or whether, as one may prefer to read it, this is still part of a dramatic study, a 'mono*drama*', as its subtitle professes. When Tennyson sent 'The Charge of the Light Brigade' to John Forster, the editor of the *Examiner* was rapturous in his praise for the poet as 'the only "muse of fire" now left to us'.[37] Like the king from the prologue to whose play this phrase is famously taken (*H*5), Tennyson was solving the particular dilemma endured by the speaker of *Maud* by busying his mind with foreign quarrels.

Let us turn in conclusion to the poem that most fully demonstrates Tennyson's creative absorption and deployment of Shakespeare: *In Memoriam A.H.H.* (1850). Its first readers compared it to Shakespeare's sonnets and to Milton's 'Lycidas'; Ricks calls the former 'important both as a source and as an analogue' (*TP*, ii, p. 313). To them we must add the spirit of Hamlet in so far as he explores with special intensity the dynamics of memory and forgetting, and their role in mourning.

The analogy with the sonnets was not always cause for admiration, for reasons sketched earlier in this chapter. *The Times* reviewer sniffed disapprovingly: 'Shakespeare may be considered the founder of this style in English. In classical and Oriental poetry it is unpleasantly familiar. . . . We really think that floating remembrances of Shakespeare's sonnets have beguiled Mr Tennyson.'[38] But his friends and admirers could also express their anxiety at his potential beguilement, his capacity, as Benjamin Jowett cautiously put it, 'perhaps in his weaker moments', to think the sonnets superior to the plays. Tennyson's poem was perhaps a form of controlled regression, the exploration of a 'phase':

> He would have seemed to me to be reverting for a moment to the great sorrow of his own mind. *It would not have been manly or natural to have lived in it always.* But in that peculiar phase of mind he found the sonnets a deeper expression of the never to be forgotten love which he felt more than any of the many moods of many minds which appear among his dramas. *The love of the sonnets which he so strikingly expressed was a sort of sympathy with Hellenism.* (my italics; quoted in *TP*, ii, p. 313)

The italicized sentences were omitted by the poet's son from his *Memoir*. Charles Kingsley on the other hand thought Tennyson's poem superior to Shakespeare's sonnets, 'for the sake of the superior faith into which it rises, for the sake of the proem at the opening of the volume – in our eyes, the noblest English Christian poem which several centuries have seen' (*TCH*, p. 183).

However the one hundred and thirty-three 'Elegies', as Tennyson called them in the process of composition (the count includes the Prologue and Epilogue), are not written in sonnet form but in four-line stanzas, variable in number, with an *abba* rhyme-scheme. It is worth attending to some reflections of Tennyson's on sonnet form, as reported by a visitor in 1890. According to William Angus Knight, Tennyson considered that 'The Sonnet arrests the free sweep of genius, and if poets were to keep to it, it would cripple them.' He conceded that it was 'a fascinating kind of verse, and to excel in it ... a rare distinction'. Knight suggested to him that the movement within the sonnet to its last-line climax should be like a wave breaking on the shore. 'Not only so', Tennyson replied; 'the whole should show a continuous advance of thought and of movement, like a river fed by rillets, as every great poem, and all essays and treatises, should.'[39]

In Memoriam is like a river fed by rillets (or 'rivulets', another watery word of which Tennyson was fond). It is much concerned with the threat of being arrested and the possibility of continuous advance. Where Meredith extended the fourteen-line sonnet to create a more oppressive structure, Tennyson's little four-line stanza does not attempt to rival the daunting, potentially crippling sonnet. The stanza contains and confines, as it must, to embody the grasp of the past, the potentially paralysing force of grief, of morbid melancholy. But the modesty of this formal enclosure and the capacity of individual poems to swell to varying lengths permit the poem as a whole to advance, steadily if not always continuously, in the service of good mourning.

There are a number of specific memories of Shakespeare's sonnets. There is a triple allusion in the lines 'Or reach a hand through time to catch / The far-off interest of tears?' (I. 7–8), to sonnet 31, *The Rape of Lucrece* and *Richard III*, and in 'The herald melodies of spring'

(XXXVIII.6) to sonnet 1. Thinking of Hallam's tomb, 'Thy marble bright in dark appears' (LXVII.5), the poet recalls sonnet 43. One stanza doubly reworks images of time's motion:

> For every grain of sand that runs
> And every span of shade that steals,
> And every kiss of toothed wheels,
> And all the courses of the suns.
>
> (CXVII.9–12)

Here memories of sonnets 77 ('thy dial's shady stealth') and 59 ('five hundred courses of the sun') are made to kiss with the image of the watch or clock drawn from Tennyson's own more mechanized world. The idea of time's consuming, devouring teeth is softened but not entirely erased by the idea of a mouth that might bite – and kisses instead.

There are many other allusions to and echoes from the plays, as for example *Othello*, for the violence unleashed by thwarted passion. When the poet thinks of crushing Sorrow 'like a vice of blood' (III.15), he is explicitly remembering Othello's 'the vices of my blood' (1.3.125), and implicitly, in 'crush', the murderous violence of Act 5. Again, 'the wrath that garners in my heart' (LXXXII.14) is a painful echo of Othello's 'there where I have garnered up my heart' (4.2.58). There is a beautiful and painful echo in the 'balmy breath' – a memory of Othello bending over the sleeping Desdemona – with which dim dawn wakens

> To myriads on the genial earth,
> Memories of bridal, or of birth,
> And unto myriads more, of death.
>
> (XCIX.14–16)

But the most significant memories are of *Hamlet*. Consider this sequence, which helps to chart the slow progressive movement towards the laying of grief to rest. Note the recurrence of the hands that reach out for the lost beloved, that gently bear the body, that bid each other farewell. Here, in a famous short poem (VII), the poet haunts the 'Dark house' where he used to wait for the loved one's hand,

> A hand that can be clasped no more –
>   Behold me, for I cannot sleep
>   And like a guilty thing I creep
> At earliest morning to the door.
>
> (vii.5–8)

'Like a guilty thing' has the partial effect of turning the poet into a ghost rather than the lost beloved, recalling as it does the Ghost of Hamlet's father, who 'started like a guilty thing' (1.1.153). Tennyson said 'it was the most real ghost that ever was' (*Memoir*, ii, p. 291). (Partial, because the 'guilty thing' also reaches Tennyson from Wordsworth's 'Immortality Ode'.) Hallam's burial prompts some relief, and a memory of Laertes's prayer for his sister, that 'from her fair and unpolluted flesh / May violets spring' (5.1.237–8).

> 'Tis well; 'tis something; we may stand
>   Where he in English earth is laid,
>   And from his ashes may be made
> The violet of his native land.
>
> (xviii.1–4)

How much more decorous than the shameful travesty at Ophelia's grave is the invocation: 'Come then, pure hands, and bear the head / . . . And hear the ritual of the dead' (9, 12). As the poet increasingly accepts the finality of separation in this world, he draws a parallel between the bride leaving her parents' home and the spirit leaving the earth. She will return:

> But thou and I have shaken hands,
>   Till growing winters lay me low;
>   My paths are in the fields I know,
> And thine in undiscovered lands.
>
> (xl.29–32)

'Undiscovered lands' is from Shelley's 'Alastor', but it is hard not also to hear Hamlet's 'undiscover'd country, from whose bourn / No traveller returns' (3.1.79–80). Finally, consider this extraordinary echo of the blindman's buff to which Hamlet refers in the terrible diatribe against his mother: 'What devil was't / That thus hath cozen'd you at hoodman-blind?' (3.4.76–7). Tennyson is recalling the games the family always played at Christmas, the 'dance and song and hoodman-blind' (LXXVIII.12). As Hamlet asks 'how could you forget my father?', so Tennyson asks 'how could we forget you?' There is pain in realizing that the pain of mourning is past or passing: 'O last regret, regret can die!' (17). It is better perhaps to suppose that regret has been transformed, so that 'Her deep relations are the same, / But with long use the tears are dry' (20). Grief has been laid to rest, quietened. The 'quiet bones' of Hallam's body (XVIII.6) are remembered now as 'The quiet sense of something lost' (LXXVIII, 8).

Let me close with the poem in which Tennyson bids farewell to the old family home (CII). It harbours memories of his boyhood, and later memories of the young manhood blest by his love for the 'lost friend' (15). He imagines these as 'Two spirits of a diverse love' who 'Contend for loving masterdom' (7–8). This calls to mind Shakespeare's virulent sonnet 144: 'Two loves I have of comfort and despair / The better angel is a man right fair, / The worser spirit a woman coloured ill.' But Tennyson's two spirits are not opposed. They are both spirits of comfort, and the gentle dispute between them ('Poor rivals in a losing game', 19) is closer to the mutuality Juliet anticipates as she waits for her beloved Romeo ('And learn me how to lose a winning match', 3.2.12). At the end of his beautiful farewell to the past, Tennyson's two spirits 'mix in one another's arms / To one pure image of regret' (24).

It seems an appropriate image for the issue of Tennyson's own dialogue with Shakespeare: unrivalrous, unanxious, grateful.

Chapter Six

THE GREAT IMAGE OF AUTHORITY

KING AND QUEENS: CARLYLE AND RUSKIN

'S hakespeare' was for the Victorians a way of expressing all sorts of
beliefs, ideals, desires and fears about authority, including
monstrous visions of its travesty such as the fallen King Lear imagines
when he says: 'There thou mightst behold the great image of authority:
a dog's obey'd in office' (*KL*, 4.6.158–9). They were particularly
interested in the fate of kings and fathers, and in the various kinds of
challenge and submission to authority by subjects, servants, wives and
children. They also looked outwards to countries, races and languages
other than their own, to the nature of the authority carried by England,
the English language and their prime literary export Shakespeare, for
other European nations, especially France, Germany and Italy. They
looked west to America and east to India; they looked to all four corners
of the empire. To look out was also to look in and to question what
England and Englishness was composed of. For all these enquiries
Shakespeare was a key point of reference.[1]

Four years after Victoria came to the throne there was another
coronation. A queen was all very well (and so was her consort) but the
nation needed a King – King Shakespeare. Thomas Carlyle began his
lecture on 'The Hero as Poet' by nominating Dante and Shakespeare as
his exemplars, and saw no difficulty about going on to hail them as
Saints of Poetry.[2] If Dante represented the Inner Life, Faith and Soul,
Shakespeare embodied the Outer, Practice and Body. The former was
'fierce as the central fire of the world', the latter 'wide, placid, far-seeing,

193

as the Sun' (p. 86). If Dante suffered and expressed misery, the key to Shakespeare was his 'joyful tranquillity' (p. 92). This made him the greater of the two, so Carlyle claimed, because he was a man who had known sorrows and triumphed over them. Shakespeare was sovereign not just over himself but over the world across which his fellow-countrymen were extending their dominion. Forced to choose between the Indian Empire and Shakespeare, no true-born Englishman would hesitate to surrender the former. But the beauty of Shakespeare's heroic saintly sovereignty was that it was not only spiritual; it was also 'real, marketable, tangibly-useful' (p. 96), the instrument of worldly power. With Shakespeare at its head, the imperial race that gave him birth would develop into 'a Saxondom covering great spaces of the globe' (p. 96). King Shakespeare would preside over it even more durably than Queen Victoria.

Carlyle's triumphalist rhetoric is not entirely convincing. For one thing he has to slide over the massive differences between Dante and Shakespeare in their relation to what he calls 'our Modern Europe'. Whereas Dante sings the Inner Life of the Middle Ages, Shakespeare is poised on the edge of their turbulent breakdown. This does not square well with Carlyle's characterization of the two poets' temper, of Dante's misery and Shakespeare's serenity. Further, there is something troubling about Shakespeare's serene sovereign vision. Shakespeare can see far and wide and deep into the heart of things, but we cannot see him. Carlyle thinks of his works as windows through which we get just a glimpse of their author, for they are all 'comparatively speaking, cursory, imperfect, written under cramping circumstances' (p. 94). What a shame that he had to write for the theatre, that 'his great soul had to crush itself, as it could, into that and no other mould' (p. 94). This makes him sound more thwarted than triumphant. It is one thing to dream up a king of infinite space and time before whom to prostrate yourself; he might as well be called a god. But supposing the king were still human, what would it mean to *be* that man? Carlyle cannot imagine a real living Shakespeare. Dante is different, a being with whom Carlyle can deeply identify. Look at the portrait by Giotto, he says: 'The face of one wholly in protest, and life-long unsurrendering battle, against the world' (p. 74). Carlyle could be looking at himself. It is ironic, then, to find that as he looks into the mirror of Dante, it is a phrase from Shakespeare that wells up in his mind, from Claudio's great speech on the fear of death and the hereafter (*MM*, 3.1.117–31): 'A soft ethereal soul looking-out so stern, implacable, grim-trenchant, as from imprisonment of thick-ribbed ice!' (p. 74).

One of the difficulties in associating Shakespeare with the idea of heroic saintly kingship is that we might remember all the kings he actually puts on stage in his plays. Some of them, such as Richard II and Claudius, utter fine ideas about the divinity that is supposed to hedge them, but not when they are alone in the middle of the night. In *Macbeth* Edward the Confessor seems magically good, but he remains offstage while we listen to Malcolm pondering the weight of all the kingly virtues. The Victorians took a keen interest in Shakespeare's English kings and what their plays had to say about English history. It was for this reason that *King John* and *Henry VIII* figured prominently in the nineteenth-century repertoire, along with the *Henry IV* plays and *Henry V* (as well of course as the perennially popular *Richard III*). *Richard II* is striking for its lack of hold on the stage, despite Charles Kean's landmark production of 1857, and the salience Pater gives it in his essay on 'Shakespeare's English Kings' towards the end of the century (1888). As regards the identification of Shakespeare himself with any of his own regal figures, however, Prince Hamlet is one obvious choice, from the Romantics onwards. The other, though, emerges with particular prominence only towards the end of the century: Prospero.

For those who looked in the plays for ideal authority, one alternative to Shakespeare's troubled kings was his queens. We have already seen the extraordinary reverence his women could inspire. In 1865 Ruskin gave famous expression to the view that 'Shakespeare has no heroes – he has only heroines' (Ruskin, XVIII, p. 112). He went on to blame the catastrophe of every play on the folly or fault of a man. Poor Ophelia is singled out as the only weak woman, for failing Hamlet at the critical moment. There are three wicked witches – Lady Macbeth, Regan and Goneril – but they are 'frightful exceptions'. (He does not mention

Cleopatra, Gertrude or Cressida.) The aberrations apart, Shakespeare's women are 'infallibly faithful and wise counsellors ... strong always to sanctify, even when they cannot save' (XVIII, p. 114). This is a hard act to live up to. Some years later, in *Proserpina*, Ruskin modified his verdict on Shakespeare's faulty men with the surprising declaration that Desdemona, Ophelia and Rosalind had all been given 'entirely heroic and faultless persons to love' (XXV, p. 418). But his attention here was on distinguishing the nine different levels of 'loving temper' displayed by the women, on a scale that starts with the least earthly (Isabella – Shakespeare's only 'Saint'), descends through Cordelia, Portia, Desdemona and others to Perdita and Miranda ('Rather mythic visions of maiden beauty than mere girls'), and concludes with Viola and Juliet ('Love the ruling power in the entire character: wholly virginal and pure, but quite earthly, and recognizing no other life than his [*sic*] own') (XXV, pp. 416–19).

Ruskin's is a rarefied fantasy. No wonder Mary Cowden Clarke and others wanted to imagine some flesh and blood, and Shaw railed at the impossible angels (though like Ruskin he admired Isabella, albeit for different reasons). But angels and saints are much to the point when we realize the strength of religious feeling behind Ruskin's reading. For all the high-flown admiration, Shakespeare troubled him as he troubled Carlyle, and many others who looked to him and his work for infallible counsel. For the tragedies were perplexing. In May 1868 Ruskin delivered a lecture in Dublin on 'The Mystery of Life and its Art'; in 1871 he published it as the third lecture of *Sesame and Lilies*, but in some later editions he omitted it because of the questions it raised about tragedy. He coupled Shakespeare with Homer, and characterized the two of them thus:

> Men ... of so unrecognized personality, that it disappears in future ages, and becomes ghostly, like the tradition of a lost heathen god. Men, therefore, to whose unoffended, uncon-demning sight, the whole of human nature reveals itself in a pathetic weakness, with which they will not strive; or in mournful and transitory strength, which they dare not praise.

And all Pagan and Christian Civilization thus becomes subject
to them. It does not matter how little, or how much, any of us
have read, either of Homer or Shakespeare; everything round
us, in substance, or in thought, has been moulded by them.
(XVIII, p. 159)

This is a remarkable passage. One might think that Homer and
Shakespeare should be separated by the difference between paganism
and Christianity. But Ruskin links them through their shared
resemblance to 'a lost heathen god', and a power of vision ('unoffended,
uncondemning') from which the sense of justice normally associated
with both pagan and Christian deities has been purged. The Homeric
gods do at least provide 'consolation' of some kind. But Shakespeare at
his bleakest does not: he makes Ruskin stare into an abyss where 'the
strongest and most righteous are brought to their ruin, and perish
without word of hope' (XVIII, p. 161). This was not a vision with which
Ruskin could live. Returning to the topic some years later, we find him
taking desperate refuge in the 'so-called poetical justice' revealed in the
world by 'the great masters' (XXIX, pp. 266–7). *Othello*, for example:
'"*She hath deceived her father*, – and may thee." The root of the entire
tragedy is marked by the mighty master in that one line – the double
sin, namely, of daughter and father' (XXIX, pp. 265–6). It is a desperate
reading of the play that would find the root of the tragedy here, in
the double sin of father and daughter, as who should say with the
protagonist, 'It is the cause, it is the cause.' But when the *Cornhill*
published an article, 'Why did Shakespeare write Tragedies?' (August
1880), Ruskin was certain of his answer. He was convinced of 'the
spirit of faith in God, and hope in Futurity, which, though unexpressed,
were meant by the master of tragedy to be felt by the spectator'. This
spirit, he believed, was summed up in the line from *Romeo and Juliet*,
'For Nature's tears are Reason's merriment' (XXIX, p. 447). Friar
Laurence's words can rarely have received such a credulous welcome
(*RJ*, 4.5.83).

There are no heroes in Shakespeare nor are there heroines, at least
not in the sense that Ruskin intends, of flawless infallible beings. Emilia

acts heroically at the end of *Othello* but no one has ever thought of calling her a 'heroine': she has a lot to make up for. Carlyle, Ruskin and others sought the heroic in Shakespeare and his creations as a sovereign remedy against the menace of flesh-and-blood turmoil, political, religious, ethical, sexual.

MULTITUDINOUS POWERS

For the first half of the nineteenth century this turmoil was embodied in the all too real events of the French Revolution. This gave particular salience to the play of Shakespeare's most centrally concerned with the act of regicide: *Macbeth*. The play and its two principal characters are the model for individual murder and guilt in many nineteenth-century writers, especially novelists such as Bulwer-Lytton, Dickens, Thackeray, Wilkie Collins and Mrs Braddon. They provide a powerful vocabulary not only for murderous passion but also for consequent guilt, particularly in its socially isolating and maddening effects.

In its political aspect *Macbeth* found itself associated with other plays that involve the murder or assassination of heads of state, especially *Hamlet* and *Julius Caesar*. This latter, along with *Coriolanus*, works with *Macbeth* to produce images of the murderous power of the mob, 'the many-headed multitude'. Shakespeare repeated for Caius Martius, and for him alone, the great coinage he discovered for Macbeth's nightmare vision of a blood-letting so prolific and indelible that it would 'The multitudinous seas incarnadine, / Making the green one red' (*Mac*, 2.2.59–60).[3] A couple of years later he created in Martius another murderous warrior spurred on by a powerful woman. Martius pits himself against 'the many-headed multitude', and urges his fellow patricians to 'at once pluck out the multitudinous tongue' (*Cor*, 3.1.156). What if he were to be absorbed into them and his violence were to become theirs? Add to this from *Julius Caesar* the vision of an indiscriminate civil violence unleashed by the murder of the head of state, and nineteenth-century writers have the right Shakespearean brew on which to draw when they think of a revolutionary mob. In America two of the three sons of the tragedian Junius Brutus Booth effected a further specific conjunction between *Julius Caesar* and *Hamlet*. John Wilkes Booth played Brutus for real when he assassinated Lincoln in 1865, while his brother Edwin became the American Hamlet, an identification all the more powerful for the sense that it answered his criminal sibling's.[4]

The word 'multitudinous' resonates through Carlyle's history of *The French Revolution*, published the same year that Victoria came to the throne. By the time Ruskin wrote the following in the mid-1860s, the idea of the mob was beginning to lose some of the nightmare urgency it had once had: 'No nation can last, which has made a mob of itself, however generous at heart. It must discipline its passions, and direct them, or they will discipline *it*, one day, with scorpion whips' (*Ruskin*, XVIII, p. 84). But for readers in the first decade or so of Victoria's reign, the vision of rampant multitudinous passion was all too vivid. In Paris just after the September massacres, Wordsworth had heard a voice cry 'Sleep no more',[5] though the great poem in which he described his experience was only published posthumously in 1850. Thirteen years earlier, Carlyle had also echoed Macbeth's cry in a present tense that made the events of the 1790s live again in the here and now: 'How the whole People shakes itself, as if it had one life; and, in thousand-voiced rumour, announces that it is awake, suddenly out of long death-sleep, and will thenceforth sleep no more!'[6] (I, iv, 2). They are 'this multitudinous French People' (I, iv, 2), 'the seas of people still hang multitudinous' (I, v, 2), there is a 'general outburst of multitudinous Passion' (I, vii, 10) and the Champ-de-Mars is 'multitudinous with men' (II, iii, 1).

Macbeth is not only a play about regicide; it is also a play about mass murder. Listen to this description of a painting.

> Purple and blue, the lurid shadows of the hollow breakers are cast upon the mist of night, which gathers cold and low, advancing like the shadow of death upon the guilty ship as it labours amidst the lightning of the sea, its thin masts written upon the sky in lines of blood, girded with condemnation in that fearful hue which signs the sky with horror, and mixes its

flaming flood with the sunlight, and, cast far along the desolate
heave of the sepulchral waves, incarnadines the multitudinous
sea. (*Ruskin*, III, p. 572)

The young Ruskin is trying to express the tumultuous effect of J.M.W.
Turner's *Slave Ship*, exhibited at the Royal Academy in 1840 (or to give
it its full title, *Slavers Throwing Overboard the Dead and Dying, Typhoon
Coming On*). This painting has been described as 'the only indisputably
great work of Western art ever made to commemorate the Atlantic
slave trade'.[7] In the build-up to this culminating sentence, Ruskin
speaks of the sunset dyeing the sea 'with an awful but glorious light', of
'the intense and lurid splendour which burns like gold, and bathes like
blood', of the water 'now lighted with green and lamp-like fire, now
flashing back the gold of the declining sun' (III, p. 572). In the
references to gold, blood, green, water and sea, the reader may sense
the imaginative presence of *Macbeth*, but they rise to clinching
magnificence in the final words: 'incarnadines the multitudinous
sea'. This is not a casually ornamental allusion. Ruskin is drawing to
wonderful effect on the deep associations that meet in his imagination
between Shakespeare's play and Turner's painting. All three, in their
different media, seek to realize the idea of massacre, of immeasurable,
unthinkable – multitudinous – guilt.

   A word of caution is required about the extent to which a specifically
Shakespearean resonance can ever be claimed for a single word, albeit
one that Shakespeare takes the credit for inventing. 'Multitudinous' is a
remarkably popular word in nineteenth-century literary contexts,
especially in poetry, and its connotations are not simply or even mainly
inauspicious. It is frequently applied to natural or cosmic phenomena,
from mountains and leaves to stars and angels. It is particularly
associated with sounds, with music, melody, clang, hum, bells, voices,
silences, echo. It suggests a rapture at the sheer fecundity of the world.
This is not the monopoly of poets. In *The Principles of Psychology* (1855)
Herbert Spencer writes of 'the hypothesis that Life in its multitudinous
and infinitely-varied embodiments, has arisen out of the lowest and
simplest beginnings' (p. 532).[8]

Yet such enormity poses a challenge to the consciousness drawn to taking its measure. It requires nothing less than the 'multitudinous powers' that A.C. Bradley believed Shakespeare had most fully exhibited in *King Lear* (Bradley, p. 243). When George Eliot produces her famous image in *Middlemarch* for the relativity of the patterns we impose on the raw data of experience, she thinks of a pier-glass 'minutely and multitudinously scratched in all directions' (*M*, ch. 27). Henry James praised her capacity to create characters as positively 'Shakespearean' – 'characters that are born of the *overflow* of observation – characters that make the drama seem multitudinous, like life'.[9] But when writers think of human beings in the mass, as opposed to stars or leaves or sounds, the word is likely to express fear, if not horror, at the impossibilility of controlling the multitude. It is at this point that the word excites memories of its murderous Shakespearean origins. Shelley writes of 'multitudinous anarchy' ('Ode to Liberty'); Elizabeth Gaskell of the 'multitudinous sound' of the rioters in *North and South* (i, ch. 22); George Eliot of the 'multitudinous gaze' that the Coriolanian Felix Holt endures at his trial (*FH*, ch. 46, p. 393); Anna Jameson of 'that multitudinous Moloch termed Opinion' that would immolate a modern Portia.[10] Meanwhile the everyday urban masses could make the poet James Thomson think of 'the pulse and breath / Of multitudinous lower life' ('In the Room', 1872),[11] and the prostitutes thronging the city streets prompted an Edinburgh Professor of Surgery to warn readers of 'a multitudinous amazonian army the devil keeps in constant field service, advancing his own ends'.[12] Confronted with the 'blank confusion' and 'unmanageable sight' of London, including the times when half the city broke out 'Full of one passion, vengeance, rage, or fear', Wordsworth had been stirred to 'multitudinous' thoughts that only the memory of more natural landscapes could help to compose.[13] Yet even in the mountains a man can think dark thoughts. In 'Echo, upon the Gemmi', from 'Memorials of a Tour on the Continent, 1820', the 'multitudinous' harmony the poet hears turns out to derive from a solitary wolf: 'So, from the body of one guilty deed, / A thousand ghostly fears, and haunting thoughts, proceed!' So from one word a thousand haunting echoes for a fearful century.

THEATRE AND EDUCATION:
PHELPS AND KEAN

The theatre is a multitudinous place, and many of the Victorians' fears and desires about authority found a focus in the power of theatre to tame and to inflame. In the early Victorian years Macready exerted his authority to make it more respectable. Admirers often spoke of him as a Hercules cleansing the Augean stables, by which they meant he had cleared the prostitutes out of Covent Garden and Drury Lane. His former colleague Samuel Phelps performed what seemed to some a comparable task at Sadler's Wells. Like many others, Macready's friend Charles Dickens made the journey to North London to see what Phelps was making of his Shakespeare productions. In 1847 he wrote Phelps a fan letter about his production of *Cymbeline*, and ten years later he praised him in public as 'the mind of the theatre in which the English drama has found a home'.[14] Between the two, Dickens had published a significant piece lauding Phelps's achievements, entitled 'Shakspeare and Newgate' (co-authored with R.H. Horne).[15] It is a moral tale about the purging of multitudinous passion.

When Phelps took over Sadler's Wells it had been overrun by 'as ruffianly an audience as London could shake together', so *Household Words* asserted in 1851 (p. 344). It had been much less companionable than the theatres in the Waterloo Road and Hoxton patronized by Joe Whelks and his friends in 'The Amusements of the People' (which Dickens had written the previous year).[16]

> Without, the Theatre, by night, was like the worst part of the worst kind of Fair in the worst kind of town. Within, it was a bear-garden, resounding with foul language, oaths, catcalls, shrieks, yells, blasphemy, obscenity – a truly diabolical clamour.
> (p. 344)

Typical fare at Sadler's Wells had been the improving melodrama *Jack Ketch*, the tale of the legendary hangman, whose services, so Dickens and Horne imply, would have been usefully employed on most of the audience. When Phelps opened there with *Macbeth* in 1844, the performance was received with the usual violent uproar, so he decided the only way to 'humanise the place' was to have the riff-raff outside the theatre moved on, to eject the beer-sellers and children-in-arms, and to silence the cursing and swearing. *Household Words* strongly approved. Now that 'order and silence' had been established, the audience was as disciplined as if it were in a lecture-room. Men could take their wives and daughters; 'staid and serious people of the neighbourhood who once abhorred the name of a Theatre, are frequenters of this one; and ... the place which was a Nuisance, is become quite a household word' (p. 349).

This sounds depressingly like Peter Brook's Deadly Theatre, and readers who have never had their entertainment ruined by truly diabolical clamour might be tempted to lament the demise of the bear-garden and wax indignant at the emasculation of proletarian revelry. Fortunately there is reason to believe that the *Household Words* account is a fantasy, and that sufficient appetite for Phelps's improving fare amongst respectable members of the Islington working classes made the stringent measures hailed by Dickens and Horne unnecessary.[17] *Household Words* was promoting a lurid myth about the antagonism between 'high drama' and 'low sensual enjoyments', between 'the beauties of the poem' and 'truly diabolical clamour', between the bear-garden and the family, between *Macbeth* and *Jack Ketch*. The multitude had to be a riotous anarchic mob or a regiment of virtue. In 1851 the memory of riotous assemblies was still a vivid one for writers and readers keen to see nuisances transformed into household words, and the poet's wand supported by the policeman's truncheon.

No policemen were needed to keep audiences at the Royal Princess's Theatre in Oxford Street under control. This was the theatre run by Charles and Ellen Kean (née Tree) from 1851 to 1859. It was where Queen Victoria most happily took her Shakespeare in public.[18] In private she revived the office of Master of the Revels and regularly invited the Keans to perform at Windsor over the Christmas season from 1848 to 1857. In this last year *Richard II* was performed in St George's Hall at Windsor under the eyes of royal portraits and arms of Knights of the Garter dating back to 1348. It was a curious experience, the Queen reflected, to see in such a setting 'a Play, in which all my ancestors figured'.[19] Not many people can say this.

The combination of Queen Victoria and King Shakespeare gave a mighty fillip to the Keans, but it also bolstered the social acceptability of theatre-going itself. Charles's brilliant, wild father Edmund had sent him to Eton in the hope that this would stop him going on the stage. Instead Charles followed his father and laboured to make it a career neither brilliant nor wild but thoroughly respectable. He capitalized on Macready's strivings (though the two men never liked each other) and anticipated Irving's social triumph as the first theatrical knight. Kean's painstaking research into authentic historical costume and design won the respect of the intelligentsia and secured his election in 1857 as a Fellow of the Society of Antiquaries.[20] Audiences were made to feel they were being educated. In his farewell address in 1859 Kean said that he had been 'anxious to make the theatre a school as well as a recreation'.[21]

The most important lessons were to do with history and its 'realization'. The pseudo-authenticity of Kean's staging sought a form of physical revival for which the statue scene in *The Winter's Tale* stood as Shakespeare's own paradigm. When Mrs Kean took the role of the Chorus in *Henry V* and identified it with Clio, the Muse of History, it was with Hermione that critics made the connexion. Richard Schoch has argued a convincing case for seeing these productions as a serious contribution to ideas about history and Englishness that begin to solidify in the 1850s and 1860s. The combination of preparatory scholarship and executive technique created for audiences the illusion of history made real, much as cinema and television do for audiences now. There is nothing like seeing and believing, however much of a shock it may be (as it is for George Eliot's Dorothea in Rome, 'the city of visible history' (*M*, ch. 20)). Kean's was the theatre of visible history. The *Literary Gazette* hailed his *King John* as the successor to Scott's novels, bringing 'before our eyes the living pages of history'; the *Theatrical Journal* thought the interpolated scene of Bolingbroke's entry into London in *Richard II* 'breathed and pulsed in all the perfection of historic truth'.[22] Kean gave currency to a vision of Englishness rooted in the Middle Ages, 'the homestead of history' as he called it in his playbill for *Richard II*. The Middle Ages were for the Victorians a precious and contested property that writers of various political affiliations sought to claim for their version of history, from Scott, Pugin, Carlyle and Disraeli to William Morris. Kean's theatre joins hands with more conventional forms of historiography interested in the ethnic composition of 'Englishness', particularly its Anglo-Saxon inheritance, from Sharon Turner's *The History of the Anglo-Saxons* (1799–1805, used by Scott for *Ivanhoe*) to J.M. Kemble's *The Saxons in England* (1849), and beyond.[23] The designs for Kean's *Macbeth* sought to draw on this interest in the Nordic and Germanic elements of the British past, though it was much less warmly welcomed than the productions of the English plays, the four key ones being *King John* (1852), *Henry VIII* (1855), *Richard II* (1857) and *Henry V* (1859).

Henry V provided a logical culmination to the vision, and Kean sought to clinch its climax with a particular effect. His *Richard II* had famously realized the scene described in Shakespeare's text by York, in which the defeated King trails disconsolately through the streets of London at the heels of the victorious Bolingbroke. In this way Kean (and others) sought to fill up some of the gaps that Shakespeare had so carelessly left. This was the Victorian equivalent to the Restoration 'improvements' to Shakespearean texts which smoothed over their lacunae and confusions. In his 1899 production of *King John* Beerbohm Tree actually staged the signing of Magna Carta unaccountably omitted by Shakespeare (Kean had merely referred to it in his playbill). In his *Henry V* Kean was making a specific point when he complemented the interpolated scene in *Richard II* with one that answered it. This showed the triumphant return Henry makes to London after Agincourt, alluded to by the Chorus in the prologue to Act 5 (Figure 19). This Henry is no longer a guilty usurper like his father but a legitimate king, so Kean's preface to the printed edition of the play insists: 'The victor of Agincourt is hailed, not as a successful usurper, but as a conqueror; the adored sovereign of his people; the pride of his nation; and apparently the chosen instrument of heaven, crowned with imperishable glory.'[24] It was a good moment for Kean to call it a day.

FIGURE 19 *'Historical Interlude' of Henry's Return to London after Agincourt,* from Charles Kean's production of *Henry V* at the Princess's Theatre, 1859.

GERMAN RELATIONS

The Keans used Shakespeare's authority to promote a particular idea of English history rooted in the Middle Ages. But there were other ways in which Shakespeare incited thoughts about what it meant to be English (or British), and to speak and write English, in the second half of the nineteenth century. As the English-speaking peoples spread themselves over the globe it became a matter of increasing urgency to know where they stood in relation to other world powers both ancient and modern. Shakespeare provided the Victorians with a way of comparing themselves, with Greeks and Romans, with Germans, French and Italians. To ask how our national poet and dramatist measured up to Sophocles, Dante, Racine and Goethe was to ask how *we* measured up. What impression had he made on them and what had they made of him, our Continental rivals, allies, relations?

They had made a good deal. In the main this was for the Victorians a matter of pride, verging on vainglory; it was the note struck by Carlyle at the end of 'The Hero as Poet'. Even the French, or at least some of them, such as Stendhal, Berlioz and Victor Hugo, had decided there might be something in Shakespeare. The Italians too had embraced Shakespeare as a symbol of more than artistic freedom in their fight to throw off the foreign yoke, as for example in Verdi's *Macbeth* (1847). And although news travelled more slowly from Russia, towards the end of the century it began to dawn on the English what a massive impact Shakespeare had had on their writers and composers, on Pushkin, Lermontov, Tolstoy, Dostoevsky and Tchaikovsky.

Carlyle had spoken of Saxondom, and it was the Saxon connection with our German relations that fuelled the most intense reflections. The Victorian appreciation of Shakespeare owes a great debt to German criticism and philosophy right up to the last and most eminent of Victorian academic Shakespeareans, A.C. Bradley. There was gratitude of course, not just for the deep perception of Shakespeare's supreme genius displayed by writers and critics from Goethe onwards, but also for the labours of critics, scholars and commentators from A.W. Schlegel to Delius, Ulrici and Gervinus. Gratitude could be tinged by resentment, but if there was friction it was still within the family, despite the increasing menace of Prussian military might after 1870. The family was Anglo-Saxon, Teutonic, Northern, Protestant. In 1875 Edward Dowden declared in the most widely read book on Shakespeare of his generation that '*King Lear* is ... the greatest single achievement in poetry of the Teutonic, or northern genius.'[25] At the Tercentenary celebrations of 1864 in Stratford-upon-Avon the Germans had been prominent guests. A deputation was led by Professors Max Müller and G.W. Leitner, and the latter made a speech at the official banquet, in which he dwelt on the bond between Goethe and Shakespeare. The two of them together, he said, represented the 'most perfect embodiment of the highest aspirations of Saxon poetry'. He expressed the hope that the kindred blood between England and Germany should 'once more assert its power by uniting into one fellow-feeling all the members of the race of the Saxons on this or that side of every sea'.[26] We do not know if the applause was more than polite. But as we shall see, even on the brink of the Great War there were those who wanted to see Stratford-upon-Avon as the English Bayreuth.

For English readers the pre-eminent German critic of Shakespeare was A.W. Schlegel, whose *Lectures* (1815) were widely available in translation throughout the century. There is no play on which Schlegel's pronouncements were more frequently cited than *Romeo and Juliet*. The following was a particularly popular passage. It gives some sense of the intoxication, the voluptuous rapture and despair, the 'fulness of life and self-annihilation' that *Romeo and Juliet* epitomized for the Victorians. Note that Schlegel calls it a 'poem'.

> All that is most intoxicating in the odour of a southern spring, – all that is languishing in the song of the nightingale, or voluptuous in the first opening of the rose, all alike breathe forth from this poem. But even more rapidly than the earliest blossoms of youth and beauty decay, does one from the first timidly-bold declaration and modest return of love hurry on to the most unlimited passion, to an irrevocable union; and then hastens, amidst alternating storms of rapture and despair, to the fate of the two lovers, who yet appear enviable in their hard lot, for their love survives them, and by their death they have obtained an endless triumph over every separating power. The sweetest and the bitterest love and hatred, festive rejoicings and dark forebodings, tender embraces and sepulchral horrors, the fulness of life and self-annihilation, are here all brought close to each other; and yet these contrasts are so blended into a unity of impression, that the echo which the whole leaves behind in the mind resembles a single but endless sigh.[27]

This is an idea of tragedy that exercised immense influence on the nineteenth century. In imagining the triumph of love over death it brings Romeo and Juliet as close to Wagner's Tristan and Isolde as anyone could dare. It looks ahead to Bradley's belief, expressed in the conclusion to his essay on 'Hegel's Theory of Tragedy', that in some sense we 'exult' in the death of the tragic hero.[28] Schlegel's final sentence here seems to adumbrate the story of Shakespeare's own creative progress through the conflict of genres to their reconciliation, leaving not a rack behind but an echo in the mind.

This is of course a highly Romantic Shakespeare. But German Romanticism was no more homogeneous than any other Romanticisms, and there was another way of viewing Shakespeare that marked a sharper challenge. The German dignitaries at Stratford in 1864 emphasized the bond between Shakespeare and Goethe, but they could also be measured against each other. Here is his English biographer, G.H. Lewes, reflecting on Goethe's 'objectivity', his eschewal of 'extraneous imagery', and contrasting him in this respect with Shakespeare.

> Most poets describe objects by metaphors or comparisons; Goethe seldom tells you what an object is *like*, he tells you what it *is*. Shakespeare is very unlike Goethe in this respect. The prodigal luxuriance of his imagery often entangles, in its overgrowth, the movement of his verse. It is true, he also is eminently concrete; he sees the real object vividly, and he makes us see it vividly; but he scarcely ever paints it save in the colours of metaphor and simile. Shakespeare's imagery bubbles up like a perpetual spring: to say that it repeatedly *overflows*, is only to say that his mind was lured by its own sirens away from the direct path. He did not master his Pegasus at all times, but let the wild careering creature take its winged way. Goethe, on the contrary, always masters his; perhaps because his steed had less of restive life in its veins. Not only does he master it, and ride with calm assured grace, he seems so bent on reaching the goal, that he scarcely thinks of anything else.[29]

Prodigally luxuriant, entangled in overgrowth, bubbling, overflowing and lured away by sirens, a wild careering creature: this is a Shakespeare at whom the French had flung up their hands in distaste – until Stendhal and Hugo. But the English too have always needed alternatives to Shakespeare, even if it has more often been Milton than Racine. In this sense Goethe comes to stand for Victorian critics as one exemplary alternative to Shakespeare, that paradoxical thing, a modern classic, whose Pegasus never gets out of control. It is instructive, however, that just as Lewes is about to award the laurel to Goethe, he casts doubt on the comparative vitality of their two steeds, and the desirability of heading single-mindedly for your destination. As it happens Goethe tried to rewrite *Romeo and Juliet*. The result, Lewes judged, was disastrous: 'Profoundly as he appreciated the poet, he seems to me wholly to have misunderstood the dramatist.'[30]

ARNOLD, PATER AND CAPRICE

Along with Lewes and George Eliot, and Coleridge and Carlyle before them, Matthew Arnold was a key figure for the importation to England of German ideas.[31] In 1854 he confessed that Goethe was one of the two moderns for whom he cared most, the other being Wordsworth. In his poetry Arnold praised Goethe's 'wide / And luminous view', and appealed to the judgments passed upon the present 'by the two men, the one of strongest head, the other of widest culture, whom it has produced; by Goethe and Niebuhr'. In his first critical essay he named Goethe as 'the greatest poet of modern times, the greatest critic of all times'.[32] Arnold was more directly concerned than Lewes with what an aspiring young poet might learn from the great models of the past. For him this meant comparing Shakespeare not directly with Goethe so as much as with the ancient Greeks by whom Goethe had himself been powerfully influenced. It was on the Greeks that he had drawn, as it seemed to his English admirers, for an aesthetic of objectivity, discipline and restraint.

'The confusion of the present times is great', wrote Arnold, in *On the Classical Tradition*, 'the multitude of voices counselling different things bewildering, the number of existing works capable of attracting a young writer's attention and of becoming his models, immense.'[33] Young English writers naturally looked to Shakespeare. Arnold's own early sonnet, 'Shakespeare' (1844), had looked *up* as at a mountain peak, 'Out-topping knowledge', a state of being beyond comprehension, 'Self-school'd, self-scann'd, self-honour'd, self-secure'. If Shakespeare was not an impossible model, then the mature Arnold judged him a dangerous one. Like all great poets Shakespeare possessed the 'power of execution, which creates, forms, and constitutes'. But he had an extra gift of his own, the power of 'happy, abundant, and ingenious expression' (p. 9). This could lead the unwary astray – a poet like Keats, for example, whose 'Isabella', Arnold said, was 'a perfect treasure-house of graceful and felicitous words and images'. But it was so feebly conceived as a whole, its action so loosely constructed, that the total effect was 'absolutely null' (p. 10). For the young writer, Arnold concluded, Shakespeare might be infinitely 'suggestive', but Sophocles was more 'instructive' (p. 12). One helps us to see life steadily and see it whole; the other tempts us to see it erratically and in fragments – by flashes of lightning, as it were.

There are several words on which Arnold puts particular weight. 'Caprice' and 'capricious' are particularly dangerous; so are 'multitude' and 'multitudinous' (see pp. 198–201). In 1848 Arnold described the effect of Browning's poetry as 'a confused multitudinousness'. Poets like Keats and Browning did not 'understand that they must begin with an Idea of the world in order not to be prevailed over by the world's multitudinousness'.[34] Arnold is also nervous about 'curiosity', as if the Horatio in him were constantly putting the Hamlet firmly in his place. ("Twere to consider too curiously, to consider so' (*Ham*, 5.1.205–6).) For Horatio/Arnold, curiosity is a secretly exorbitant quality in things which excites a correspondingly excessive interest in the observer. Nothing beginning with 'ex-' is going to be good for us. What we need in the face of confused multitudinousness is not curiosity about its seductive particulars, he told the audience for his inaugural lecture in the Chair of Poetry at Oxford, but 'the general ideas which are the law of this vast multitude of facts'. Without these we shall be left in a permanent state of pleasureless suspense, awaiting 'deliverance' from 'an immense, moving, confused spectacle which, while it perpetually excites our curiosity, perpetually baffles our comprehension'.[35] If only the world would stop for us to grasp it; if only poets would stop colluding with its confusion. Shakespeare sets such a bad example. Look how difficult his language can be, 'so artificial, so curiously tortured', such 'over-curiousness of expression'.[36] Sophocles is not like that.

But Euripides is, as admirers of Sophocles, Plato and the Elgin Marbles have regularly deplored. According to Arnold's brand of Hellenism, Shakespeare was an incitement to literary delinquency. But as Victorian ideas of Hellenism suffered a sea-change in the last quarter of the nineteenth century, delinquency began to seem rather attractive. For Swinburne, Pater, Symonds, Wilde, Burne-Jones and Leighton, ancient Greek culture provided incentives to more and more curious practices, not only in writing and art. Both Arnold and Pater saw in the very word 'curious' the call of the sirens; but one of them wanted to carry on listening.

It is a pity that Walter Pater did not go through with the idea he had in 1874 for a whole book on Shakespeare. In the three essays he completed he fastened on plays that had been caviare to the general, *Measure for Measure*, *Love's Labour's Lost* and *Richard II*.[37] Though Isabella was a favoured 'heroine' (or 'saint'), *Measure for Measure* itself found few champions. *Love's Labour's Lost* found none. And of the English history plays he surveys, Pater's prime focus is on the unadmired and rarely performed *Richard II*. Pater was not much interested in performance, but he does pause to commend the one major revival by Charles Kean in the 1850s, which in its archaeological fidelity had 'afforded much more than Shakespeare's play could ever have been before'. The London of Chaucer had confronted its vulgar modern counterpart, and the play became in Charles Kean's hands, thought Pater, 'like an exquisite performance on the violin' (p. 195).

This would be one way of describing Pater's own performance. It is no wonder he chooses to write about the most precious of Shakespearean comedies. But this would be to underrate the intelligence of his interest in 'the playthings of grown-up people, their vanities, their fopperies even, their lighter loves' (p. 164). We have to understand *Love's Labour's Lost* as a play about fashion, Pater says, and specifically about the allure of words, 'that pride of dainty language and curious expression' (p. 165) so characteristic of the Elizabethans and their greatest poet. This is exactly what Arnold had so disapproved of in Shakespeare. Pater flaunts a litany of words designed to irritate the traditional moralist, words like 'exquisite', 'curious', 'peculiar', 'quaint', 'delicate' and 'dainty'. These are chosen with care, as the roots of the word 'exquisite' itself suggest. There is, Pater says, a 'peculiar happiness' in the drawing of some Shakespearean characters, such as Biron (or 'Berowne' to most modern readers) – 'never quite in touch, never quite on a perfect level of understanding, with the other persons of the play' (p. 169). If *Measure for Measure* is full of the 'peculiarities' of Shakespeare's poetry, these are intimately related to its sense of justice, 'in its essence a finer knowledge through love' (p. 183). True justice, Pater concludes, 'is dependent on just those finer appreciations which poetry cultivates in us the power of making, those peculiar valuations of action and its effect which poetry actually requires' (p. 184).

Every one is 'peculiar'. This is what fascinates Pater about Biron, Claudio and Richard, the three men on whom he dwells most attentively. Shakespeare can depict heroic natures in heroic circumstances, but in the history plays it is the 'irony of kingship' that is his special concern, 'average human nature, flung with a wonderfully pathetic effect into the vortex of great events' (pp. 185–6). Hence his particular attraction to Richard II, and his general sympathy with frailty rather than strength. Richard tries to mask this frailty from others and from himself, through ceremony and ritual, through his own eloquence, through his vain belief in 'divine right', a belief that Pater shrewdly says is found in kings 'to act not such much as a secret of power over others, as of infatuation to themselves' (p. 197). This belief or superstition or sentiment is like 'any other of those fantastic, ineffectual, easily discredited, personal graces, as capricious in its operation on men's wills as merely physical beauty' (p. 197).

'Capricious' is a key word here. Whereas Arnold saw 'caprice' as a dereliction of the will, Pater sees it as an authority there is no possibility of predicting or resisting, whether it manifests itself through the will of others, accident or untimely death. It is the principle of blind chance that so unnerved Arnold. Euripides had called it *tyche* and Thomas Hardy would call it 'Hap'. Pater writes with extraordinary sympathy of the way it afflicts the brother and sister he takes to be at the centre of *Measure for Measure* (rather than Isabella and Angelo). In the stress of the terrible dilemma into which she is thrown, he reflects, Isabella 'develops a new character'. Pater writes with great insight of Isabella's 'dangerous and tigerlike changefulness of feeling' (p. 178), but it is the image of Claudio that stands for him at the centre of the play. How is it that this 'gilded, witless youth' is suddenly gifted with thoughts as profound as Hamlet's, that he 'gives utterance to some of the central truths of human feeling, the sincerely concentrated expression of the recoiling flesh' (p. 181)? Pater has a deep feeling for the force of words that can take us by surprise, for better and worse, revealing capacities in us we did not know we had and the absence of others we supposed that we did. Biron is intrigued by the things he can do with words; so too is Richard, quite fatally so. But Claudio never knew he had it in him; he is shocked out of his witlessness by the prospect of death, as if there were a grace that could answer caprice.

Pater is pleasantly unshocked by the seedier aspects of *Measure for Measure*, cheerfully describing the cast as 'a group of persons, attractive, full of desire, vessels of the genial, seed-bearing powers of nature, a gaudy existence flowering out over the old court and city of Vienna' (p. 173). He similarly admires Falstaff and Faulconbridge for the way they bear witness to the force of 'nature'. But each of his essays selects a single figure and claims them as the play's central focus to the progressive exclusion of others and of the world outside his own private sensations. Is kingship more than a piece of theatre and politics more than child's play? In his conclusion to the 'English Kings', we see the general tendency which dominates critical and academic writing through the nineteenth century (and beyond) reach something of a climax. It is one which exalts the single self over the multitude, the spirit over the body, the poet over the dramatist, the reader over the spectator. Drama for Pater aspires to the condition of lyric, which the solitary reader alone can truly appreciate. This is the Reader as King.

AMERICA AND THE ANGLO-SAXON MECCA

Kings are not generally popular in America. In 1847 audiences in Manchester and London could have heard a series of lectures by an eminent American visitor that challenged comparison with Carlyle's

On Heroes and Hero-Worship some years earlier. Ralph Waldo Emerson did not use the metaphors of royalty as freely as Carlyle. But he did appeal to the same sense of racial identity, describing Shakespeare as 'the man who carries the Saxon race in him by the inspiration which feeds him' (p. 717).[38] Lecturing to British and American audiences he made no difference between them when he proclaimed that their literature, philosophy and thought had all been 'Shakspearized': 'His mind is the horizon beyond which, at present, we do not see' (p. 718). Not all his fellow-countrymen would have been content with that 'we'. For many of them, Shakespeare was too deeply embroiled with ideas of monarchy and hereditary privilege belonging to a past their ancestors had tried to leave behind. Shakespeare was an obstacle *blocking* the horizon. Nineteenth-century America replicates many of the debates surrounding Shakespeare in Victorian Britain, including the oppositions between poetry and the theatre, the reader and the multitude, the patrician and the popular, gentility and physical force.[39] Shakespeare served English readers and audiences as a focus for debates about what it meant to be English – or British. But for Americans, Shakespeare posed even more urgent questions about their own literary, cultural and political loyalties. Did not Shakespeare belong to an English past that was at best a distraction from the task of building the American future?

The questions were not always as simple as this, nor is the history of their answers.[40] Nevertheless, we can discern two broad contrary tendencies in the period that concerns us. The first was for Americans to claim that Shakespeare was no less American than English, or even more so. Thus Fenimore Cooper in 1833: 'Shakespeare is, of course, the great author of America, as he is of England.'[41] In 1898 the author of *Shakespeare and America* argued that it was the discovery of the New World that aroused the Anglo-Saxon mind 'with its revelations, its marvels, its riches, its promises and possibilities', and thus America had helped 'to Shakespearize English thought and language'.[42] There was enthusiasm for the view that in the portrayal of his women Shakespeare had left a legacy which only the modern American woman, fearless and independent, was fit to enjoy. On the other side were the nativist Anglophobes. The most eloquent was Whitman, who famously declared in 1871:

> The great poems, Shakspere included, are poisonous to the idea of pride and dignity of the common people, the life-blood of the democracy. The models of literature, as we get it from other lands, ultramarine, have had their birth in courts, and bask'd and grown in castle sunshine.[43]

British art and culture were still tied to a gorgeous feudalism. The poetry of the future would have to reject the black magical arts of Shakespeare, Scott and Tennyson. How hard it was, he continued in 1882, to escape 'the flavor, the conviction, the lush-ripening culmination, and last honey of decay (I dare not call it rottenness) of that feudalism which the mighty English dramatist painted in all the splendors of its noon and afternoon'.[44]

Henry James was prepared to give the honey a try. So too were other Americans who chose to spend time or even settle in the decaying Old World. The Grand Tour was an English institution they could take over and adapt to their purposes, and the English sights and scenes they knew from books were no less the object of their curiosity than Paris, the Alps, Florence and Rome. Where Shakespeare was concerned, Americans were prime movers in the creation of what would become known as 'the Anglo-Saxon Mecca'. In 1820 Washington Irving reported on his search for the Boar's Head Tavern in Eastcheap and his 'poetical pilgrimage' to Stratford-upon-Avon, where he found the walls of the birthplace covered with the names of pilgrims 'of all nations, ranks, and conditions, from the prince to the peasant'.[45] Writers and actors who by the 1864 Tercentenary had left their mark included Scott, Tennyson, Rogers, Dickens, Thackeray, Edmund Kean, Charles Kean, Madame Vestris and Helen Faucit.[46] In the late 1840s there were rumours that P.T. Barnum, of Barnum and Bailey's Circus, was going to buy the Birthplace and have it shipped over to America; this stirred up a campaign to keep it British, and in 1847 it was bought for the nation. But an assault of a different kind was soon to be launched from across the Atlantic.

Questions were beginning to be asked about the man behind the great image of authority. Could he be a dog in office? How could an illiterate, third-rate actor have passed himself off as our Bard? Were the immortal works not more likely to have been written by Francis Bacon? Armed with an introduction from Emerson, and perhaps inspired by her own name, Delia Bacon (who was no relation) was received in June 1853 by the Carlyles and their friend James Spedding, and over tea and scones she explained her theory that the man from Stratford was an impostor: they laughed in her face.[47] Others listened more sympathetically. Increasing interest in the archaeological vestiges of Shakespeare's life and times had combined with veneration of the Poet as Hero–Saint–King to create the Authorship Question. How could the two images of the peasant and the poet be reconciled? The question drove poor Delia to Stratford, madness and an early grave. Two years before her death in 1859, Nathaniel Hawthorne was persuaded to write a preface to her manic magnum opus, *The Philosophy of the Plays of Shakspere*, and in 1863 he confessed his belief that it must have taken a miracle for genius to survive the blighting squalor of an upbringing in Elizabethan Stratford. The Tercentenary celebrations of the following year were designed to quash the blight of doubt and give the miracle a local habitation and a name. From this date on Victorian Stratford becomes one of the essential destinations for all English-speaking tourists.[48] Yet Henry James was not alone in his scepticism. In 1903 he told a correspondent that he was '"sort of" haunted by the conviction that the divine William is the biggest and most successful fraud ever practised on a patient world'. True, he found it '*almost* as impossible to conceive that Bacon wrote the plays as to conceive that the man from Stratford, as we know the man from Stratford, did'.[49] Almost, but not quite. Out of this haunting lack of conviction he created two eloquent homages to the mystery of Shakespeare, a fine comic fable titled 'The Birthplace' (1903) and an astonishing essay on *The Tempest* (1907), one of his most impassioned meditations on the difference between the Man and the Artist.[50]

Shakespeare and Stratford are never named in 'The Birthplace'. They do not need to be because no one could mistake the references to 'temple' and 'shrine', 'the early home of the supreme poet, the Mecca of the English-speaking race'. Mecca was a widely favoured metaphor: it connoted a world religion while avoiding blasphemous rivalry with Jerusalem. The unsigned introduction to an illustrated album cashing in on the 1864 Tercentenary, *A Shakespeare Memorial*, reflects on how much better one understands the Bible when one reads it in 'the Holy Land'.[51] It is the same with Shakespeare. If you talk to Warwickshire locals, they will almost quote Shakespeare's familiar phrases, sometimes unconsciously, 'as Bedouins quote the Bible'. Warwickshire is a Holy Land for 'all the descendants of that great Anglo-Saxon family which is now rapidly extending itself over far-distant lands'. As they reach out to the four corners of the globe, they are summoned back by the voice of Shakespeare, 'back to the very heart of their mother country'.

> Many a 'passionate pilgrim' from the forests of Canada, and many devotees from amongst the Shakspeare-loving Americans, are irresistibly attracted to the room in Henley Street, in which our Poet was born three hundred years ago. In that room they meet wanderers from our Indian Empire, shepherds from the vast plains of Australia, and settlers from New Zealand and the Cape.

For those who could not make the pilgrimage to 'this literary Mecca', the book itself would seek to transport them in imagination. The few known facts about the founder of this religion could be strung together 'as a precious rosary'.

Orthodox religion might have had a few qualms about this rival brand, and the continuing threat of hell-fire was indeed regularly voiced by the anti-theatrical lobby, from provincial pulpits to the bishops in the House of Lords. But for those to whom the theatre was a school of vice, Shakespeare could still be read with a clear conscience in private or within the family. He could also be enjoyed without scandal at the public readings that became increasingly popular in the second half of the century. Shakespeare was an important component in the courses of study devised for the new Working Men's Colleges by F.D. Maurice; readings were thought more suitable than performance.

Nevertheless, the story of the relation between stage and church in Victorian times is one of progressive *rapprochement*, and it is symptomatic of the alliance forged with Shakespeare by the established church that the Tercentenary celebrations at Stratford should have been marked by strong religious elements, including weighty sermons by the Archbishop of Dublin, Richard Chevenix Trench, and the Bishop of St Andrew's, Charles Wordsworth.[52] The latter was the poet's nephew and author of one of the innumerable works devoted to proving the bonds between Shakespeare and Holy Scripture, *On Shakespeare's Knowledge and Use of the Bible* (1864). Shakespeare's growing attraction for many was precisely that he could be read as a secular Scripture, complementing without challenging its sacred counterpart. Or, indeed, the beliefs of non-Christians. This was why English literature was so useful, Government administrators in India emphasized, as a means of 'inclining the reader's thoughts towards religion while maintaining its secular character'.[53] This could bring them into conflict with the missionary schools, for whom 'inclination' was not good enough. The missionaries were fighting a losing battle. David Masson echoed the dominant orthodoxy when he cited the influential German scholar Hermann Ulrici. Shakespeare's ethics were to be identified 'with the *moral* essence of Christianity, and even occasionally with the doctrines with which the morality is bound up'. Sonnet 146 and Isabella's impassioned speeches to Angelo were favoured illustrations.[54]

Some of the connexions between religion and race that attached themselves to Stratford can be gauged from a book by Reginald R. Buckley entitled *The Shakespeare Revival and the Stratford-upon-Avon Movement* (1911). Buckley is looking back on the 'Stratford movement' effectively inaugurated in 1864, and marked by the opening of the Shakespeare Memorial Theatre in 1879. From 1886 the annual Stratford Festival was usually entrusted to the Bensons and their company, and Frank Benson contributed a Foreword to Buckley's book. It is an alarmingly lyrical epitome of turn-of-the-century racial fantasies. No longer the Anglo-Saxon Mecca, Stratford is now 'a temple dedicated to the genius of the Anglo-Celtic race' (p. xix). Ruskin, Emerson, Pater and Yeats are among the intellectual sponsors mentioned, and Yeats's essay 'At Stratford-on-Avon' is quoted at length.[55] Matthew Arnold is another key influence here, perhaps *the* key influence in the Celticizing of Shakespeare. The Bard's handling of nature expressed 'the Celtic note in him', claimed Arnold, without which ancestral strain 'Germanic England' would never have been able to produce a Shakespeare.[56]

Benson and Buckley preach the cause of an Anglo-Celtic federation that must join hands with 'the subtle strength of India', a blending of East and West and reconciliation of Black and White that will ensure 'the triumph of the Aryan Empire'. It will include 'the fervour of the Romance nations, the discipline of the Teuton, the primitive vigour of the Slav, the enterprise of the Scandinavian, the mystic reverence of the Oriental'. Benson could hear 'in the great peace of the night . . . the call of the higher Humanity'; he could feel the throb of 'the note of nature that makes the whole world kin'. The whole world does not, however, include Africans, and Jews are specifically excluded. Buckley says with evident approval that when he drew Shylock, Shakespeare 'showed his race feeling'. Those who believe that Reason has broken down the barriers of nationality and race are, Buckley argues, entirely mistaken; Cosmopolitanism is 'the common enemy' (p. 105). As for Shakespeare's role in all this: 'The entire significance of the Stratford Movement lies in the race question' (pp. 107–8). This is to make Stratford akin to Wagner's Bayreuth, and Buckley does indeed describe the theatre of his dreams in which the dramas of Shakespeare and Wagner would be performed in alternation.

CALIBAN AND IRELAND

Mystic reverential Orientals would have found it hard to make their way in great numbers to the Anglo-Saxon or Anglo-Celtic Mecca at the turn of the century. But in India there was plenty of Shakespeare to be seen and read.[57] At one extreme there was a Shakespeare sponsored by the colonial authorities, both on stage and page, and assimilated by the more privileged and upwardly mobile members of Indian society: this was not merely 'King' but 'Emperor Shakespeare'. At the other there were the fruits of a Shakespeare assimilated into indigenous theatrical and narrative forms, involving much interpolated song and dance. This activity resembles the traditions of burlesque and travesty on the popular stage back home in Victorian Britain itself. In between there were all sorts of hybrid, including the appearance of a 'Native Gentleman' as Othello at an English theatre in Calcutta in 1848, a Bengali called Bustomchurn Addy,[58] and the success of an English-woman, Mary Fenton, on the Parsi stage in Bombay. If the British thought India could be Shakespearized, it was even more certain that Shakespeare could be Indianized. Typical products were a popular Gujarati version of *Othello* as a tragicomedy in three acts with songs, and the transformation of *Hamlet* into an Urdu musical in 1898.

For the nineteenth-century imagination the equation between Ireland and the Orient was powerfully fostered by the popularity of Tom Moore's *Irish Melodies* (1808–34) and *Lalla Rookh* (1817).[59] Closer to home than the Oriental jewel in the crown was the Celtic thorn in the side. The history of Shakespeare and Ireland goes at least as far back as the first production of the plays themselves, if not to the history of the events they represent or refer to. With its multinational cast list of English, French, Scots, Welsh and Irish, *Henry V* bristles with questions about what it means to have or belong to a 'nation', questions that theatrical performance and two well-known films have frequently tried to assuage. But to English eyes in the latter decades of the nineteenth century the play and the figure that reflect most temptingly on Ireland and the Irish are *The Tempest* and Caliban.

The Irish do not come well out of Shakespeare. Apart from the signal appearance of Captain Macmorris in *Henry V* and his demand to know 'what ish my nation?' (*H5*, 3.2.124), references to Irish bogs, wolves and rough rug-headed kerns reinforce the Elizabethan stereotype of them as dirty dangerous brutes. But whether it is a precious stone or a paltry farm, Ireland is unignorably *another* island set in the silver sea, close to the one the dying John of Gaunt had in mind (*R2*, 2.1.40–60) – as the title of Shaw's 1904 play has it, *John Bull's Other Island*. Andrew Hadfield has argued that the ghostly presence of Ireland haunts Shakespeare's plays after 1599, and David J. Baker has questioned where Ireland might be in *The Tempest*.[60] By the middle of

the nineteenth century the ghostly presence had materialized, and it
took the shape of Caliban.

As one might expect from an era that saw the movements in Britain
and North America to abolish slavery, Caliban elicited more sympathy
in this century than he had in the previous. Coleridge described him as
a noble being and Hazlitt argued that he was the island's legitimate
ruler.[61] In 1876 George Eliot has Daniel Deronda demur at Grandcourt's
description of the Jamaican negro as 'a beastly sort of baptist Caliban',
saying that 'he had always felt a little with Caliban, who naturally had
his own point of view and could sing a good song' (DD, ch. 29). Political
and evolutionary ideas begin to make their mark. The year of
revolution, 1848, saw the first overtly republican Caliban in The
Enchanted Isle, a burlesque by Robert and William Brough;[62] in 1864
Browning published his 'Caliban upon Setebos'; and in 1873 Daniel
Wilson made an explicit connexion with Darwinian theory in Caliban:
The Missing Link.[63] Wilson is careful to insist that both the
Shakespearean and Darwinian creatures are equally fanciful, but his
scrupulous agnosticism did little to stop the fictions reinforcing each
other. A couple of years earlier the evolutionary perspective had
coloured George Rignold's impersonation on stage, at least in the eyes
of an observer who thought him 'exactly what Shakespeare intended,
fierce, strong, hideous, almost all animal, but with glimmerings of
human intellect, the undeveloped soul feeling up for the light through
the mass of brute instinct in which it is encased'.[64] Witnesses could
differ on just how strong were the glimmerings and developed the soul,
but the terms continue their relevance to the effects created by two
major players of the role at the end of the century, F.R. Benson and
Beerbohm Tree. It was no longer a foregone conclusion that the leading
player would take Prospero. Benson had read Wilson's Missing Link and
studied great apes at the zoo: the result was 'an astonishingly athletic
performance that audiences found both disturbing and hilarious'.[65]
Tree did for Caliban what Irving had done for Shylock, emphasizing his
dignity as a potentially or actually tragic figure. Irving's Shylock and
Tree's Caliban complement each other in the sense that they are the
two Shakespearean scapegoats with ruefully viewed but unmistakable

connexions to the contemporary British ruling class, the alien 'within' and the alien 'without'.[66] (As it happens, they are the only two characters to whom Shakespeare gives a 'gaberdine'.) Tree's production closed with a famously elaborate tableau, in which Caliban stretched his arms out towards the departing ship in mute despair: 'The night falls, and Caliban is left on the lonely rock. He is a King once more.'[67]

But Shakespeare on stage can be a world elsewhere, and Tree's fantastic productions ensured that it was. In the real world of contemporary America and Ireland, Caliban was less often sentimentalized. The *Punch* for 24 January 1863 showed a notorious cartoon entitled 'Scene from the American "Tempest"'. Lincoln is handing the Emancipation Proclamation to a grateful and obsequious black Caliban who gestures derisively over his shoulder at a scowling Robert E. Lee. *Punch* also had a cartoon that makes explicit the connexion between Shakespeare's play and contemporary Ireland. 'The Irish "Tempest"' appeared in the issue for 19 March 1870 (Figure 20). Around this time Ireland was never much out of the news, but in the first half of 1870 the turmoil surrounding land reform ensured its regular association with images of violence and menace. On 12 February 'Hercules and the Hydra' saw Gladstone in a loincloth preparing to tackle the multitudinous serpent with heads labelled 'Fenianism', 'Irish Land Question', 'Sanitary Reform', 'Trades Unions', 'Education', 'Emigration' and others. On 12 March a cartoon with the caption 'Where's the (Irish) Police?' showed a rioting mob marked with the usual degenerate apelike features. The *Tempest* cartoon shows a disturbingly well-armed Caliban sporting the names of the warring Irish factions (as who should say, 'a plague on *all* your houses!'), most prominently the 'Ultramontani' on his sash, and 'Ribandism', 'Orangeism' and 'Fenianism' on his chest. Fortified only with the staff of his 'Irish Land Bill', Gladstone/Prospero clasps the shrinking maidenly Hibernia. As applied by the English to Ireland, this familiar trope goes at least as far back as Spenser's *Faerie Queene* (bk v, cantos xi–xii), with the virgin Irene and the violent woodkerne Grantorto from whom she needs to be delivered by the British knight Artegall.[68]

FIGURE 20 'The Irish "Tempest"'. Caliban (Rory of the Hills) – 'This Island's mine, by Sycorax my Mother, which thou tak'st from me.' *Punch*, 19 March 1870.

DOWDEN, BRADLEY AND
SOVEREIGN INDEPENDENCE

We get some sense of Edward Dowden's political position from his sonnet 'King Mob' (*Poems*, 1876). The prospect of King Mob surrounded by 'foot-lickers' and drinking in the poison of flattery does not inspire him with confidence. 'I love you too, big Anarch, lately born', he protests,

> Half beast, yet with a stupid heart of man,
> And since I love, would God that I could warn
> Work out the beast as shortly as you can,
> Till which time oath of mine shall ne'er be sworn,
> Nor knee be bent to you, King Caliban.

Tennyson had sung of moving upward, 'working out the beast' (*In Memoriam*, CXVIII), as if it were a task for us all. In Dublin in the 1870s it could seem a matter of urgency – for *you*.[69]

Dowden had ambitions as a poet, but he had to settle at the tender age of twenty-four for the first Chair of English at Trinity College Dublin. He was one of a new breed: at his death no fewer than thirty of his students held Chairs of English literature in various countries.[70] In 1875 Dowden published the first critical book on Shakespeare by what we would now call a professional academic. *Shakspere: A Critical Study of His Mind and Art* went through twelve British editions before 1901 and established his authority as the leading British Shakespearean critic of his generation. His shorter and more popular *Shakspere* (1877) was even more widely read.

Dowden had no sympathy for Irish nationalism, vehemently opposed the Home Rule Bill of 1886 and, despite an old friendship with W.B. Yeats's father, saw little to welcome in the 'local group' (his phrase) leading the Irish Literary Revival.[71] When he came to discuss Shakespeare's politics, Dowden conceded that the dramatist was 'not in a modern sense democratic' (Dowden, p. 319), but what could one expect? 'In the Tudor period the people had not yet emerged. The people, like Milton's half-created animals, is still pawing to get free its hinder parts from the mire' (p. 320). Shakespeare had no choice but to show 'the people' as it then was: 'at worst it appeared as Caliban' (p. 325). So, *pace* Hazlitt, *Coriolanus* has nothing to tell us about politics. It has much to tell us about the individual, says Dowden, about the 'bonds of duty and of affection which attach man to fellow-man', about the 'passion of patriotism' and 'the national life, to which the individual surrenders himself with gladness and with pride' (p. 329). The business of the people is to paw their way out of the mire, not to ask with Captain Macmorris 'what is my nation?' It is possible for them to do so, Dowden believes, for the modern world affords 'proof of power ... that moral dignity, the spirit of self-control and self-denial, the heroic devotion of masses of men to ideas and not merely interests, could begin to manifest themselves' (p. 320). This is a startlingly blithe way of describing the French Revolution, not much like the violent multitudinous world of the 1790s portrayed by Carlyle. Dowden sounds here more like George Eliot, and it comes as no surprise that he admired the cautious belief in 'progress' expressed by her fiction.

Dowden's Shakespeare tells his countrymen stuck in the mire what they need to look up to. We find it above all in Prospero: 'self-mastery', 'a harmonious and fully developed *will*', 'complete possession of himself', 'an altitude of thought from which he can survey the whole of human life, and see how small and yet how great it is' (p. 418). Matthew Arnold was fond of heights, and Dowden shared his attraction to an ideal of lofty 'serenity'. 'On the heights' is the influential motto Dowden found for the fourth and final phase of Shakespeare's spiritual journey, as it can be discerned in his works: the preceding three are 'In the workshop', 'In the world' and 'Out of the depths'.[72] The plays abound with bad examples of characters still stuck in the mire, unconscious of the road out of it, or even that they are on a road at all – Falstaff, Jaques, Richard II. They all fail to face facts. 'Fact' is one of Dowden's key terms, of elastic interpretation but metaphysical validity. It was this, he thought, that the great Elizabethans had in common, Hooker and Bacon and Shakespeare, '*a rich feeling for positive, concrete fact*' (p. 23, his italics). Romeo and Hamlet represent the two great diseases of youth, abandonment to passion and to brooding thought;

they are both guilty of 'the one supreme crime in Shakspere's eyes, want of fidelity to the fact' (p. 47). The great thing about Henry V is 'his noble realisation of fact' (p. 212). He is the antithesis of the Richard II over whom Pater crooned so absurdly, and when Dowden calls him 'aesthetic' (p. 209), it is not a compliment. Shakespeare himself was determined to bring his spiritual being 'into harmony with the highest facts and laws of the world' (p. 384). For this he needed 'will', the other most important term in Dowden's sparsely conceived ethical vocabulary. Shakespeare possessed this will in supreme measure: only its force enabled him to overcome the passion and temptations that assailed him, for let no one suppose that the serenity he finally achieved came, as one might say, naturally. 'Strenuous Will' would have served Dowden well as his title.

A.C. Bradley acknowledged his debt to Dowden, but his work on Shakespeare far outweighs his predecessor's in the philosophic reach of its thinking and the scrupulous finesse of its expression. He is a critic whom it is easy to misrepresent by selective quotation, and to whom it is hard to do justice in a brief space. *Shakespearean Tragedy* (1904) has been taken to consummate a Victorian tradition of homage to Shakespeare as supreme moral authority, arbiter of difficult questions about suffering, good and evil, implicit counsellor in matters of judgment and conduct.[73] For much of the past century he was mocked for this old-fashioned seriousness, as well as for asking allegedly irrelevant questions about Lady Macbeth's children, usually by critics who had at best read him less carefully than he had written, and at worst simply jeered at a useful straw man.[74] The anxiety of influence to which real creative artists may be prone pales into insignificance by comparison with that suffered by scholars and critics. Given that he was born in 1851, there is ample justification for viewing Bradley as Victorian, yet it is not just the technicality that *Shakespearean Tragedy* was published three years after Queen Victoria's death that invites us to think of his work as looking forward as much as it looks back. He has certainly had more influence on subsequent writings on Shakespeare, even or especially in the often misconceived reactions against what he is thought to have written and stood for, than any other 'Victorian' critic.

There is one aspect of Bradley's thinking about Shakespeare that links up directly with Dowden's and displays a distinctly Victorian colouring. It is an anxiety, that we have already seen afflicting Ruskin, about how tragedies end. It is an essential part of Dowden's argument that the creator of Hamlet, Lear and Timon had seen and felt 'a darker side to the world and to the soul of man' (Dowden, p. 384). Timon was especially significant, Dowden stressed, because he could only have been created by a man who had successfully passed through Timon's bleak misanthropy and attained or regained his own serenity. This in turn is what it should mean to read the dark tragedies. We should identify with the will of their creator and take heart from his self-mastery. We shall never know if Hamlet finally achieves deliverance from his disease of will; but we do know that Shakespeare had thoroughly understood his malady and thereby 'gained a further stage in his culture of self-control' (p. 160). The most difficult case is *King Lear*, where Dowden admits that we can only guess at the spiritual significance of the great tragic facts of the world. Yet even here we can find this assurance: 'Shakspere discovers the supreme fact, – that the moral world stands in sovereign independence of the world of the senses' (p. 227).

Carlyle had hailed King Shakespeare; Dowden proposes the sovereign independence of the moral world. This is a powerful belief, and Bradley was not the only Victorian to be deeply attracted to it. His account of the end of *King Lear* is an elaborate meditation on Dowden's blunt statement of 'the supreme fact'. But whereas Dowden speaks of 'fact', Bradley points us to 'feeling', and to the 'impression' left by the death of Cordelia. This includes, he says, an immediate sense of shock, of bewilderment, dismay and protest. It is only after this shock that there flashes on us something else, 'the conviction that our whole attitude in asking or expecting that goodness should be prosperous is wrong; that, if only we could see things as they are, we should see that the outward is nothing and the inward is all' (Bradley, p. 326). If only: it is easy to override Bradley's scrupulous hesitations and attribute to him a certainty that he refrains from expressing. It would be good to believe with Dowden in the supreme fact of sovereign independence. But it is harder to separate the moral world from the world of the senses than Dowden allows.

SHAW AND BARDICIDE

Dowden and Bradley are nevertheless at one in their determination to repudiate the charge of 'pessimism' which this tragedy of Shakespeare's above all others attracts. Bradley firmly dissociates himself from the intoxicatedly pagan Swinburne, for whom the 'fatalism' of *King Lear* – 'for here is very Night herself' – is something to be acclaimed rather than deplored (Bradley, pp. 276–8). But there was another critic close to hand convinced of Shakespeare's pessimism and determined to oppose it, the man responsible for inventing the word 'Bardolatry', George Bernard Shaw.

Shaw denounces Shakespeare with such noisy eloquence that it is hard to notice that he also admired him. There are at least two Shaws on Shakespeare. There is the one who fair-mindedly distinguishes between the Shakespeare whom he loves from his intimate reading and the gaudy travesties perpetrated by Irving and Daly and Beerbohm Tree which he heartily deplores. There is another who rages indiscriminately at the absence of sovereign intellect both from the plays and the way they are performed. Yet when Frank Harris claimed that the secret to Shakespeare and his works was a heart broken by a love affair, Shaw was moved to protest. Shakespeare might be damned, but he was still a Titan.

> That Shakespear's soul was damned (I really know no other way of expressing it) by a barren pessimism is undeniable; but even when it drove him to the blasphemous despair of Lear and the Nihilism of Macbeth, it did not break him. He was not crushed by it: he wielded it Titanically, and made it a sublime quality in his plays. He almost delighted in it: it never made him bitter: to the end there was mighty music in him, and outrageous gaiety. (Shaw, pp. 199–200)

To this extent Shaw is in accord with Dowden, that Shakespeare's art is a testament to his sanity. Indeed Shaw waxes more lyrical than the monotone Dowden when he speaks of mighty music and outrageous gaiety.

But music and gaiety were not enough. Shakespeare may have been a master of word-music, but blank verse was easy, and his was a treacherous, seductive gift. Look at what he puts into his characters' mouths, Shaw railed. These people possess 'no religion, no politics, no conscience, no hope, no convictions of any sort' (p. 3). And their author had no real ideas, or too many. He certainly had no sovereign idea of his own, and no grasp of the supreme fact. Shaw's sense of supreme facts was about as different as it could be from Dowden's and Bradley's, and he would have scorned the thought of separating the moral world from the world of the senses. What about the world of ideas? Like that other great popular writer, Charles Dickens, Shakespeare could do nothing with a serious positive character, Shaw contended. Ruskin was right: there are no heroes. As for *Othello*, it was pure melodrama, and *Cymbeline* was stagey trash. The only plays worth salvaging were those bold experiments in realism that anticipate the best modern drama (his own): *All's Well, Measure for Measure* and *Troilus and Cressida*. The last play Shaw wrote near the end of his long life was a little puppet show called 'Shakes Versus Shav' (reprinted in Shaw, pp. 265–9). It concludes with Shav saying 'Peace, jealous Bard: / We both are mortal. For a moment suffer / My glimmering light to shine.' To which Shakes replies 'Out, out, brief candle', gives a puff, and the play ends in darkness.

The story told by this chapter began with Carlyle and King Shakespeare. Shakespeare proved a precious resource to the Victorians in their claims for various forms of sovereignty. But for the rising generation of writers near the end of the century the great image of authority was on the wane. Shaw dared to say what others may have thought, that there was something to be said for Bardicide.

DUBLIN EPILOGUE

The best way of marking an end to Victorian Shakespeare is to look towards Dublin. A number of important Irish figures start out from there, though all except one end up elsewhere. The eldest is the exception: born in Cork in 1843, Edward Dowden became rooted to the Chair of English at Trinity College Dublin that he held from 1867 until his death in 1913. The others migrated to London or further afield: Bram Stoker (1847–1912), Oscar Wilde (1854–1900), George Bernard Shaw (1856–1950), W.B. Yeats (1865–1939) and James Joyce (1882–1941). Their dealings with Shakespeare are of very different kinds, but they help to draw a line that separates a Victorian from a post-Victorian Shakespeare. Dowden, Stoker and Wilde fall on one side of this line; Shaw, Yeats and Joyce on the other.[1] It is no coincidence that the older ones exhibit a more or less powerful attachment to the actor-manager who dominated late-Victorian Shakespeare on stage, while the younger shake themselves free of Irving's influence or remain untouched by it.

There are of course other prominent migrants and vagrants on the late nineteenth-century scene who straddle the distinctions between 'Victorian', 'Edwardian' and 'Modernist' – Henry James and Joseph Conrad, to take two salient examples. Both have important dealings with Shakespeare that cannot be pursued here. James alludes freely to Shakespeare throughout his career. Near the end of their respective novels, both Roderick Hudson and Christopher Newman have the thought attributed to them that like Othello their 'occupation was gone' (*Oth*, 3.3.360).[2] In 'The Aspern Papers' (ch. 9) the anonymous

231

narrator confesses that he has been 'too full of stratagems and spoils', referring to the passage about 'the man that hath no music in himself' in *The Merchant of Venice* (*MV*, 5.1.83–8);[3] in *The Tragic Muse* (ch. 19), Miriam Rooth tests her potential on a famous speech of Constance's from *King John*;[4] *The Wings of the Dove* is suffused with echoes of *The Tempest* and its marine magic, while the novel's London and Venice invert Shakespeare's opposition of Venice and Belmont, with the heiress Milly Theale as a tragically betrayed and tortuously triumphant Portia.[5] Conrad's Captain Whalley in 'The End of the Tether' has been compared to King Lear, Lord Jim owes a great deal to Hamlet (and 'Hamletism'), *Nostromo* boasts an epigraph from *King John*, *Chance* makes significant use of *Othello* and *Victory* of *The Tempest*.[6] But however one tries to categorize it, *Victory* (1915) is not a Victorian novel, and neither is *The Wings of the Dove* (1902). They belong to a post-Victorian story.

James does, however, have a passing light to throw on Victorian Dublin, and it has a slight Shakespearean colouring. James may have been a supersubtle cosmopolitan, but amongst other things he was partly Irish. His grandfather William had emigrated from County Cavan to make his fortune in America. In 1895 the grandson caught a glimpse of his ancestral land from a double coign of vantage that could scarcely have been more privileged. He spent a few days as a guest first of the Viceroy, young Lord Houghton, at Dublin Castle, and then of his old friends the Garnet Wolseleys at the Royal Hospital, residence of the Commander-in-Chief of the English forces. James was miserable at the former: the contrast between its lavish extravagance and the squalor at the gates made for 'a most depressing, haunting, discomfort'.[7] He was much more at home with the military man and his artistic wife. Like his elder brother William but unlike his two younger brothers Wilkie and Bob, James had spent the American Civil War as a non-combatant. He was correspondingly fascinated by the precarious, glorious life of the soldier, the epitome of conventional manliness. It often made him think of Othello, not just for the dangers the soldier might pass but also for the stories he had to tell. One line from Othello's speech before the senate held for him a particular magic: 'This only is the witchcraft

I have used' (*Oth*, 1.3.170).[8] A few years later James consumed Wolseley's memoirs with avidity, confessing envy for his friend's 'infinite acquaintance ... with superlative *men*', and describing himself by contrast as a 'poor worm of peace'.[9] This is a cross between the 'moth of peace' Desdemona fears she will become if she is left behind (*Oth*, 1.3.258) and the 'poor worm' Prospero perceives to be 'infected' by love (*Tem*, 3.1.31). A good deal more could be said about the way James divided himself between a loving Desdemona and a treacherous Iago in his representation of the power embodied, in Dublin as elsewhere, by the English ruling classes.

Henry Irving also had a warm reception in Dublin. As a twenty-two-year-old in 1860 he had endured a baptism of fire at the Queen's Royal Theatre when he replaced a local favourite who inspired a claque against him. His roles had included Laertes, Cassio and Florizel – and Nicholas Nickleby. In 1871 he enjoyed a less troubled reception from an audience at the Theatre Royal that included a young civil servant called Bram Stoker and a lad of sixteen called George Bernard Shaw. (Shaw much preferred Barry Sullivan, for Shakespeare.) Irish friends told Irving he was the image of Robert Emmet, and in due course he commissioned a play about the Irish patriot which was about to go into production in 1884 when the Lord Chamberlain intervened.[10] By this time he was firmly installed as a darling of the Dublin establishment, his *Hamlet* in the autumn of 1876 having sealed this conquest. He was formally acclaimed by the students and Fellows of Trinity College, hauled through the streets in triumph, entertained by the Lord Lieutenant and given a long-haired terrier called 'Trin'. If there was a moving spirit behind this reception it was Stoker, who was rewarded late in 1878 by Irving's invitation to join him at the Lyceum as his business manager. The rest is history and the myth of Irving – to which Stoker largely contributed and on which he drew for the fiction by which he is himself now remembered, *Dracula* (1897).

Dowden admired Irving and recognized him as a kind of equal when he remarked, 'After all an actor's commentary is his acting' (Stoker, I, p. 27). The academic recognition he received from Trinity College was precious to Irving. The connexion was fortified by the 'Life of

Shakespeare' that Dowden contributed to the eight-volume edition of *The Henry Irving Shakespeare*, and an article on *King Lear* for the *Illustrated London News* published to coincide with the Lyceum production of 1892 (Hughes, p. 121). It was the actor who needed the academic. Dowden's critical writings betray no interest in the theatre, but the alliance between his readings and Irving's performance was none the less firm for the one-sidedness of its public acknowledgment. In the 1890s Shakespeare was no less good box-office in Dublin's most respectably patronized venues – the Theatre Royal, the Queen's Royal, the Gaiety – than in London's West End. It meant that for Dubliners and others who were fired with visions of a new theatre for a new drama, Dowden–Irving was the enemy.

This was not the case for the gifted classical scholar at Trinity College Dublin in 1871–4, even though his enthusiasm for the Pre-Raphaelites, Swinburne, aestheticism and fancy dress cannot have been to Professor Dowden's taste. (They did share an admiration for Whitman.) Oscar Wilde pretended to complain (in French) that 'I am Irish by race, and the English have condemned me to speak the language of Shakespeare.'[11] It was a sentence that he bore more lightly than the two years' hard labour handed down by the judge on 25 May 1895, the same day that Irving's knighthood was announced in the Queen's Birthday Honours List.[12] Wilde was on good terms with Irving. The sonnet 'Fabien Dei Franchi' gently rebukes him for wasting his talents on third-rate melodrama and insists that he is made for 'more august creation!', for Lear and Romeo and Richard III, concluding 'Thou trumpet set for Shakespeare's lips to blow!' (Wilde, p. 860). Wilde celebrated the Lyceum stagings for their living archaeology, the past brought back to life, and he admired their master-spirit for realizing 'his own perfection as an artist', and thus not merely appealing to the few, but also educating the many: 'He has created in the public both taste and temperament' (p. 1190).

But it was on the Lady of the Lyceum that Wilde doted. Ellen Terry had been married to the midwife of aestheticism, Edward William Godwin,[13] who would redecorate Wilde's house in Tite Street. In 'The Truth of Masks' Wilde praised Godwin as 'one of the most artistic spirits of this century in England' (p. 1163). Wilde wrote fervent sonnets to Terry – 'O Portia! Take my heart: it is thy due: / I think I will not quarrel with the Bond' (p. 839). He failed to persuade her to act in his plays, teased her Lady Macbeth for looking as if she did her own shopping in Byzantium, and hailed the glory she shed when she came to sit for his neighbour Sargent, 'the vision of Lady Macbeth in full regalia magnificently seated in a four-wheeler'.[14] Chelsea would never be the same again.

Shakespeare was a prominent contributor to Wilde's developing conception of life as art, as theatre, show, play. On the strength of 'The Truth of Masks' one might say that Shakespeare was its onlie begetter, so rich an array of examples does his drama provide to support the idea that we are what we wear. What relish we take in the power of illusion, says Wilde, the effect of a dress, a cloak, a bracelet, a handkerchief, a plume. Look how Shakespeare understood this, how the great actors demonstrate it. How dull are those beautiful players off-stage when they take off their make-up and cease to pretend, like poor Sibyl Vane in *The Picture of Dorian Gray*. Why bother to wade through Carlyle when 'the whole of the Philosophy of Clothes is to be found in Lear's scene with Edgar – a passage which has the advantage of brevity and style over the grotesque wisdom and somewhat mouthing metaphysics of *Sartor Resartus*' (p. 1161)? The best way to understand Shakespeare and the world around you, certainly the quickest, was not to read Carlyle but to watch Irving and Terry – or Sarah Bernhardt. Her 1884 production of *Macbeth* in Paris, Wilde told a journalist, was her finest creation. And he meant *her* creation, 'because to my mind it is utterly impertinent to talk of Shakespeare's *Macbeth* or Shakespeare's *Othello*. Shakespeare is only one of the parties. The second is the artiste through whose mind it passes'.[15] Onlie begetters were all very well, but performing artists were even better. Wilde's Shakespeare was a charming colleague. He was not an icon, a genius, a king, not one of 'the authorities'.

Shaw was every bit as impertinent as Wilde; he also doted on Ellen Terry. But unlike Wilde, he saw Shakespeare as a rival (and Irving too). Wilde would have been happy to drink champagne with Shakespeare:

Shaw would have thrown it in his face. From 1888 to 1898 he campaigned fiercely against the spectacular Shakespeare dominating the late-Victorian theatre, as drama critic successively for the *Star*, the *World* and the *Saturday Review*. Shakespeare had had a good run for his money, Shaw believed, and he had given actor-managers like Irving and impresarios like Augustin Daly more than a good run for theirs. It was time to promote new models of what drama could and should be. Besides the new home-based initiatives associated with J.T. Grein's Independent Theatre and its successor the Stage Society, with figures such as Archer, Poel, Granville-Barker and Shaw himself, this meant looking abroad to Scandinavia, Paris and Berlin, to the plays of Ibsen, to the practical experiments of André Antoine's *Théâtre Libre* and Otto Brahm's *Freie Bühne*.[16] By the time Barker took a lease on the Royal Court Theatre in 1904 these developments were bearing fruit. The author of the then recently published *Shakespearean Tragedy* enjoyed *Candida* so much that he was 'ready to forgive Shaw a good deal for it'. A few months later A.C. Bradley was off to a Hauptmann comedy with Bertrand Russell and his wife.[17]

1904 was also the year that saw the opening of the Abbey Theatre in Dublin. Through the 1890s there had been growing opposition to the dominance of the London-based touring companies, and the Irish Literary Theatre developed out of a shared contempt for the English commercial theatre.[18] Yeats, Lady Gregory, Edward Martyn and George Moore had something else in mind, and this made its first appearance in 1899 at the Antient Concert rooms with Martyn's *The Heather Field* and Yeats's *The Countess Cathleen*. When the Abbey Theatre company opened its doors a few years later Yeats invited Shaw to write his next play for the company. It was over a decade later before they staged the resulting *John Bull's Other Island*, but in 1909 another play of Shaw's, *The Shewing-up of Blanco Posnet*, featured as a *cause célèbre* in the history of censorship on the British stage, when the Abbey went ahead with it against instructions from Dublin Castle.[19] Meanwhile Shakespeare was out in the cold. It was nearly thirty years before a play of his was staged at the Abbey (*King Lear*, in 1928), and in the first fifty years of its history, only two more were added to it (*Macbeth*, 1934, and *Coriolanus*, 1936).[20]

Irving's Hamlet had made a strong impression on the young Yeats, who saw in Shakespeare's character 'an image of heroic self-possession for the poses of youth and childhood to copy'.[21] He also knew Dowden, who was an old college friend of his father's.[22] For a few years after the family moved back to Dublin in 1880 Dowden's cultivated existence and dark good looks provided the young Yeats with another image, 'the image of romance'. His faith in Dowden was shaken when the Professor urged him to read George Eliot, who disturbed and alarmed him, until his father tossed her aside and started praising *Wuthering Heights*. Years later Yeats discovered that his father had always thought Dowden put too much faith in the intellect, and that for all his cosmopolitan learning, the one man of letters Dublin Unionism possessed was really a provincial.[23] As the young Yeats grew in confidence, he came to identify Dowden with everything he hated in the Protestant Establishment of Victorian Ireland. By the time he went to Stratford-upon-Avon in the spring of 1901 to see Benson's company perform the histories, he was ready to dislike Dowden as a critic of Shakespeare, and he did. 'The more I read the worse does Shakespeare criticism become. And Dowden is about the climax of it', he told Lady Gregory.[24] Dowden had turned Shakespeare into 'a British Benthamite'.[25] In 1909 a performance of *Hamlet* reminded him of how badly Dowden had misprised the great creative artist. In his last years, said Yeats, Shakespeare was 'no quiet country gentleman, enjoying, as men like Dowden think, the temporal reward of an unvalued toil'. How could he have subsided to this level, the man whose *Hamlet* made Yeats feel that he was 'in the presence of a soul lingering on the storm-beaten threshold of sanctity'?[26] Dowden had never got near such a threshold; he probably did not know it existed.

Like Yeats, James Joyce takes us well beyond the Victorian age, though he reflects back on the distinctly Victorian Dublin of his childhood and young manhood. He too knew Dowden, though more distantly, from his student days at University College Dublin, and he put Dowden into the crazed conversation about Shakespeare in the National Library on 16 June 1904 that features in Episode 9 of *Ulysses* (1922), 'Scylla and Charybdis'. In September 1903 Joyce had tried to get a job at the Library and called on Dowden for his support; the Professor is supposed to have thought him 'extraordinary' and 'quite unsuitable'.[27]

In 1899 the unsuitable young Joyce had been in the audience for the riotous first performance of Yeats's *Countess Cathleen*, and he took the side of the insurgents against his friends. Early the following year he read a paper on 'Drama and Life' to the Literary and Historical Society at University College in which he disparaged the great drama of the past, including the Greeks and Shakespeare. Joyce thought, like Shaw, that Shakespeare had had his day. Writers of the future should look across to what was happening in Europe now, to Ibsen, Wagner, Hauptmann, D'Annunzio. He rounded off a bravura performance by quoting Lona Hessel's famous speech from *The Pillars of Society* about opening the windows and letting in the fresh air.[28] A few months later the *Fortnightly Review* printed his review of Ibsen's last play, *When We Dead Awaken* – quite a coup for an eighteen-year-old. Joyce's youthful enthusiasm for Ibsen became tempered, and he was never devoid of interest in Shakespeare. In Trieste in 1912 he lectured on *Hamlet*, and he remained intrigued by the idea of Shakespeare as both King and Prince.[29] He gave to Stephen Dedalus theories about the real-life models behind the poems and plays: Anne Hathaway (Venus in *Venus and Adonis*), the younger brothers Richard and Edmund she slept with (the villains in *Richard III* and *King Lear*), the dead son (Arthur in *King John*) and his mother (Volumnia in *Coriolanus*). His friends said Joyce took this more seriously than his fictional character.[30] He suffered from no particular awe or even respect for Shakespeare, by comparison with Dante, and as for drama, on at least one occasion he stuck to his guns about the modern Norwegian's superiority. In 1936 a Danish journalist asked him if he placed Ibsen higher than Shakespeare? 'He towers head and shoulders above him', Joyce replied.[31]

Challenged by Shakespearean tragedy in 1877, Ruskin had expressed his belief in a 'poetical justice' that showed the proper rewards of virtue and vice, 'the manifestation of the Father in this world, no less than in that which is to come' (*Ruskin*, XXIX, p. 266). Challenged by *Coriolanus* in the aftermath of Waterloo, Hazlitt had written sardonically that the history of mankind 'was a romance, a mask, a tragedy, constructed upon the principles of *poetical justice*; it is a noble or royal hunt, in which what is sport to the few is death to the many'.[32] Challenged by an examiner to answer the question 'How is poetic justice exemplified in the play of *King Lear?*' a Dublin undergraduate in 1900 said he did not know. 'Oh, come, Mr. Joyce, you are not fair to yourself. I feel sure you have read the play', barked the Professor. Mr Joyce conceded that he had indeed done so, but that he failed to understand the question: 'The phrase "poetic justice" is unmeaning jargon so far as I am concerned.'[33]

Not bliss to be alive perhaps, but a dawn to be sure, taking Joyce and many others beyond the Victorians, and beyond the Victorian Shakespeare.

NOTES

INTRODUCTION

1. G.R. Elliott, 'Shakespeare's significance for Browning', *Anglia. Zeitschrift für Englische Philologie*, 32 [n.s. 20] (1909), 111.
2. See Danny Karlin's forthcoming essay on this enigmatic and neglected poem, '"The Names": Robert Browning's "Shaksperean Show"', in *Victorian Shakespeare: Literature and Culture*, ed. Gail Marshall and Adrian Poole (Basingstoke, 2003).
3. 'Frances Anne Kemble' (1893), in *Literary Criticism: Essays on Literature, American Writers, English Writers*, ed. Leon Edel, Library of America (Cambridge, 1984), p. 1079.
4. For a concise overview, see Russell Jackson, 'Victorian editing of *As You Like It* and the purposes of editing', in *The Theory and Practice of Text-Editing: Essays in Honour of James T. Boulton*, ed. Ian Small and Marcus Walsh (Cambridge, 1991), pp. 142–56.
5. G.H. Lewes, *On Actors and the Art of Acting* (1875).
6. 'Shakspeare; or, the Poet', *Representative Men* (1850), in *Essays and Lectures*, Library of America (Cambridge, 1983), p. 718.

1: THEATRE

1. For the 'provincial' theatre in Britain, see Russell Jackson, 'Shakespeare in Liverpool: Edward Saker's revivals, 1876–81', *Theatre Notebook*, 32.3 (1978), 100–9, and Douglas Reid, 'Popular theatre in Victorian Birmingham', in *Performance and Politics in Popular Drama*, ed. David Bradby, Louis James and Bernard Sharratt (Cambridge, 1980), pp. 65–89; also Arnold Hare, 'Shakespeare in a Victorian provincial stock company', Jeremy Crump, 'The popular audience for Shakespeare in nineteenth-century Leicester' and Kathleen Barker, 'Charles Dillon: a provincial tragedian', all in *Shakespeare and the Victorian Stage*, ed. Richard Foulkes (Cambridge, 1986), pp. 255–94. For Australia, Canada and India, see Dennis Bartholomeusz, 'Shakespeare on the Melbourne stage, 1843–61', *SS 35* (Cambridge, 1982), pp. 31–41; Alan Brissenden, 'Australian Shakespeare', in *Shakespeare Performed: Essays in Honor of R.A. Foakes*, ed. Grace Ioppolo (Newark and London, 2000),

pp. 240–59; John Golder and Richard Madelaine, eds, *O Brave New World: Two Centuries of Shakespeare on the Australian Stage* (Sydney, 2001); Herbert Whittaker, 'Shakespeare in Canada before 1853', *Stratford Papers on Shakespeare*, ed. B.W. Jackson (Toronto, 1965), pp. 71–89; Ania Loomba, 'Shakespearian transformations', in *Shakespeare and National Culture*, ed. John J. Joughin (Manchester and New York, 1997), pp. 109–41; and Jyotsna Singh, 'Different Shakespeares: the bard in colonial/postcolonial India', *Theatre Journal*, 41.4 (December 1989), 445–58. For America, see Charles H. Shattuck, *Shakespeare on the American Stage: from the Hallams to Edwin Booth* (Washington, D.C., 1976); also George B. Churchill, 'Shakespeare in America' (1906), and Ashley Thorndike, 'Shakespeare in America' (1927), in *Americans on Shakespeare 1776–1914*, ed. Peter Rawlings (Aldershot, 1999), pp. 418–48, 512–26.

2. For a convenient selection of contemporary views of these and other leading performers, see *Victorian Actors and Actresses in Review*, ed. Donald Mullin (Westport, Conn. and London, 1983), and *Shakespeare in the Theatre: An Anthology of Criticism*, ed. Stanley Wells (Oxford, 2000), pp. 67–178.

3. For Poel, see William Poel, *Shakespeare in the Theatre* (1913), and Robert Speaight, *William Poel and the Elizabethan Revival* (1954). For the transition from 'Victorian' to 'Early Modern' Shakespeare, see J.L. Styan, *The Shakespeare Revolution* (Cambridge, 1977); Russell Jackson, 'Before the Shakespeare revolution: developments in the study of nineteenth-century Shakespearian production', *SS* 35 (Cambridge, 1982), pp. 1–12; and Jean Chothia, 'Variable authenticities: staging Shakespeare in the early modern period', in *English Drama of the Early Modern Period, 1890–1940* (1996), pp. 227–47.

4. Webster experimented with a neo-Elizabethan staging of *The Taming of the Shrew* that anticipates the revolutionary movement gathering force towards the end of the century. See Jan McDonald, '*The Taming of the Shrew* at the Haymarket Theatre, 1844 and 1847', in *Nineteenth-Century British Theatre*, ed. Kenneth Richards and Peter Thomson (1971), pp. 157–70.

5. For a useful survey of London theatres in the period through contemporary views (not specifically focused on Shakespeare), see *Victorian Theatre*, ed. Russell Jackson (1989), pp. 9–78.

6. 'The Amusements of the People', *Household Words*, 30 March and 13 April 1850; reprinted in *Dickens' Journalism*, Dent Uniform Edition, II, ed. Michael Slater (1996), pp. 179–85, 193–201.

7. M. Willson Disher, *Greatest Show on Earth* (1937), pp. 210–17.

8. Theodor Fontane, *Shakespeare in the London Theatre 1855–58*, trans. Russell Jackson (1999), p. 16.

9. See Richard W. Schoch, *Not Shakespeare: Bardolatry and Burlesque in the Nineteenth Century* (Cambridge, 2002), and *Nineteenth-Century Shakespeare Burlesques*, 5 vols, ed. Stanley Wells (1977–8).

10. *The Plays of W.S. Gilbert*, ed. George Rowell (Cambridge, 1982), pp. 172–85.

11. Richard Brown, '"Shakespeare Explained": James Joyce's Shakespeare', in *Shakespeare and Ireland*, ed. Mark Thornton Burnett and Ramona Wray (1997), pp. 99–104.

12. Geoffrey Ashton, *Catalogue of Paintings at the Theatre Museum, London*, ed. James Fowler (1992), p. 59. See also Mollie Sands, *Robson of the Olympic* (1979), and 'P.T.' [Peter Thomson], in *The Cambridge Guide to Theatre*, ed. Martin Banham (Cambridge, 1992), p. 835.

13. You could see him exceptionally at Sadler's Wells in mid-century, and in Poel's scholarly productions at the end.

14. On Phelps's audience, see Shirley S. Allen, *Samuel Phelps and Sadler's Wells Theatre* (Middleton, Conn., 1971), pp. 94–7.

15. Fontane, *Shakespeare*, p. 74.

16. In this he differed from his author, who went on to supply the grateful Macready with two of the most popular plays of the century, *The Lady of Lyons* (1838) and *Richelieu* (1839).

17. Playbills from the Theatre Museum, Covent Garden, London.

18. J.S. Bratton, introduction to her edition of *King Lear: Plays in Performance* (Bristol, 1987), p. 3.

19. Laurence Irving, *Henry Irving: The Actor and his World* (1951), p. 403.

20. I owe this point to Hughes, p. 72.

21. See Allen, *Phelps*, Appendix I, pp. 314–15.

22. For a shrewd account of the 'late Victorian popular obsession' with *The Merchant of Venice*, see Linda Rozmovits, *Shakespeare and the Politics of Culture in Late Victorian England* (Baltimore and London, 1998).

23. See Richard Foulkes, 'Charles Kean's *King Richard II*: a Pre-Raphaelite drama', in *Shakespeare and the Victorian Stage*, pp. 39–55; also C.E. Montague, 'Montague on Benson as Richard II', in *Shakespeare in the Theatre*, ed. Wells, pp. 165–70.

24. See Carol J. Carlisle, 'Macready's production of *Cymbeline*', in *Shakespeare and the Victorian Stage*, ed. Foulkes, pp. 138–52; Russell Jackson, '"Cymbeline" in the Nineteenth Century', MA dissertation, University of Birmingham (1971); and Ann Thompson, '*Cymbeline*'s other endings', in *The Appropriation of Shakespeare: Post-Renaissance Reconstructions of the Works and the Myth*, ed. Jean I. Marsden (New York and London, 1991), pp. 203–20.

25. Quoted by Margaret Lamb, '*Antony and Cleopatra*' on the English Stage (London and Toronto, 1980), p. 92; for a useful acccount of productions from Macready's (1833) to Tree's (1906), see pp. 60–98.

26. Eugene M. Waith, introduction to his edition of *Titus Andronicus* (Oxford, 1984), pp. 47–9.

27. Thompson, '*Cymbeline*', p. 211.

28. See Michael R. Booth, *Victorian Spectacular Theatre 1850–1910* (1981), pp. 30–59.

29. Richard Foulkes, *Performing Shakespeare in the Age of Empire* (Cambridge, 2002), p. 131.

30. One of these has survived and recently been released on video in a compilation from the British Film Institute Archives, *Silent Shakespeare* (1999). Tree also made a silent film of five scenes from his 1910 production of *Henry VIII*; F.R. Benson promptly followed with films of four productions from the Stratford-upon-Avon Memorial Theatre. Tree's *Henry VIII* has been hailed as 'the first really important British film' (Rachel Low, *The History of British Film 1906–1914* (1973), p. 95).

31. *William Charles Macready's 'King John': A Facsimile Prompt-Book*, ed. Charles H. Shattuck (Urbana, 1962), p. 1.

32. The concept of 'realization' provides the title for Martin Meisel's important book, *Realizations: Narrative, Pictorial, and Theatrical Arts in Nineteenth-Century England* (Princeton, N.J., 1983).

33. *Macready's 'King John'*, p. 12.

34. *Ellen Terry's Memoirs* (1932), p. 13.

35. Henry James, *The Scenic Art: Notes on Acting and the Drama 1872–1901*, ed. Allan Wade (1949), p. 163.

36. Sullivan also contributed to the vast Victorian output of Shakespearean song five settings for voice and piano. See Arthur Jacobs, 'Sullivan and Shakespeare', in *Shakespeare and the Victorian Stage*, ed. Foulkes, pp. 196–206.

37. The essential biographies are Carol Jones Carlisle, *Helen Faucit: Fire and Ice on the Victorian Stage* (2000), and Nina Auerbach, *Ellen Terry: Player in Her Time* (1987).

38. Henry James, 'The London theatres' (1880), in *The Scenic Art*, p. 144.

39. Henry James, 'Frances Anne Kemble' (1893), in *Literary Criticism*, p. 1082.

40. Carlisle, *Faucit*, p. 200.

41. See Auerbach, *Terry*, pp. 230–7.

42. Laurence Irving, *Irving*, p. 389.

43. Auerbach, *Terry*, pp. 261–5.

44. Roger Manvell, *Ellen Terry* (1968), Appendix I, 'Ellen Terry's notes for the interpretation of Lady Macbeth', pp. 356–62.

45. *Victorian Actors and Actresses*, ed. Mullin, p. 362.

46. *Victorian Actors and Actresses*, p. 366.

47. William Charles Macready, *Reminiscences and Selections from his Diary and Letters*, ed. F. Pollock (1875), pp. 441–2.

48. Helena Faucit, Lady Martin, *On Some of Shakespeare's Female Characters*, 6th edn (Edinburgh and London, 1899), p. 295.

49. Quoted in Laurence Irving, *Irving*, p. 442.

50. James, *Scenic Art*, p. 36. Some twenty years later James delivered his final verdict on what Irving did best: 'a big, brave general picture, and then, for the figure, [he] plays on the chord of the sinister-sardonic, flowered over as vividly as may be with the elegant-grotesque' (*Scenic Art*, p. 287).

51. The critical comments on Sullivan in this paragraph are culled from *Victorian Actors and Actresses*, ed. Mullin, pp. 426–31.

52. See Adrian Poole, 'Northern Hamlet and southern Othello? Irving, Salvini and the whirlwind of passion', in *Shakespeare and the Mediterranean: Proceedings of the Seventh World Shakespeare Congress*, ed. Tom Clayton, Susan Brock and Vicente Forès (Newark, 2003).

53. Laurence Irving, *Irving*, p. 377.

54. Sir Henry Irving, *Theatre, Culture and Society: Essays, Addresses and Lectures*, ed. Jeffrey Richards (Keele, 1994), p. 239.

55. Henry Irving, *Theatre, Culture and Society*, p. 240.

56. Edward Gordon Craig, *Henry Irving* (1930), p. 84.

57. Henry Arthur Jones, *The Shadow of Henry Irving* (1931), p. 49.

58. Craig, *Irving*, p. 19.

59. See Clement Scott, *Some Notable Hamlets of the present time* (1900). The most notable anglophone cross-dressed Hamlet of the period was probably Alice Marriott, who first essayed the role in 1859 in Glasgow. For an appreciation (also of Emma Waller's Iago), see Frank W. Wadsworth, 'Hamlet and Iago: nineteenth-century breeches parts', *SQ*, 17.2 (Spring 1966), 129–39.

2: THE VISUAL ARTS

1. In the second half of the eighteenth century the most popular plays for representation had been *Macbeth, King Lear, As You Like It, Romeo and Juliet* and the two *Henry IV* plays. In the nineteenth century, *Romeo and Juliet* rose to the top of the list, and *As You Like It* was joined in the premier league by *The Tempest, Hamlet, The Merchant of Venice* and *A Midsummer Night's Dream*. It is significant that *Hamlet* overtakes *Macbeth, King Lear* and *Othello*, which subside, along with the Falstaff plays, *Twelfth Night, The Taming of the Shrew, Cymbeline* and *The Merry Wives* to a 'middle category' (Altick, pp. 259–60).

2. Geoffrey Ashton, *Shakespeare's Heroines in the Nineteenth Century*, exhibition catalogue (Buxton Museum and Art Gallery, 1980), p. 48.

3. See Meisel, *Realizations*, especially chs 3, 'Speaking pictures: the drama', and 19, 'Irving and the artists'.

4. For a suggestive account of the influence of Maclise's Shakespearean paintings on Dickens, especially his portrayal of murderous and vengeful phantoms, see Gager, pp. 78–94.

5. Reprinted in *Paris Sketchbook and Art Criticisms*, Oxford Thackeray (1909), p. 576; quoted in Christopher Forbes, *The Royal Academy (1837–1901) Revisited*, exhibition catalogue (Metropolitan Museum of Modern Art, 1975), pp. 102–3.

6. Ruskin took a different line, complaining that Hamlet looked like an Irish ruffian, and that Ophelia's maudlin expression would have been explained by an empty gin bottle on her lap (Ruskin, III, p. 619).

7. There is, however, a watercolour version of the scene from *Hamlet* belonging to the Forbes Magazine Collection, brightly reproduced as colour plate XV in Forbes, *The Royal Academy (1837–1901) Revisited*, p. 173.

8. See [C.R. Smith,] 'Pictorial illustrations of Shakespeare', *Quarterly Review*, 142 (1876), 457–79, and Peter Holland, '"Counterfeit presentments": illustrating Shakespeare and performance', in *Victorian Shakespeare: Theatre, Drama, Performance*, ed. Gail Marshall and Adrian Poole (Basingstoke, 2003).

9. Besides the Staunton illustrations, Gilbert painted many Shakespearean scenes, including the *Apotheosis* (1871; see Figure 7), and several aspects of the Wolsey of *Henry VIII*, from his disgrace (1845) to the height of his power at the start of the play, in the celebrated *Cardinal Wolsey Going in Procession to Westminster Hall*, or *Ego et Rex Meus* (1889).

10. See Helen O. Borowitz, '*King Lear* in the art of Ford Madox Brown', *Victorian Studies*, 21 (1978), pp. 309–34.

11. In a Harvard lecture of 1895, picked up by Peter Thomson,'"Weirdness that lifts and colours all": the secret self of Henry Irving', in Richard Foulkes (ed.) *Shakespeare and the Victorian Stage* (Cambridge, 1986), p. 100.

12. Bown has some good pages on Scott and his two Shakespeare paintings of 1837, *Puck Fleeing Before the Dawn* and *Ariel and Caliban*, in *Fairies in Nineteenth-Century Art and Literature* (Cambridge, 2000), pp. 56–63.

13. First exhibited at the Salon of 1831, Paul Delaroche's painting of *Les Enfants d'Edouard* made a great impression on the young Henry James amongst others. Millais had his own children model for his *Princes in the Tower* (1878): their golden hair and innocent features float appealingly, even seductively, out of the surrounding darkness.

14. Heath's first collection had forty-five plates by eleven different artists, amongst whom Kenny Meadows predominated. In 1848 (the year he died) Heath issued a second, more popular, collection with the same number of plates but a smaller and more distinguished group of artists, led by John Massey Wright, and including Augustus Egg and W.P. Frith. This went through several editions up to 1883, and some of the plates were used in

editions of the complete works. It includes most of the women one would expect to find and some more, such as Mopsa from *The Winter's Tale* and Lady Grey from *3 Henry VI*. There is no Tamora, no Juliet's Nurse nor Mistress Quickly nor Doll Tearsheet, no Emilia nor Paulina, no Goneril nor Regan. More surprisingly, perhaps, there is no Gertrude, no Volumnia and no Hermione.

15. Meadows and Frith both use this moment in Heath's first and second *Galleries*; Frith painted the scene in 1874 (it is now in the Folger) and again in 1898 at the age of nearly eighty. Baxter's Olivia wears a jewel with three pendants similar to theirs.

16. William L. Pressly, *A Catalogue of Paintings in the Folger Shakespeare Library*: "*as imagination bodies forth*" (New Haven and London, 1993), p. 54.

17. For a helpful account of this painting, including Dadd's own identification of the characters, see Patricia Allderidge, *The Late Richard Dadd: 1817–1886*, exhibition catalogue (Tate Gallery, 1974), pp. 125–6. Bown reads the painting as partially determined by contemporary anxieties about science, nature and the supernatural, in *Fairies*, pp. 150–62.

18. Russell Jackson, 'Shakespeare's fairies in Victorian criticism and performance', in *Victorian Fairy Painting*, ed. Jane Martineau (1997), p. 40.

19. For an appreciation of its significance, see Trevor Griffiths, 'A neglected pioneer production: Madame Vestris' *A Midsummer Night's Dream* at Covent Garden, 1840', *SQ*, 30.3 (Summer 1979), 386–96. Vestris was not quite the first female Oberon, but her striking success established a tradition (on the London stage) broken only in Frank Benson's 1889 production, when Otho Stuart took the role; he was the only male Oberon on the London stage between 1816 and 1900. See Judith M. Kennedy, 'Oberon viewed in the nineteenth century', in *Shakespeare and the Visual Arts, Shakespeare Yearbook*, 11, ed. Holger Klein and James L. Harner (Lewiston, N.Y., 2000), pp. 336–53.

20. Paton also painted *The Fairy Raid: Carrying off a Changeling – Midsummer Eve*, and an *Oberon and the Mermaid*, where Oberon gazes wistfully down at a gorgeous creature reclining on a dolphin's back as Puck stares knowingly out at the viewer (the moment the artist is recalling is *MND*, 2.1.148–54).

21. Shortly after this Paton produced a small work based on a detail in the *Quarrel*, *Elves and Fairies: A Midsummer Night's Dream* (*c.*1850; now at the Yale Center for British Art); it is described and reproduced in Geoffrey Ashton, *Shakespeare and British Art*, exhibition catalogue (New Haven, 1981), no. 99. Puck here presides over the group of grotesque elves (and one shapely nymph) making music. Bown discusses the *Reconciliation* and the *Quarrel*, *Fairies*, pp. 91–7.

22. *The Mount* (1878), p. 253; quoted by Kennedy, 'Oberon', p. 345.

23. *Edinburgh Review*, 87 (April 1848); quoted by Kennedy, 'Oberon', p. 343.

24. These include Ford Madox Brown's *Lear and Cordelia* (1849), *Romeo and Juliet* (1870) and *Cordelia's Portion* (1872); Walter Howell Deverell's *Twelfth Night* (1850) and *A Scene from 'As You Like It'* (1853); Arthur Hughes's *Ophelia* (1852) and *Scenes from 'As You Like It'* (1873); William Holman Hunt's *Valentine Rescuing Sylvia from Proteus* (1851) and *Claudio and Isabella* (1853); John Everett Millais's *Ferdinand Lured by Ariel* (1849), *Ophelia* (1852) and *Rosalind in the Forest* (c.1868); Dante Gabriel Rossetti's *Hamlet and Ophelia* (1858?), *Mariana* (1870) and *The Death of Lady Macbeth* (c.1875); and Lucy Rossetti's *Romeo and Juliet* (1870). See Christine Poulson, 'A checklist of Pre-Raphaelite illustrations of Shakespeare's plays', *Burlington Magazine*, 122 (April 1980), 244–50.

25. Meisel, *Realizations*, p. 363.

26. *The Journals of George Eliot*, ed. Margaret Harris and Judith Johnston (Cambridge, 1998), p. 54.

27. Gager makes some telling points, however, about the role it could play in writing about love, friendship and betrayal, notably in *David Copperfield*, where Steerforth plays Proteus to David's Valentine (Gager, pp. 229–34).

28. An earlier study (1850) had her clasping her hands more strenuously round his neck (Meisel, *Realizations*, p. 364).

29. 'J.B.', in *The Pre-Raphaelites*, exhibition catalogue (Tate Gallery, 1984), p. 103.

30. Letter to Charles Eliot Norton, 23 April 1869; quoted by J.A. Gere, *Pre-Raphaelite Drawings in the British Museum* (1994), p. 43. The date of composition is uncertain. Gere believes it to have been begun in 1865 and completed in 1867. 'A.G.' assigns it to the previous decade, c.1854–9, in *The Pre-Raphaelites*, pp. 275–6.

31. Nothing can save the damned madwoman of Rossetti's other important Shakespearean drawing, a Lady Macbeth consumed by introspection. (It is a late work, from about 1875 or thereabouts, one of several studies for a never-completed painting: see 'A.G.''s entry in *The Pre-Raphaelites*.) She is a crazy androgyne still radiating force on the point of expiry, with streaming hair, a mouth of misery and ceaseless hands. She is not, as so often, alone. On the contrary, she is surrounded with helpless caring figures: a doctor who sponges her forehead, a waiting-woman who catches her turbulent hair, a holy man who prays, a maidservant who has fallen asleep with exhaustion. It is a busy death-chamber, yet not quite a chamber because the sheltering canopy gives onto the world of battle outside. This recalls another famous and frequently visualized scene of regal madness-unto-death. But unlike King Lear, this Lady Macbeth has no Cordelia – no child at all – to escort her back from the extreme verge.

32. Henry James, *The Painter's Eye: Notes and Essays on the Pictorial Arts*, ed. John L. Sweeney (1956), p. 250.

33. At the Royal Exhibition of 1852 there were two other Ophelias, by Arthur Hughes and Henry Nelson O'Neil, and subsequent versions of the scene included paintings by Richard Redgrave, William Orchardson, John William Waterhouse and Henrietta Rae. See Martha Tuck Rozett, 'Drowning Ophelias and other images of death in Shakespeare's plays', and B.R. Siegfried, 'Ethics, interpretation, and Shakespeare's Ophelia: the re-emergence of visual phronesis in the works of Maclise, Rossetti, Préault, and Abbey', in *Shakespeare and the Visual Arts*, ed. Klein and Harner, pp. 182–96, 197–226.

34. His Shakespearean paintings include *Lorenzo and Jessica, Bassanio Commenting on the Caskets, The Defeat of Shylock* and *Othello's First Suspicion*.

35. Pressly, *Paintings in the Folger*, p. 86.

36. There is a print of the 'Seven Ages' from the 1790s showing Shakespeare surrounded by seven oval vignettes, and Thomas Stothard published a set in 1799. Robert Smirke's treatment for Boydell was well known, and there is a humorous Regency treatment by Henry Alken (1824; Victoria and Albert Museum). When Charles Kemble retired in 1837 he was presented with a magnificent silver cup ornamented with scenes representing the 'seven ages of man' in high relief.

37. Gary Taylor points out the discrepancy between Shakespeare's Seven Ages and the Four Ages of Shakespeare popularized by Edward Dowden in his *Shakspere* (1877), in *Reinventing Shakespeare: A Cultural History from the Restoration to the Present* (1989), pp. 174–80. For more on Dowden, see pp. 225–8.

38. For most of his life Mulready was a single parent, and his mature works are often concerned with childhood and education. He anticipated some of the Pre-Raphaelites' technical innovations, and as a teacher in the Royal Academy life class he may well have had a direct influence on Millais and Holman Hunt. He illustrated Scott's Waverley Novels and Goldsmith's *Vicar of Wakefield*, and contributed to the Moxon edition of Tennyson (1857). See Christopher Wood, *Victorian Painting* (1999), pp. 35–6; also Kathryn Moore Heleniak, *William Mulready* (New Haven and London, 1980), and Marcia Pointon, *Mulready*, book with exhibition catalogue (Victoria and Albert Museum, 1986).

39. *Fraser's Magazine* (June 1838), 759. A steel engraving by H. Bourne is included in Charles Knight's Imperial Edition of *The Works of Shakespere* (1873–6).

40. See Nina Auerbach, *Woman and the Demon: The Life of a Victorian Myth* (Cambridge, Mass., 1982), pp. 200–3.

41. The secretary of the Garrick Club is recalling the speech Dickens made there on 22 April 1854 ('Some uncollected speeches by Dickens', ed. Philip Collins, *The Dickensian*, 73 (1977), 91).

42. M. Kimberley, *Lord Ronald Gower's Monument to Shakespeare*, Stratford-upon-Avon Papers, 3 (Stratford-upon-Avon, 1989), p. 2.

43. Philip Ward-Jackson, 'Lord Ronald Gower, Gustave Doré and the genesis of the Shakespeare Memorial at Stratford-on-Avon', *Journal of the Warburg and Courtauld Institute*, 50 (1987), 165.

44. Ward-Jackson, 'Gower', 169.

45. 'Now' because originally Hal stood directly in front of Shakespeare, Lady Macbeth behind him, with Falstaff and Hamlet to the two sides, and the 1933 relocation has shifted them forty-five degrees – and further away from the central rotunda – to very good effect. But because of the angle at which Shakespeare himself is sitting, Hal still enjoys the most favoured position, under his author's gaze.

3: CHARACTER, STORY AND PLOT

1. First published as 'Shakspeare Papers.–No.I: Sir John Falstaff', *Bentley's Miscellany*, 1 (May 1837), 494–508; reprinted in William Maginn, *Shakspeare Papers: Pictures Grave and Gay* (1859).

2. D.J. Taylor, *Thackeray* (1999), p. 285.

3. Harry Esmond and his beloved patroness Lady Castlewood are both 'oldened' early on (*Henry Esmond*, bk 1, chs 9, 11); Clive Newcome's cousin Ethel describes him as 'terribly ill, pale, and oldened' (*The Newcomes*, ch. 68); in six weeks Amelia Sedley's ruined father 'oldened more than he had done for fifteen years before', and only Dobbin's feelings for Amelia are 'not in the least changed or oldened' (*Vanity Fair*, chs 18, 43).

4. Extract from *The Times*, 25 April 1906, in *The Literary Notes of Thomas Hardy*, 2 vols, ed. Lennart A. Björk (1985), II, p. 253.

5. See Adrian Poole, 'Falstaff's belly, Bertie's kilt, Rosalind's legs: Shakespeare and the Victorian Prince', *SS 56* (Cambridge, 2003), pp. 126–36.

6. Stanley Weintraub, *The Importance of Being Edward: King in Waiting 1841–1901* (2000), p. xiv.

7. See Jonathan Bate, *Shakespearean Constitutions: Politics, Theatre, Criticism 1730–1830* (Oxford, 1989), pp. 75–84.

8. *Blackwood's Magazine* (January 1853), 105.

9. The visual history of Falstaff includes Hogarth's *Falstaff Examining His Recruits* (1730), a fine painting of *Falstaff Rebuked* (c.1795) by Robert Smirke, who did others for Boydell, and his own *Illustrations to Shakespeare*

(1825). Thomas Stothard was another artist in the early decades of the nineteenth century particularly associated with Falstaff, and this association was still very much alive seventeen years after his death when Anna Eliza Bray published her *Life* in 1851. His pupil John Massey Wright devoted several of his fine Shakespearean watercolours to Falstaff. Of the one hundred and eighteen paintings in the Folger collection almost a quarter feature Falstaff, the great majority drawing on the *Henry IV* plays. See Pressly, *Paintings in the Folger*, p. 18; also the considerable number of Falstaff paintings at the Yale Center for British Art, described (and some of them reproduced) by Ashton, *Shakespeare and British Art*.

10. *Athenaeum* (23 May 1857), 667.

11. He followed his father and elder brother in political caricature and established himself as Gillray's leading successor. The private life of the Prince Regent was one of his targets. See Robert L. Patten, *George Cruikshank's Life, Times, and Art*, 2 vols (1992), II, p. 504.

12. In 1840 David Scott had painted Queen Elizabeth at the theatre, watching a performance with an antlered Falstaff. Queen Victoria never saw the play, having been told how very coarse it was.

13. Robert Nye makes a valiant effort in his novel *Falstaff* (1976).

14. Reginald R. Buckley describes it as 'a fair picture of what England was and might well become again without deterioration', *The Shakespeare Revival and the Stratford-upon-Avon Movement* (1911), p. 116. See further on Buckley, pp. 219–20.

15. This is an aspect of Shakespeare's afterlives, especially in opera and song, too extensive to be pursued here, but it is worth noting the following. In England, there is William Balfe's opera of 1838, and Vaughan Williams's of 1929 (*Sir John in Love*). Elgar's symphonic poem of 1913 is firmly based on the Falstaff of the *Henry IV* plays; so too is Gustav Holst's fine 'musical interlude' *At the Boar's Head* (1925), which revolves round the opposition (literary, musical and historical) between Falstaff and a Hal who sings several of the sonnets. Abroad there is Otto Nicolai's *Die Lustigen Weiber von Windsor* (1849) and, supremely, Verdi's *Falstaff* (1893).

16. Examples include Elizabeth Macauley's *Tales of the Drama* (1833), Amelia E. Barr's *The Young People of Shakespeare's Dramas: For Youthful Readers* (1882), and Mary Macleod's *The Shakespeare Story-Book* (1902).

17. See Megan Lynn Isaac, *Heirs to Shakespeare: Reinventing the Bard in Young Adult Literature* (Portsmouth, N.H., 2000), p. 95.

18. Susan J. Wolfson calls persuasive attention, for instance, to her management of the Helena of *All's Well that Ends Well* in 'Explaining to her sisters: Mary Lamb's *Tales from Shakespear*', in *Women's Re-Visions of Shakespeare*, ed. Marianne Novy (Urbana and Chicago, 1990), pp. 16–40.

19. See Rozmovits, *Shakespeare and the Politics of Culture*, pp. 97–107, for discussion of editions of and commentaries on *The Merchant of Venice* designed for schoolchildren and young readers from the 1860s onwards.

20. References here are to the fourth edition of 1846. Extracts can be found in the useful anthology, *Women Reading Shakespeare 1660–1900*, ed. Ann Thompson and Sasha Roberts (Manchester and New York, 1997), pp. 66–80. See also Auerbach, *Woman and the Demon* (Cambridge, Mass., 1982), pp. 210–15; Christy Desmet, '"Intercepting the dew-drop": female readers and readings in Anna Jameson's Shakespearean criticism', in *Women's Re-Visions of Shakespeare*, ed. Novy, pp. 41–57; and Judith Johnston, *Anna Jameson: Victorian, Feminist, Woman of Letters* (1997).

21. See Ann Thompson and Sasha Roberts, 'Mary Cowden Clarke: marriage, gender and the Victorian woman critic of Shakespeare', in *Victorian Shakespeare: Literature and Culture*, ed. Marshall and Poole (Basingstoke, 2003); also Rozmovits, *Shakespeare and the Politics of Culture*, pp. 41–8.

22. For a spirited defence of the long tradition of thinking about Shakespearean characters as if they were real, see Michael D. Bristol, 'Vernacular criticism and the scenes Shakespeare never wrote', *SS 53* (Cambridge, 2000), pp. 89–102.

23. See Rozmovits, *Shakespeare and the Politics of Culture*, pp. 31–58.

24. Faucit's essays took the form of letters to named individuals who included Browning, Ruskin and Tennyson. They were published at first piecemeal and then gathered (without Tennyson's Hermione, who came later) into the first edition of 1885. This was well received and went through six further editions, the last in 1904 six years after her death. References here are to the 6th edn (Edinburgh and London, 1899).

25. Carol Jones Carlisle, *Helen Faucit: Fire and Ice on the Victorian Stage* (2000), p. 250.

26. These extracts include Shaw's review of the Lyceum production (1896) entitled 'Blaming the Bard', and his malicious rewriting of Act 5, 'Cymbeline Refinished' (1945).

27. For *Othello*'s role in Scott's popular novel, see Diana Henderson, 'Othello Redux? Scott's *Kenilworth* and the trickiness of race on the nineteenth-century stage'; for its role in Trollope's, see John Glavin, '"To make the situation natural": *Othello* at mid-century'; both in *Victorian Shakespeare: Literature and Culture*, ed. Marshall and Poole.

28. Note in his edition of *Pendennis* (Oxford, 1994), p. 1031.

29. Thackeray was regularly drawn to these lines about poppy and mandragora: see *The History of Henry Esmond* (1852), bk 1, ch. 13; *The Newcomes* (1854), ch. 40; *The Virginians* (1858), ch. 35; and *Lovel the Widower* (1861), chs 5, 6. In *He Knew He Was Right*, Trollope's Emily Trevelyan echoes them when she laments to her dementedly jealous husband: 'Alas, Louis, . . . neither can

the law, nor medicine, nor religion, restore to you that fine intellect which foolish suspicions have destroyed' (ch. 60).

30. Anna Jameson, *Characteristics of Women: Moral, Political, and Historical* (1832), II, p. 309.

31. The title of a study by Helen Small that notes the Shakespearean models and references, above all to Ophelia, on which the earlier nineteenth-century novel draws: *Love's Madness: Medicine, the Novel, and Female Insanity, 1800–1865* (Oxford, 1996).

32. Small, *Love's Madness*, p. 123.

33. See Frank McCombie, 'Scott, *Hamlet*, and *The Bride of Lammermoor*', *Essays in Criticism*, 25 (1975), 419–36.

34. Christine Alexander, *The Early Writings of Charlotte Brontë* (Buffalo, 1983), p. 22.

35. There is more to be said about the uses to which Brontë puts Shakespeare in *Jane Eyre*, especially *King Lear*. See Marianne Novy, *Engaging with Shakespeare: Responses of George Eliot and Other Women Novelists* (Iowa City, 1998), pp. 32–43.

36. See Margaret J. Arnold, 'Coriolanus transformed: Charlotte Brontë's use of Shakespeare in *Shirley*', in *Women's Re-Visions of Shakespeare*, ed. Novy, pp. 76–88.

37. Macready first played Coriolanus at Covent Garden in 1819, and some twenty years later, in 1838, he gave it a major revival. On his retirement in 1851 he was temporarily commemorated as a waxwork Coriolanus in 'Madame Tussaud and Son's Great Room'. For reviews of Kemble and Macready, see *Shakespeare in the Theatre*, ed. Wells, pp. 33–7, 59–61, 77–84. Though *Coriolanus* was not a widely popular play, its appeal was renewed from time to time by signal performances that engaged with contemporary history. Richard Schoch has an illuminating account of the 1846 burlesque by James Morgan that directly engages with the activities of the Anti-Corn Law League (*Not Shakespeare*, pp. 163–74).

38. 'Characters of Shakespear's Plays', *Complete Works of William Hazlitt*, ed. P.P. Howe (1930), IV, p. 216.

39. This was the phrase she used in an essay written at the Pensionnat Héger in Brussels, contrasting Wellington favourably with the modern Prometheus, Napoleon (Elizabeth Gaskell, *The Life of Charlotte Brontë* (1857), ed. Angus Easson (Oxford and New York, 1996), p. 204).

40. Mrs Braddon was staggeringly productive, even by Victorian standards, and she maintained her hold over a wide readership. By 1898 no less than fifty-seven of her novels had appeared as the yellowbacks sold at railway bookstalls from the late 1850s onwards. See John Sutherland, *The Longman Companion to Victorian Fiction* (Harlow, 1988), pp. 80–1.

41. Ellen Terry, *Four Lectures on Shakespeare* (1914), pp. 125, 162–3.

42. W.F. Rae, 'Sensation Novelists: Miss Braddon', *North British Review*, n.s. 4 (1865), 186–7; quoted in David Skilton's introduction to his edition of *Lady Audley's Secret* (Harmondsworth, 1987), p. xviii.

43. Braddon was herself an avid reader of contemporary French fiction, including Balzac and Flaubert; her novel *The Doctor's Wife* (1864) was the first Englishing enjoyed by *Madame Bovary*. See Skilton, introduction to *Lady Audley's Secret*, pp. xiii–xv.

4: THREE NOVELISTS: DICKENS, ELIOT, HARDY

1. The case for seeing George Eliot as the Victorian Shakespeare is made by Philip Davis, 'Implicit and explicit reason: George Eliot and Shakespeare', in *Victorian Shakespeare: Literature and Culture*, ed. Gail Marshall and Adrian Poole (Basingstoke, 2003).

2. *Thomas Hardy: Interviews and Recollections*, ed. James Gibson (1999), p. 127.

3. My account of Dickens is indebted to Valerie L. Gager's valuable study, *Shakespeare and Dickens: The Dynamics of Influence* (Cambridge, 1996).

4. Charles Haywood, 'Charles Dickens and Shakespeare: or, The Irish Moor of Venice, *O'Thello*, with Music', *Dickensian* 73 (1977), pp. 67–88.

5. *Selected Journalism 1850–1870*, ed. David Pascoe (Harmondsworth, 1997), pp. 193–203.

6. See Jonathan Arac, 'Hamlet, *Little Dorrit*, and the history of character', in *Critical Conditions: Regarding the Historical Moment*, ed. Michael Hays (Minneapolis, 1992), pp. 82–96.

7. Review of *Middlemarch* (1873), in *Literary Criticism: Essays on Literature, American Writers, English Writers*, p. 958.

8. I draw in the following paragraphs on my essay, 'The shadow of Lear's "houseless" in Dickens', *SS* 53 (Cambridge, 2000), pp. 103–13.

9. See Jerome Meckier, 'Dickens and *King Lear*: a myth for Victorian England', *South Atlantic Quarterly*, 71.1 (Winter 1972), 75–90; Alexander Welsh, *From Copyright to Copperfield: The Identity of Dickens* (Cambridge, Mass., and London, 1987), pp. 87–103; John Harvey, 'Shakespeare and the ends of time: the illustrations', *Cambridge Review*, 117 (May 1996), 25–48.

10. For a helpful account of the influence of Opie's dramatized fiction, see J.S. Bratton, 'The Lear of private life: interpretations of *King Lear* in the nineteenth century', in *Shakespeare and the Victorian Stage*, pp. 124–37.

11. Harvey, 'Shakespeare and the ends of time', pp. 32–3.

12. Quoted in D.J. Taylor, *Thackeray* (1999), p. 403.

13. Dickens, *Selected Journalism*, ed. Pascoe, pp. 73–80.

14. 'Love in the Drama', *Leader*, 6 (25 August 1855), in *George Eliot: A Writer's Notebook 1854–1879 and Uncollected Writings*, ed. Joseph Wiesenfarth (Charlottesville, 1981), pp. 254–5.

15. This is Touchstone, slightly misquoted: 'more dead than a great reckoning in a little room' (*AYL*, 3.3.13–14).

16. 'In a London Drawing-Room', in *George Eliot: Collected Poems*, ed. Lucien Jenkins (1989), p. 41.

17. John Lyon argues for 'the profoundly anti-literary, anti-textual basis of her creative energy. George Eliot's creativity is in large part hostile and negative ... and such hostility extends into her relationship with Shakespeare'. See his 'Shakespearian margins in George Eliot's "working-day world"', *SS* 53 (Cambridge, 2000), pp. 114–26.

18. Marianne Novy, *Engaging with Shakespeare: Responses of George Eliot and Other Women Novelists* (Iowa City, 1998), pp. 12–21, 48–56, 109–14, 126–33.

19. *Coriolanus* supplies mottoes for chs 27 and 30 in *Felix Holt*, and contributes to a passage in the latter which uses Menenius's fable of the belly. For Hamlet and *Daniel Deronda*, see Novy, *Engaging with Shakespeare*, pp. 124–32. See also the conversation-poem 'A College Breakfast-Party' (*Collected Poems*, pp. 160–84), which features a group of students at 'our English Wittenberg', including young Hamlet ('Blond, metaphysical, and sensuous'), Horatio, Osric, Laertes, Rosencranz, Guildenstern and a 'polished priest'. Eliot composed it in March–April 1874, as the novel was taking shape.

20. See, in addition to Novy's *Engaging with Shakespeare*, the volume of essays edited by her, *Women's Re-Visions of Shakespeare* (Urbana and Chicago, 1990).

21. A point made by Novy, *Engaging with Shakespeare*, p. 106.

22. In 'The Marchioness of Stonehenge' (*A Group of Noble Dames*, 1891) Thomas Hardy replays Eliot's fable in miniature. The sexes are reversed so that there are two mothers and one son, and the final punishment is given a less merciful edge when Lady Caroline is rejected by her son and learns like King Lear the 'anguish that is sharper than a serpent's tooth'.

23. See David Leon Higden, 'George Eliot and the art of the epigraph', *Nineteenth-Century Fiction*, 25.2 (September 1970), 127–51; A.G. van den Broek, 'Shakespeare at the heart of George Eliot's England', *George Eliot – George Henry Lewes Studies*, 24–5 (September 1993), 36–64, and his entry on 'epigraphs' in the *Oxford Reader's Companion to George Eliot*, ed. John Rignall (Oxford, 2000), pp. 100–1.

24. *George Eliot's 'Middlemarch' Notebooks: A Transcription*, ed. John Clark Pratt and Victor A. Neufeldt (1979), especially pp. 209–13, from which quotations in the rest of this paragraph are taken. See also Otice C. Sircy, '"The fashion of sentiment": allusive technique and the sonnets of *Middlemarch*', *Studies in Philology*, 84.2 (Spring 1987), 219–44.

25. [Peter Bayne], 'Shakespeare and George Eliot', *Blackwood's*, 133 (April 1883), 524–38. Page references in this and the following paragraph are to this article. It was first brought to my attention by Philip Davis, who puts it to very good use in his paper 'Implicit and explicit reason: George Eliot and Shakespeare' (see n. 1).

26. Thomas Hardy, *The Literary Notes of Thomas Hardy*, ed. Lennart A. Björk, II (1985), p. 375.

27. For Hardy's dealings with Shakespeare, including helpful listings of specific allusions, see the following: Carl J. Weber, 'Twin-voice of Shakespeare', *Shakespeare Association Bulletin*, 9 (1934), 91–7, 'Shakespeare's twin-voice again', ibid., 162–3, and *Hardy of Wessex* (1940), pp. 33–8; E.P. Vandiver, Jr, 'Hardy and Shakespeare again', *Shakespeare Association Bulletin*, 13 (1938), 87–95; F.B. Pinion, *A Hardy Companion* (1968), pp. 215–17; Marlene Springer, *Hardy's Use of Allusion* (1983); Ralph W.V. Eliott, *Thomas Hardy's English* (Oxford, 1984), pp. 120–6; Michael Thorpe's entry on 'Shakespeare, William', in the *Oxford Reader's Companion to Hardy*, ed. Norman Page (Oxford, 2000), pp. 390–2.

28. *Thomas Hardy's Personal Writings*, ed. Harold Orel (1967), p. 189.

29. Hardy copied this passage from Symonds's *Essays Speculative and Suggestive* (London, 1890): '"The great poems – Shakespeare included – are poisonous to the idea of the pride & dignity of the common people. ... The models of our literature ... have had their birth in courts, & basked & grown in castle sunshine; All smells of princes' favours ... As now taught, accepted, & carried out, are not the processes of culture rapidly creating a class of supercilious infidels, who believe in nothing"' (W. Whitman)' (*The Literary Notes of Thomas Hardy*, II, p. 40).

30. *Literary Notes*, ed. Björk, I, pp. 147–8.

31. See William F. Hall, 'Hawthorne, Shakespeare and Tess: Hardy's use of allusion and reference', *English Studies*, 52.6 (December 1971), 536–9.

5: POETRY

1. Christopher Murray, 'James Sheridan Knowles: the Victorian Shakespeare?', in *Shakespeare and the Victorian Stage*, ed. Foulkes, pp. 164–79.

2. *The Diaries of William Charles Macready 1833–1851*, 2 vols, ed. William Toynbee (1912), I, p. 355.

3. Thus G.R. Elliott: '*Othello*, with its terrible soul struggle concentrated in one character, evidently made a deeper impression on Browning's mind and work than any other of Shakespeare's plays.' ('Shakespeare's significance for Browning', *Anglia. Zeitschrift für Englische Philologie*, 32, n.s. 20 (1909), 133.)

4. *The Poetical Works of Robert Browning*, II, ed. Ian Jack and Margaret Smith (Oxford, 1984), p. 500.

5. *Poetical Works*, IV, ed. Ian Jack, Rowena Fowler and Margaret Smith (Oxford, 1991), p. 263.

6. *Aurora Leigh*, ed. Margaret Reynolds (Athens, Ohio, 1992).

7. Baron de Tabley's two Ophelia poems can be found in *Glimpses of Antiquity* (1862) and *Collected Poems* (1903), Cory's 'Prospero' in *Ionica* (1891), and Benson's in *Le Cahier Jaune* (1892).

8. 'Will These Hands Ne'er Be Clean?', and '"Cannot sweeten"', in *The Complete Poems*, text by R.W. Crump, notes and intro. Betty S. Flowers (Harmondsworth, 2001), pp. 628–9, 829–30. Other poems of Rossetti's prompted by lines or moments in Shakespeare include 'Books in the Running Brooks' (1852) and 'Look on this Picture and on This' (1856).

9. See Leah Price, *The Anthology and the Rise of the Novel: from Richardson to George Eliot* (Cambridge, 2000).

10. References here are to the 1854 octavo edition published by Edward Moxon.

11. Hallett Smith, 'The nondramatic poems', in *Shakespeare: Aspects of Influence*, ed. G.B. Evans (Cambridge, Mass., 1976), pp. 43–53.

12. *The Memoirs of John Addington Symonds*, ed. Phyllis Grosskurth (Chicago, 1984), p. 62. For reflections on Symonds's relations with Wilde, see Lawrence Danson, 'Oscar Wilde, W.H., and the unspoken name of love', *ELH*, 58.4 (Winter 1991), 979–1000.

13. As reported by Henry Taylor in his *Autobiography* (1885), quoted by Christopher Ricks, *Tennyson* (New York, 1972), pp. 160–1.

14. Another trendsetter around this time was James Boaden's *On the Sonnets of Shakespeare identifying the person to whom they are addressed; and elucidating several points in the poet's history* (1837).

15. *The Trials of Oscar Wilde*, ed. H. Montgomery Hyde (1948), p. 129.

16. *Trials*, p. 236.

17. First published in *Blackwood's Magazine* (July 1889), a subsequently expanded version remained unpublished until 1921. This latter is the text referred to here. See Kate Chedgzoy, '"Strange worship": Oscar Wilde and the key to Shakespeare's *Sonnets*', in *Shakespeare's Queer Children: Sexual Politics and Contemporary Culture* (Manchester and New York, 1995), pp. 135–76.

18. *Trials*, p. 112.

19. Arline Goldin, 'Victorian renascence: the revival of the amatory sonnet sequence, 1850–1900', *Genre*, 7 (1974), 133–47.

20. Douglas Murray, *Bosie: A Biography of Lord Alfred Douglas* (2000), p. 275.

21. E.C. Stedman, 'Elizabeth Barrett Browning', *Scribner's*, 7 (1983), 109, and Edmund Gosse, introduction to his edition of *Sonnets from the Portuguese*

(1894), p. 10; quoted by Tricia Lootens, *Lost Saints: Silence, Gender, and Victorian Literary Canonization* (Charlottesville and London, 1996), p. 143.

22. Review of George Barnett Smith, *Poets and Novelists: A Series of Literary Studies* (1975), in *Literary Criticism: Essays on Literature, American Writers, English Writers*, p. 1229.

23. *The Poems of George Meredith*, ed. Phyllis B. Bartlett, 2 vols (New Haven and London, 1978).

24. On the poems' 'bewildering textual surface', see Stephen Regan, introduction to his edition (Peterborough, 1988), p. 12.

25. C. Day Lewis, introduction to his edition of *Modern Love* (1948), p. xxiii.

26. See Cynthia Grant Tucker, 'Meredith's broken laurel: *Modern Love* and the Renaissance sonnet tradition', *Victorian Poetry*, 10.4 (Winter 1972), 351–65.

27. Quoted by Day Lewis, pp. xi–xii.

28. John Maynard, *Browning's Youth* (Cambridge, Mass., and London, 1977), p. 227.

29. This and all subsequent references to Browning's poetry are to *RBP* unless stated otherwise.

30. All references to *The Ring and the Book* are to the edition by Richard D. Altick (Harmondsworth, 1971).

31. All references to Tennyson's poetry are to *The Poems of Tennyson*, 2nd edn, 3 vols, ed. Christopher Ricks (Harlow, 1987). I have drawn gratefully on the many allusions to and echoes of Shakespeare noted by Ricks. See also his important essay, 'Tennyson inheriting the earth', in *Studies in Tennyson*, ed. Hallam Tennyson (1981), pp. 66–104.

32. *Gerard Manley Hopkins: Selected Letters*, ed. Catherine Phillips (Oxford, 1990), pp. 23–6.

33. *Keats: The Complete Poems*, ed. Miriam Allott (Harlow, 1970).

34. *Tennyson*, ed. Ricks (1972), pp. 49–50.

35. The 'rot' recurs at 280 with 'Why, if man rot in dreamless ease'. It is the (Folio) Ghost who urges Hamlet that 'duller shouldst thou be than the fat weed / That rots itself in ease on Lethe wharf' (1.5.32–3). (In the quartos the weed does not 'rot' but 'roots'.) See Robert Douglas-Fairhurst, 'Shakespeare's weeds', in *Victorian Shakespeare: Literature and Culture*, ed. Marshall and Poole.

36. See T.P. Harrison, '*Maud* and Shakespeare', *Shakespeare Association Bulletin*, 17 (1942), pp. 80–5.

37. *The Letters of Alfred Lord Tennyson*, ed. Cecil Y. Lang and Edgar F. Shannon, Jr, II, 1851–1870 (Oxford, 1987), p. 102.

38. *In Memoriam: A Casebook*, ed. John Dixon Hunt (1970), p. 104.

39. William Angus Knight, 'A Reminiscence of Tennyson', *Blackwood's* (August 1897), quoted in *Letters of Tennyson*, III (Oxford, 1990), p. 415.

6: THE GREAT IMAGE OF AUTHORITY

1. See Richard Foulkes, *Performing Shakespeare in the Age of Empire* (Cambridge, 2002).

2. *On Heroes, Hero-Worship and the Heroic in History* (1841), notes and intro. Michael K. Goldberg (Berkeley, Los Angeles and Oxford, 1993).

3. 'Multitude' has an ancient pedigree, but the first occurrence of 'multitudinous' recorded by the *OED* is Shakespeare's in *Macbeth* (1605), narrowly anticipating Thomas Dekker (1606) and John Donne (1629).

4. See Albert Furtwangler, *Assassin on Stage: Brutus, Hamlet, and the Death of Lincoln* (Urbana and Chicago, 1991).

5. *The Prelude: A Parallel Text*, ed. J.C. Maxwell (Harmondsworth, 1971), l. 87. This and subsequent references are to the 1850 text.

6. *The French Revolution* (1837), ed. K.J. Fielding and David Sorensen (Oxford and New York, 1989). References here are to part, book and chapter.

7. Marcus Wood, *Blind Memory: Visual Representations of Slavery in England and America 1780–1865* (Manchester and New York, 2000), p. 41.

8. Quoted by Gillian Beer, *Darwin's Plots: Evolutionary Narrative in Darwin, George Eliot and Nineteenth-Century Fiction* (1983), p. 140.

9. '*Daniel Deronda*: A Conversation' (1876), in *Literary Criticism: Essays on Literature, American Writers, English Writers*, p. 991.

10. *Characteristics*, I, p. 95.

11. *Poems and Some Letters of James Thomson*, ed. Anne Ridler (1963).

12. James Miller, *Prostitution Considered in Relation to Its Cause and Cure* (Edinburgh, 1859), p. 5; quoted by J.B. Bullen, *On the Pre-Raphaelite Body* (Oxford, 1998), p. 61.

13. *The Prelude* (1850), bk VII, ll. 722, 732, 673.

14. In a speech to the Royal General Theatrical Fund, 6 April 1857, quoted in Gager, p. 260.

15. 'Shakspeare and Newgate', *Household Words*, 4 October 1851, in *The Uncollected Writings of Charles Dickens: Household Words 1850–1859*, ed. Harry Stone (1969), I, pp. 343–9.

16. *Household Words*, 30 March and 13 April 1850; reprinted in *Dickens' Journalism*, II, ed. Michael Slater (1996), pp. 179–85, 193–201.

17. See Shirley S. Allen, *Samuel Phelps and Sadler's Wells Theatre* (Middletown, Conn., 1971), pp. 96–7. Allen notes that in his biography Phelps's nephew specifically denies the *Household Words* account.

18. See George Rowell, *Queen Victoria Goes to the Theatre* (1978).

19. Rowell, *Queen Victoria*, p. 50.

20. Richard W. Schoch, *Shakespeare's Victorian Stage: Performing History in the Theatre of Charles Kean* (Cambridge, 1998), p. 46.

21. Nancy J. Doran Hazelton, *Historical Consciousness in Nineteenth-Century Shakespearean Staging* (Ann Arbor, 1987), p. 99.

22. Schoch, *Victorian Stage*, pp. 51, 106.

23. See J.W. Burrow, 'The German inheritance: a people and its institutions', in *A Liberal Descent: Victorian Historians and the English Past* (Cambridge, 1981), pp. 97–125.

24. Quoted by Hazelton, *Historical Consciousness*, p. 97.

25. Edward Dowden, *Shakspere: A Critical Study of His Mind and Art* (1975), p. 257.

26. Robert E. Hunter, *Shakespeare and Stratford-upon-Avon, … together with A Full Record of the Tercentenary Celebration* (1864), pp. 191, 170–1.

27. A.W. Schlegel, *A Course of Lectures on Dramatic Art and Literature*, trans. John Black (1846), pp. 400–1.

28. Bradley writes of 'that strange double impression which is produced by the hero's death. He dies, and our hearts die with him; and yet his death matters nothing to us, or we even exult', in 'Hegel's Theory of Tragedy', *Oxford Lectures on Poetry* (1909), p. 91.

29. G.H. Lewes, *The Life of Goethe*, 3rd edn (1875), pp. 53–4.

30. *Life of Goethe*, p. 434.

31. See Rosemary Ashton, *The German Idea: Four English Writers and the Reception of German Thought 1800–1860* (Cambridge, 1980).

32. *Letters of Matthew Arnold*, ed. Cecil Y. Lang, I, 1829–1859 (Charlottesville and London, 1996), p. 241; 'Stanzas in Memory of the Author of "Obermann"', in *The Poems of Matthew Arnold*, 2nd edn, ed. Miriam Allott (Harlow, 1979); 'Preface to Poems (1853)', in *On the Classical Tradition*, ed. R.H. Super (Ann Arbor, 1960), p. 14.

33. *On the Classical Tradition*, p. 8; subsequent page references are also to this work.

34. *Letters*, I, p. 128.

35. 'On the Modern Element in Literature' (1869), in *On the Classical Tradition*, p. 20.

36. *On the Classical Tradition*, p. 12.

37. The essays on *Measure for Measure* and *Love's Labour's Lost* date from 1874 and 1878 respectively; they were collected along with 'The English Kings' (1889) in *Appreciations: with an Essay on Style* (1889). References here are to the Library Edition (1910; repr. Oxford and New York, 1967).

38. 'Shakspeare; or, the Poet', in *Representative Men* (1850), in *Essays and Lectures*, The Library of America (New York, 1983), pp. 710–26.

39. In the development of American theatre there was a symbolic contrast in the performance styles represented by the two native-born male tragedians

who respectively dominated the American stage during the middle and later decades of the century, Edwin Forrest (1806–72) and Edwin Booth (1833–93). See Lisa Merrill, 'Acting like a man: national identity, homoerotics, and Shakespearean criticism in the nineteenth-century American press', in *Victorian Shakespeare: Theatre, Drama, Performance*, ed. Marshall and Poole. 'What a mountain of a man!' Fanny Kemble exclaimed on first meeting Forrest (quoted by Charles Shattuck, *Shakespeare on the American Stage: from the Hallams to Edwin Booth* (Washington, D.C., 1976), p. 65). In Shakespeare Forrest was only at ease as Othello and Lear (and, late in his career, as Coriolanus). Fiercely patriotic, he was more generally at home in American plays such as Stone's *Metamora* and Conrad's *Jack Cade*. The slight, intellectual and introspective Booth was by contrast the American Hamlet. In the rivalry between Forrest and Macready, however, the conflict of styles between force and intellect assumed an overtly political hue around the time Emerson was delivering his lectures. In Edinburgh in 1846 Forrest openly hissed Macready's *Hamlet*; in Cincinatti in 1848 Macready was in the middle of the scene with the recorders when half a dead sheep was thrown onto the stage; the following year thirty-one people died in the Astor Place riots sparked off by the hostility between the two actors. The leading English tragedian of the time was not popular in America, at least with 'the people' to whom Forrest was a national hero.

40. For a valuable anthology of writings on Shakespeare in this period, see *Americans on Shakespeare 1776–1914*, ed. Peter Rawlings (Aldershot, 1999); for the institutionalizing of Shakespeare in nineteenth-century America, see Gary Taylor, *Reinventing Shakespeare: A Cultural History from the Restoration to the Present* (1989), pp. 196–204, and Michael D. Bristol, *Shakespeare's America, America's Shakespeare* (1999), *passim*.

41. *Americans on Shakespeare*, p. 59.

42. Frank M. Bristol, in Rawlings (ed.), *Americans on Shakespeare*, p. 409.

43. *Americans on Shakespeare*, p. 282.

44. *Americans on Shakespeare*, p. 331.

45. Washington Irving, *The Sketchbook of Geoffrey Crayon, Gent.* (1820); extracts in *Americans on Shakespeare*, pp. 32–41, 42–55.

46. Hunter, *Shakespeare and Stratford-upon-Avon*, p. 68.

47. S. Schoenbaum, *Shakespeare's Lives*, revised edn (Oxford, 1991), p. 387. Schoenbaum gives a succinct account of Delia Bacon (pp. 385–94), and of the whole 'Anti-Stratford' movement, in 'Part VI: Deviations', pp. 385–454.

48. See Richard Foulkes, *The Shakespeare Tercentenary of 1864* (1984), and *Performing Shakespeare in the Age of Empire*, pp. 58–81.

49. Letter to Violet Hunt, 26 August 1903, *The Letters of Henry James*, 2 vols, ed. Percy Lubbock (New York, 1920), I, p. 424.

262 SHAKESPEARE AND THE VICTORIANS

50. 'Introduction to *The Tempest*' (1907), in *Literary Criticism: Essays on Literature, American Writers, English Writers*, pp. 1205–20.
51. *A Shakespeare Memorial* (n.d.), published by S.O. Beeton, 248 Strand. The writer was probably Hepworth Dixon, editor of the *Athenaeum*. All the quotations are from p. 2.
52. The Tercentenary sermons can be read in Hunter. See also Richard Foulkes, *Church and Stage in Victorian England* (Cambridge, 1997), especially ch. 6, 'Shakespeare'.
53. Charles Trevelyan, *On the Education of the People of India* (1838), quoted by Gauri Viswanathan, *Masks of Conquest: Literary Study and the British Rule in India* (1989), p. 87.
54. David Masson, *Shakespeare Personally* (1914), p. 144. Masson in fact dissents from Ulrici's definition of Shakespeare as 'the most Christian of poets', preferring to believe in his inheritance of 'that old mythical cosmology of the Gothic race, as preserved in the Scandinavian Eddas' (p. 160).
55. First published in *Ideas of Good and Evil* (1903), though based on earlier essays in *The Speaker*, 11 and 18 May 1901. See Jonathan Allison, 'W.B. Yeats and Shakespearean character', in *Shakespeare and Ireland: History, Politics, Culture*, ed. Mark Thornton Burnett and Ramona Wray (1997), pp. 114–35.
56. Matthew Arnold, *On the Study of Celtic Literature* (1867), in *Lectures and Essays in Criticism*, ed. R.H. Super (Ann Arbor, 1962), pp. 378, 341. See John V. Kelleher, 'Matthew Arnold and the Celtic revival', in *Perspectives of Criticism*, ed. H. Levin (1950; repr. Chicago, 1971), pp. 197–221, and Terence Brown, 'Saxon and Celt: the stereotypes', in *Ireland's Literature: Selected Essays* (Mullingar, 1988), pp. 3–13.
57. English theatres in Calcutta had performed Shakespeare, Sheridan, Congreve, and Massinger from 1775 onwards, and the original Bombay Theatre dates back to 1770. But the Indian Educational Act of 1835 had installed English language and literature as a key element of the education system, and the second half of the nineteenth century saw a complex appropriation of Shakespeare by indigenous readers, translators and performers. By the early years of the twentieth century most of the plays had been translated into India's major languages and many of them adapted for performance in Bengali, Marathi, Urdu, and Gujarati. There were influential touring companies run by the Parsis in Bombay (who would promptly adapt themselves to the new opportunities of cinema). A famous Macbeth, Ganpatrao Joshi, was known as the Garrick of Maharashtra, and the manager K.P. Khatau as the Irving of India. See Singh, 'Different Shakespeares', and Loomba, 'Shakespearian transformations' (p. 242, n. 1).

58. See Sudipto Chatterjee and Jyotsna G. Singh, 'Moor or less? The surveillance of *Othello*, Calcutta 1848', in *Shakespeare and Appropriation*, ed. Christy Desmet and Robert Sawyer (London and New York, 1999), pp. 65–84.

59. Terence Brown, 'Thomas Moore: a reputation', in *Ireland's Literature*, pp. 21–7.

60. Andrew Hadfield, 'Shakespeare's "British" plays and the exclusion of Ireland', and David J. Baker, 'Where is Ireland in *The Tempest*?', in *Shakespeare and Ireland*, pp. 47–67, 68–88.

61. For the nineteenth-century Caliban, see Alden T. Vaughan and Virginia Mason Vaughan, *Shakespeare's Caliban: A Cultural History* (Cambridge, 1991), pp. 102–14, 180–9, 233–43. See also Trevor Griffiths, '"This island's mine": Caliban and colonialism', *Yearbook of English Studies*, 13 (1983), pp. 159–80; Bärbel Krömer, '"Savage and deformed slave" or "ill-used gentleman" – Caliban in eighteenth and nineteenth-century British representations', in *Shakespeare and the Visual Arts*, ed. Klein and Harner, pp. 354–88.

62. See Richard Schoch's helpful discussion in *Not Shakespeare*, pp. 174–87.

63. Gillian Beer points out that the legendary figure was far too popular to be stopped in its tracks by emphatic denials from Darwin and Huxley that any link was missing in the evolutionary process: 'The idea of the missing link becomes a way of warding off connection, keeping hypothetical the kinship of humans and animals, or of races, or even of social classes.' (*Forging the Missing Link* (Cambridge, 1992), p. 32.)

64. Richard Dickins, *Forty Years of Shakespeare on the English Stage* (1908), quoted by Griffiths, '"This island's mine", p. 164.

65. Stephen Orgel, introduction to his edition of *The Tempest* (Oxford, 1987), p. 73.

66. On Shylock, see Rozmovits, *Shakespeare and the Politics of Culture*, pp. 61–128, especially pp. 120–2 on 'plutocracy'. *Punch* had no qualms about portraying Disraeli as Shylock, as the cartoon entitled '"Permissive" Government' for 21 August 1875 demonstrates.

67. *The Tempest, as Arranged for the Stage by Herbert Beerbohm Tree* (1904), p. 63, quoted by Orgel, p. 26. For an account of American and British productions between 1889 and 1904 by McVicker, Benson, Daly, Poel, Warde and James, and Beerbohm Tree, see Mary M. Nilan, '"The Tempest" at the turn of the century', *SS* 25 (Cambridge, 1972), pp. 113–23.

68. Paul Brown remarks that 'Such a sexual division of the other into rapist and virgin is common in colonialist discourse.' ('"This thing of darkness I acknowledge mine": *The Tempest* and the discourse of colonialism', in *Political Shakespeare: New Essays in Cultural Materialism*, ed. Jonathan Dollimore and Alan Sinfield (Manchester, 1985), p. 6.) See also L. Perry Curtis Jr, *Apes and Angels: The Irishman in Victorian Caricature* (Newton Abbot, 1971) and R.F. Foster, *Paddy and Mr. Punch* (1993).

69. Dowden was not alone in making a connexion between this stanza of Tennyson's and Shakespeare's Caliban. Daniel Wilson uses it as the epigraph to ch. 5, 'The Monster Caliban', in *Caliban: The Missing Link* (1873), p. 67.
70. Terence Brown, 'Edward Dowden: Irish Victorian', in *Ireland's Literature* (Mullingar, 1988), p. 40.
71. *Letters of Edward Dowden and His Correspondents* (1914), p. 285; quoted by Brown, 'Edward Dowden', p. 44.
72. See Gary Taylor, *Reinventing Shakespeare: A Cultural History from the Restoration to the Present* (1988), pp. 173–82.
73. Further important essays delivered during his tenure as Professor of Poetry at Oxford (1900–5) are collected in *Oxford Lectures on Poetry* (1909): 'The Rejection of Falstaff', 'Shakespeare's *Antony and Cleopatra*', 'Shakespeare the Man' and 'Shakespeare's Theatre and Audience'.
74. See Katharine Cooke, *A.C. Bradley and his Influence in Twentieth-Century Shakespeare Criticism* (Oxford, 1972).

DUBLIN EPILOGUE

1. These six figures are of course also divided by the Great War, which the older ones did not live to see and the younger lived well beyond. Though Shaw was only two years younger than Wilde he outlived him by half a century. Mention should also be made here of Frank Harris (1856–1931), another Irish Shakespearean of sorts, author of *The Man Shakespeare and His Tragic Life Story* (1909): but not a Dubliner.
2. In the early texts of *Roderick Hudson* (1875) and *The American* (1877); see *Henry James: Novels 1871–1880*, Library of America (New York, 1983), pp. 511, 865. In the revised versions for the New York Edition (1907–9), Roderick loses the Shakespearean allusion but Newman keeps it.
3. The Shakespearean allusion was added to the first text of 1888 when James revised it for the New York Edition of 1908.
4. See Philip Horne, '"Where did she get hold of that?": Shakespeare in Henry James's *The Tragic Muse*', in *Victorian Shakespeare: Literature and Culture*, ed. Marshall and Poole.
5. For the role of *The Tempest* in *The Wings of the Dove*, see Daniel Mark Fogel, *Henry James and the Structure of the Romantic Imagination* (Baton Rouge and London, 1981), pp. 71–6. See also Nina Schwartz, 'The master lesson: James reading Shakespeare', *Henry James Review*, 12.1 (Winter 1991), 69–83.
6. See J.H. Stapes's entry on 'Shakespeare', in the *Oxford Reader's Companion to Conrad*, ed. Owen Knowles and Gene Moore (Oxford, 2000), pp. 340–6.

7. *Henry James Letters*, IV, 1895–1916, ed. Leon Edel (Cambridge, Mass., and London, 1984), p. 4. See also Leon Edel, 'In Ireland', in *The Life of Henry James* (1977), II, pp. 183–7.

8. See Adrian Poole, 'Henry James, war and witchcraft', *Essays in Criticism*, 41.4 (1991), 291–307.

9. *Letters*, IV, pp. 297–8.

10. Laurence Irving, *Irving*, pp. 175, 329, 332, 436–7.

11. Wilde to Edmond de Goncourt [17 December 1891]: 'Français de sympathie, je suis Irlandais de race, et les Anglais m'ont condamné à parler le langage de Shakespeare.' (*Selected Letters*, ed. Rupert Hart-Davis (Oxford, 1979), p. 100).

12. Nina Auerbach comments on the irony of the timing, that 'The theater had become respectable, but theatricality would never cease to be an offense.' (*Ellen Terry*, p. 202)

13. The figure is Auerbach's, *Ellen Terry*, p. 144.

14. Auerbach, *Ellen Terry*, pp. 171, 263.

15. Richard Ellmann, *Oscar Wilde* (1987), p. 236.

16. See John Stokes, *Resistible Theatres* (1972), and Jean Chothia, *English Drama of the Early Modern Period, 1890–1940* (1996), pp. 44–53.

17. Cooke, *A.C. Bradley*, pp. 11, 84.

18. D.E.S. Maxwell, *A Critical History of Modern Irish Drama 1891–1980* (Cambridge, 1984), p. 10.

19. Michael Holroyd, *Bernard Shaw, 1898–1918: The Pursuit of Power* (1989), pp. 227–32.

20. Brinsley MacNamara, *Abbey Plays 1899–1948* (Dublin, 1949).

21. W.B. Yeats, 'Reveries over Childhood and Youth', in *Autobiographies* (1955), p. 47.

22. For the relations between Yeats and Dowden, see Terence Brown, *Ireland's Literature* (Mullingar, 1988), pp. 29–48, and Jonathan Allison, 'W.B. Yeats and Shakespearean character', in *Shakespeare and Ireland: History, Politics, Culture*, ed. Burnett and Wray, pp. 114–35.

23. W.B. Yeats, 'Reveries', pp. 85–9, 235.

24. W.B. Yeats, *The Collected Letters*, 3 vols, ed. John Kelly (Oxford, 1986–94), III, p. 61. This spell at Stratford yielded the essay 'At Stratford-on-Avon', published in *Ideas of Good and Evil* (1903) and later in *Essays and Introductions* (1961).

25. 'The Trembling of the Veil', in *Autobiographies*, p. 235.

26. W.B. Yeats, 'The Death of Synge', in *Autobiographies*, pp. 521–2.

27. Richard Ellmann, *James Joyce*, new and revised edn (Oxford, 1982), p. 140.

28. Ellmann, *Joyce*, pp. 71–3.

29. Ellmann, *Joyce*, pp. 299, 345.

30. Ellmann, *Joyce*, p. 364.
31. Ellmann, *Joyce*, p. 694.
32. 'Characters of Shakespear's Plays', *Works*, ed. Howe, IV, p. 216.
33. Eugene Sheehy, *May It Please the Court* (Dublin, 1951), pp. 13–14; quoted by Ellmann, *Joyce*, p. 59.

SELECT BIBLIOGRAPHY

Unless stated otherwise, place of publication is London.

After the General section, this bibliography is organized by reference to the individual chapters. A limited number of items occur more than once.

GENERAL

Adler, John (ed.), *Responses to Shakespeare*, vols VI, 1830–1859, and VII, 1861–1898 (1997)

Desmet, Christy, and Robert Sawyer (eds), *Shakespeare and Appropriation* (London and New York, 1999)

Lootens, Tricia, *Lost Saints: Silence, Gender, and Victorian Literary Canonization* (Charlottesville and London, 1996)

Marsden, Jean I. (ed.), *The Appropriation of Shakespeare: Post-Renaissance Reconstructions of the Works and the Myth* (New York and London, 1991)

Marshall, Gail, and Adrian Poole (eds), *Victorian Shakespeare: Theatre, Drama, Performance* (Basingstoke, 2003)

— , *Victorian Shakespeare: Literature and Culture* (Basingstoke, 2003)

Meisel, Martin, *Realizations: Narrative, Pictorial, and Theatrical Arts in Nineteenth-Century England* (Princeton, N.J., 1983)

Schoenbaum, Samuel, *Shakespeare's Lives*, revised edn (Oxford, 1991), Part V: Victorians, and Part VI: Deviations, pp. 273–454

Stavisky, Aron Y., *Shakespeare and the Victorians: Roots of Modern Criticism* (Norman, Oklahoma, 1969)

Taylor, Gary, *Reinventing Shakespeare: A Cultural History from the Restoration to the Present* (1989)

Wells, Stanley, *Shakespeare For All Time* (2002), pp. 248–335

1: THEATRE

Allen, Shirley S., *Samuel Phelps and Sadler's Wells Theatre* (Middleton, Conn., 1971)

Auerbach, Nina, *Ellen Terry: Player in Her Time* (1987)

Banham, Martin (ed.), *The Cambridge Guide to Theatre* (Cambridge, 1992)

Bartholomeusz, Dennis, 'Shakespeare on the Melbourne stage, 1843–61', *SS* 35 (Cambridge, 1982), pp. 31–41

Booth, Michael R., *Victorian Spectacular Theatre 1850–1910* (1981)

Brissenden, Alan, 'Australian Shakespeare', in *Shakespeare Performed: Essays in Honor of R.A. Foakes*, ed. Grace Ioppolo (Newark and London, 2000), pp. 240–59

Carlisle, Carol Jones, *Helen Faucit: Fire and Ice on the Victorian Stage* (2000)

Chothia, Jean, 'Variable authenticities: staging Shakespeare in the early modern period', in *English Drama of the Early Modern Period, 1890–1940* (1996), pp. 227–47

Craig, Edward Gordon, *Henry Irving* (1930)

Downer, Alan S., *The Eminent Tragedian: William Charles Macready* (Cambridge, Mass., 1966)

Faucit, Helena, Lady Martin, *On Some of Shakespeare's Female Characters* (1885; 6th edn, Edinburgh and London, 1899)

Fontane, Theodor, *Shakespeare in the London Theatre 1855–58*, trans. Russell Jackson (1999)

Foulkes, Richard, *Church and Stage in Victorian England* (Cambridge, 1997)
— , *Performing Shakespeare in the Age of Empire* (Cambridge, 2002)
— (ed.), *Shakespeare and the Victorian Stage* (Cambridge, 1986)

Golder, John and Richard Madelaine (eds), *O Brave New World: Two Centuries of Shakespeare on the Australian Stage* (Sydney, 2001)

Griffiths, Trevor, 'A neglected pioneer production: Madame Vestris' *A Midsummer Night's Dream* at Covent Garden, 1840', *SQ*, 30.3 (Summer 1979), 386–96

Hughes, Alan, *Henry Irving, Shakespearean* (Cambridge, 1981)

Irving, Sir Henry, *Theatre, Culture and Society: Essays, Addresses and Lectures*, ed. Jeffrey Richards (Keele, 1994)

Irving, Laurence, *Henry Irving: The Actor and his World* (1951)

Jackson, Russell, '"Cymbeline" in the Nineteenth Century', MA dissertation, University of Birmingham (1971)
— , 'Shakespeare in Liverpool: Edward Saker's revivals, 1876–81', *Theatre Notebook*, 32.3 (1978), 100–9
— , 'Before the Shakespeare revolution: developments in the study of nineteenth-century Shakespearian production', *SS* 35 (Cambridge, 1982), pp. 1–12
— , 'Actor-managers and the spectacular', in *Shakespeare: An Illustrated Stage History*, ed. Jonathan Bate and Russell Jackson (Oxford, 1996), pp. 112–27
— (ed.), *Victorian Theatre* (1989)

James, Henry, *The Scenic Art: Notes on Acting and the Drama 1872–1901*, ed. Allan Wade (1949)

— , 'Frances Anne Kemble' (1893), in *Literary Criticism: Essays on Literature, American Writers, English Writers*, ed. Leon Edel, Library of America (Cambridge, 1984), pp. 1071–97

Jones, Henry Arthur, *The Shadow of Henry Irving* (1931)

Lamb, Margaret, *'Antony and Cleopatra' on the English Stage* (London and Toronto, 1980)

Lewes, G.H., *On Actors and the Art of Acting* (1875)

Loomba, Ania, 'Shakespearian transformations', in *Shakespeare and National Culture*, ed. John J. Joughin (Manchester and New York, 1997), pp. 109–41

Macready, William Charles, *Reminiscences and Selections from his Diary and Letters*, ed. F. Pollock (1875)

— , *The Diaries of William Charles Macready 1833–1851*, 2 vols, ed. William Toynbee (1912)

Manvell, Roger, *Ellen Terry* (1968)

Mullin, Donald, *Victorian Plays: A Record of Significant Productions on the London Stage, 1837–1900* (New York, 1987)

— (ed.), *Victorian Actors and Actresses in Review* (Westport, Conn. and London, 1983)

Poel, William, *Shakespeare in the Theatre* (1913)

Poole, Adrian, 'Northern Hamlet and southern Othello? Irving, Salvini and the whirlwind of passion', in *Shakespeare and the Mediterranean: Proceedings of the Seventh World Shakespeare Congress*, ed. Tom Clayton, Susan Brock and Vicente Forès (Newark, 2003)

Rawlings, Peter (ed.), *Americans on Shakespeare 1776–1914* (Aldershot, 1999)

Reid, Douglas, 'Popular theatre in Victorian Birmingham', in *Performance and Politics in Popular Drama*, ed. David Bradby, Louis James and Bernard Sharratt (Cambridge, 1980), pp. 65–89

Richards, Kenneth, and Peter Thomson (eds), *Nineteenth-Century British Theatre* (1971)

Rowell, George, *Queen Victoria Goes to the Theatre* (1978)

Sands, Mollie, *Robson of the Olympic* (1979)

Schoch, Richard W., *Shakespeare's Victorian Stage: Performing History in the Theatre of Charles Kean* (Cambridge, 1998)

— , *Not Shakespeare: Bardolatry and Burlesque in the Nineteenth Century* (Cambridge, 2002)

Shattuck, Charles H., *Shakespeare on the American Stage: from the Hallams to Edwin Booth* (Washington, D.C., 1976)

— (ed.), *William Charles Macready's 'King John': A Facsimile Prompt-Book* (Urbana, 1962)

Singh, Jyotsna, 'Different Shakespeares: the bard in colonial/postcolonial India', *Theatre Journal*, 41.4 (December 1989), 445–58

Speaight, Robert, *William Poel and the Elizabethan Revival* (1954)

Stoker, Bram, *Personal Reminiscences of Henry Irving*, 2 vols (1906)

Styan, J.L., *The Shakespeare Revolution* (Cambridge, 1977)

Terry, Ellen, *Four Lectures on Shakespeare* (1914)

— , *Ellen Terry's Memoirs* (1932)

Thompson, Ann, '*Cymbeline's* other endings', in *The Appropriation of Shakespeare: Post-Renaissance Reconstructions of the Works and the Myth*, ed. Jean I. Marsden (New York and London, 1991), pp. 203–20

Wells, Stanley (ed.), *Nineteenth-Century Shakespeare Burlesques*, 5 vols (1977–8)

— (ed.), *Shakespeare in the Theatre: An Anthology of Criticism* (Oxford, 2000)

Whittaker, Herbert, 'Shakespeare in Canada before 1853', *Stratford Papers on Shakespeare*, ed. B.W. Jackson (Toronto, 1965), pp. 71–89

2: THE VISUAL ARTS

Altick, Richard D., *Paintings from Books: Art and Literature in Britain, 1760–1900* (Columbus, Ohio, 1985)

Ashton, Geoffrey, *Shakespeare's Heroines in the Nineteenth Century*, exhibition catalogue (Buxton Museum and Art Gallery, 1980)

— , *Shakespeare and British Art*, exhibition catalogue, Yale Center for British Art (New Haven, 1981)

— , *Shakespeare: His Life and Work in Paintings, Prints and Ephemera* (1990)

— , *Catalogue of Paintings at the Theatre Museum, London*, ed. James Fowler (1992)

Borowitz, Helen O., '*King Lear* in the art of Ford Madox Brown', *Victorian Studies*, 21 (1978), 309–34

Bown, Nicola, *Fairies in Nineteenth-Century Art and Literature* (Cambridge, 2000)

Forbes, Christopher, *The Royal Academy (1837–1901) Revisited*, exhibition catalogue (Metropolitan Museum of Modern Art, 1975)

Harvey, John, 'Shakespeare and the ends of time: the illustrations', *Cambridge Review*, 117 (May 1996), 25–48

Holland, Peter, '"Counterfeit presentments": illustrating Shakespeare and performance', in *Victorian Shakespeare: Theatre, Drama, Performance*, ed. Gail Marshall and Adrian Poole (Basingstoke, 2003)

Jackson, Russell, 'Shakespeare's fairies in Victorian criticism and performance', in *Victorian Fairy Painting*, ed. Jane Martineau (1997), pp. 38–45

Kimberley, M., *Lord Ronald Gower's Monument to Shakespeare*, Stratford-upon-Avon Papers, 3 (Stratford-upon-Avon, 1989)

Klein, Holger, and James L. Harner (eds), *Shakespeare and the Visual Arts, Shakespeare Yearbook*, 11 (Lewiston, N.Y., 2000), including a bibliography, by Ken A. Bugajski and Saskia Kossak, pp. 474–92

Meisel, Martin, *Realizations: Narrative, Pictorial, and Theatrical Arts in Nineteenth-Century England* (Princeton, N.J., 1983)

Melchiori, Barbara, 'Undercurrents in Victorian illustrations of Shakespeare', in *Images of Shakespeare*, ed. Werner Habicht, D.J. Palmer and Roger Pringle (Newark, 1988), pp. 120–8

Merchant, W.M., *Shakespeare and the Artist* (1959)

Poulson, Christine 'A checklist of Pre-Raphaelite illustrations of Shakespeare's plays', *Burlington Magazine*, 122 (April 1980), 244–50

Pressly, William L., *A Catalogue of Paintings in the Folger Shakespeare Library: "as imagination bodies forth"* (New Haven and London, 1993)

[Smith, C.R.], 'Pictorial Illustrations of Shakespeare', *Quarterly Review*, 142 (1876), 457–79

Ward-Jackson, Philip, 'Lord Ronald Gower, Gustave Doré and the genesis of the Shakespeare Memorial at Stratford-on-Avon', *Journal of the Warburg and Courtauld Institute*, 50 (1987), 160–70

3: CHARACTER, STORY AND PLOT

Allott, Miriam (ed.), *The Brontës: The Critical Heritage* (1974)

Auerbach, Nina, *Woman and the Demon: The Life of a Victorian Myth* (Cambridge, Mass., 1982)

Braddon, Mary Elizabeth, *Lady Audley's Secret* (1862)

— , *Aurora Floyd* (1863)

Bristol, Michael D., 'Vernacular criticism and the scenes Shakespeare never wrote', *SS* 53 (Cambridge, 2000), pp. 89–102

Brontë, Charlotte, *Jane Eyre* (1847)

— , *Shirley* (1849)

— , *Villette* (1853)

— , *The Professor* (1857)

Brough, Robert, and George Cruikshank, *The Life of Falstaff* (1857)

Clarke, Mary Cowden, *The Girlhood of Shakespeare's Heroines* (5 vols, 1850–2; abridged version by Sabilla Novello, 1879)

Faucit, Helena, Lady Martin, *On Some of Shakespeare's Female Characters* (1885; 6th edn, 1899)

Gore, Mrs Catherine, *Mrs Armytage, or Female Domination* (1836)

Isaac, Megan Lynn, *Heirs to Shakespeare: Reinventing the Bard in Young Adult Literature* (Portsmouth, N.H., 2000)

Jameson, Anna, *Characteristics of Women: Moral, Political, and Historical* (1832; later known as *Shakespeare's Heroines*)

Lamb, Charles and Mary, *Tales from Shakespear: Designed for the Use of Young Persons* (1807)

Maginn, William, *Shakspeare Papers: Pictures Grave and Gay* (1859)

Novy, Marianne, *Engaging with Shakespeare: Responses of George Eliot and Other Women Novelists* (Iowa City, 1998)

— (ed.), *Women's Re-Visions of Shakespeare* (Urbana and Chicago, 1990)

Poole, Adrian, 'Falstaff's belly, Bertie's kilt, Rosalind's legs: Shakespeare and the Victorian Prince', *SS* 56 (Cambridge, 2003), pp. 126–36

Scott, Sir Walter, *The Bride of Lammermoor* (1819)

— , *Kenilworth* (1821)

Thackeray, William Makepeace, *Vanity Fair* (1848)

— , *The History of Pendennis* (1850)

Thompson, Ann, and Sasha Roberts (eds), *Women Reading Shakespeare 1660–1900* (Manchester and New York, 1997)

Trollope, Anthony, *He Knew He Was Right* (1869)

4: THREE NOVELISTS: DICKENS, ELIOT, HARDY

Arac, Jonathan, 'Hamlet, *Little Dorrit*, and the history of character', in *Critical Conditions: Regarding the Historical Moment*, ed. Michael Hays (Minneapolis, 1992), pp. 82–96

[Bayne, Peter], 'Shakespeare and George Eliot', *Blackwood's*, 133 (April 1883), 524–38

Broek, A.G. van den, 'Shakespeare at the heart of George Eliot's England', *George Eliot – George Henry Lewes Studies*, 24–5 (September 1993), 36–64

— , 'Epigraphs', in the *Oxford Reader's Companion to George Eliot*, ed. John Rignall (Oxford, 2000), pp. 100–1

Brontë, Emily, *Wuthering Heights* (1847)

Collins, Philip (ed.), *Dickens: The Critical Heritage* (1971)

Cox, R.G. (ed.), *Hardy: The Critical Heritage* (1970)

Davis, Philip, 'Implicit and explicit reason: George Eliot and Shakespeare', in *Victorian Shakespeare: Literature and Culture*, ed. Gail Marshall and Adrian Poole (Basingstoke, 2003)

Dickens, Charles, *Sketches by Boz* (1836)

— , *The Pickwick Papers* (1837)

— , *Oliver Twist* (1838)

— , *Nicholas Nickleby* (1839)

— , *Barnaby Rudge* (1841)

— , *The Old Curiosity Shop* (1841)

— , *Martin Chuzzlewit* (1844)

— , *Pictures from Italy* (1846)

— , *Dombey and Son* (1848)

— , *David Copperfield* (1850)

— , *Bleak House* (1853)

— , *Hard Times* (1854)

— , *Little Dorrit* (1857)

— , *Great Expectations* (1861)

— , *Our Mutual Friend* (1865)

— , *The Pilgrim Edition of the Letters of Charles Dickens*, ed. Madeline House, Graham Storey and Kathleen Tillotson, 12 vols (1965–2002)

— , *Selected Journalism 1850–1870*, ed. David Pascoe (Harmondsworth, 1997)

Eliot, George, *Adam Bede* (1859)

— , *The Mill on the Floss* (1860)

— , *Silas Marner* (1861)

— , *Felix Holt, the Radical* (1866)

— , *Middlemarch* (1872)

— , *Daniel Deronda* (1876)

— , *The George Eliot Letters*, 9 vols, ed. Gordon S. Haight (New Haven and London, 1954–78)

— , *George Eliot's 'Middlemarch' Notebooks: A Transcription*, ed. John Clark Pratt and Victor A. Neufeldt (1979)

— , *George Eliot: A Writer's Notebook 1854–1879 and Uncollected Writings*, ed. Joseph Wiesenfarth (Charlottesville, 1981)

Eliott, Ralph W.V., *Thomas Hardy's English* (Oxford, 1984), pp. 120–6

Gager, Valerie L., *Shakespeare and Dickens: The Dynamics of Influence* (Cambridge, 1996)

Gibson, James (ed.), *Thomas Hardy: Interviews and Recollections* (1999)

Hall, William F., 'Hawthorne, Shakespeare and Tess: Hardy's use of allusion and reference', *English Studies*, 52.6 (December 1971), 536–9

Hardy, Thomas, *Under the Greenwood Tree* (1872)

— , *A Pair of Blue Eyes* (1873)

— , *Far from the Madding Crowd* (1874)

— , *The Return of the Native* (1878)

— , *A Laodicean* (1881)

— , *Two on a Tower* (1882)

— , *The Mayor of Casterbridge* (1886)

— , *Tess of the D'Urbervilles* (1891)

— , *Jude the Obscure* (1896)

— , *Thomas Hardy's Personal Writings*, ed. Harold Orel (1967)

— , *The Literary Notes of Thomas Hardy,* 2 vols. ed. Lennart A. Björk (1985)

Hayden, John O. (ed.), *Scott: The Critical Heritage* (1970)

Higden, David Leon, 'George Eliot and the art of the epigraph', *Nineteenth-Century Fiction,* 25.2 (September 1970), 127–51

Lyon, John, 'Shakespearian margins in George Eliot's "working-day world"', *SS* 53 (Cambridge, 2000), pp. 114–26

Meckier, Jerome, 'Dickens and *King Lear*: a myth for Victorian England', *South Atlantic Quarterly,* 71.1 (Winter 1972), 75–90

Novy, Marianne, *Engaging with Shakespeare: Responses of George Eliot and Other Women Novelists* (Iowa City, 1998)

Pinion, F.B., *A Hardy Companion* (1968), pp. 215–17

Poole, Adrian, 'The shadow of Lear's "Houseless" in Dickens', *SS* 53 (Cambridge, 2000), pp. 103–13

Sircy, Otice C., '"The fashion of sentiment": allusive technique and the sonnets of *Middlemarch*', *Studies in Philology,* 84.2 (Spring 1987), 219–44

Southam, B.C. (ed.), *Jane Austen: The Critical Heritage* (1968)

Springer, Marlene, *Hardy's Use of Allusion* (1983)

Thorpe, Michael, 'Shakespeare, William', in *Oxford Reader's Companion to Hardy,* ed. Norman Page (Oxford, 2000), pp. 390–2

Vandiver, E.P., Jr, 'Hardy and Shakespeare again', *Shakespeare Association Bulletin,* 13 (1938), 87–95

Weber, Carl J., 'Twin-voice of Shakespeare', *Shakespeare Association Bulletin,* 9 (1934), 91–7, and 'Shakespeare's twin-voice again', ibid., 162–3

— , *Hardy of Wessex* (1940)

Welsh, Alexander, *From Copyright to Copperfield: The Identity of Dickens* (Cambridge, Mass., and London, 1987)

Williams, Ioan (ed.), *Meredith: The Critical Heritage* (1971)

5: POETRY

Anon., *The Sweet Silvery Sayings of Shakespeare on the Softer Sex, compiled by an Old Soldier* (1877)

Arnold, Matthew, *The Poems of Matthew Arnold,* 2nd edn, ed. Miriam Allott (Harlow, 1979)

Browning, Elizabeth Barrett, *Aurora Leigh,* ed. Margaret Reynolds (Athens, Ohio, 1992)

Browning, Robert, *The Ring and the Book,* ed. Richard D. Altick (Harmondsworth, 1971)

— , *Robert Browning: The Poems,* 2 vols. ed. John Pettigrew, (Harmondsworth, 1981; repr. 1996)

— , *The Poetical Works of Robert Browning*, 8 vols, ed. Ian Jack, Margaret Smith, Rowena Fowler, Robert Inglesfield, Stefan Hawlin and T.A.J. Burnett, (Oxford, 1983–2001)

Chedgzoy, Kate, '"Strange worship": Oscar Wilde and the key to Shakespeare's *Sonnets*', in *Shakespeare's Queer Children: Sexual Politics and Contemporary Culture* (Manchester and New York, 1995), pp. 135–76

Clarke, Mary Cowden, *Shakespeare Proverbs* (1848)

Dodd, William, *The Beauties of Shakespeare* (1752, and many subsequent editions)

Douglas-Fairhurst, Robert, 'Shakespeare's weeds', in *Victorian Shakespeare: Literature and Culture*, ed. Gail Marshall and Adrian Poole (Basingstoke, 2003)

Dunbar, Mary F.P., *Shakespeare Birthday Book* (1884)

Elliott, G.R., 'Shakespeare's significance for Browning', *Anglia. Zeitschrift für Englische Philologie*, 32, n.s. 20 (1909), 90–161

Goldin, Arline, 'Victorian renascence: the revival of the amatory sonnet sequence, 1850–1900', *Genre*, 7 (1974), 133–47

Harrison, T.P., '*Maud* and Shakespeare', *Shakespeare Association Bulletin*, 17 (1942), 80–5

Hunt, John Dixon (ed.), *In Memoriam: A Casebook* (1970)

Jump, John D. (ed.), *Tennyson: The Critical Heritage* (1967)

Karlin, Danny, '"The Names": Robert Browning's "Shaksperean Show"', in *Victorian Shakespeare: Literature and Culture*, ed. Gail Marshall and Adrian Poole (Basingstoke, 2003)

Litzinger, Boyd, and Donald Smalley (eds), *Browning: The Critical Heritage* (1970)

Masson, David, *Shakespeare Personally* (1914)

Meredith, George, *Modern Love* (1862)

Palgrave, F.T. (ed.), *The Golden Treasury* (1861, and later editions)

Price, Leah, *The Anthology and the Rise of the Novel: from Richardson to George Eliot* (Cambridge, 2000)

Ricks, Christopher, *Tennyson* (New York, 1972)

— , 'Tennyson inheriting the earth', in *Studies in Tennyson*, ed. Hallam Tennyson (1981), pp. 66–104

Rossetti, Christina, *The Complete Poems*, text by R.W. Crump, notes and intro. Betty S. Flowers (Harmondsworth, 2001)

Shakespeare, William, *Songs and Sonnets*, ed. F.T. Palgrave (1865)

— , *The Christ in Shakespeare: Dramas and Sonnets*, interpreted by Charles Ellis (3rd edn, 1902)

— , *The Sonnets*, ed. H.C. Beeching (1904)

— , *Shakespeare Self-Revealed in his 'Sonnets' and 'Phoenix and Turtle'*, with introduction and analyses by 'J.M.' (1904)

Smith, Hallett, 'The nondramatic poems', in *Shakespeare: Aspects of Influence*, ed. G.B. Evans (Cambridge, Mass., 1976), pp. 43–53

Tennyson, Alfred Lord, *The Poems of Tennyson*, 3 vols, 2nd edn, ed. Christopher Ricks (Harlow, 1987)

— , *The Letters of Alfred Lord Tennyson*, ed. Cecil Y. Lang and Edgar F. Shannon, Jr, 3 vols (Oxford, 1982–1990)

Tennyson, Hallam, *Alfred Lord Tennyson: A Memoir by His Son*, 2 vols (1897)

Tucker, Cynthia Grant, 'Meredith's broken laurel: *Modern Love* and the Renaissance sonnet tradition', *Victorian Poetry*, 10.4 (Winter 1972), 351–65

Wilde, Oscar, 'The Portrait of Mr. W.H.' (1889), in *Collins Complete Works of Oscar Wilde*, Centenary Edition, ed. Merlin Holland (Glasgow, 1999)

6: THE GREAT IMAGE OF AUTHORITY

Arnold, Matthew, *On the Classical Tradition*, ed. R.H. Super (Ann Arbor, 1960)

— , *Lectures and Essays in Criticism*, ed. R.H. Super (Ann Arbor, 1962)

Ashton, Rosemary, *The German Idea: Four English Writers and the Reception of German Thought 1800–1860* (Cambridge, 1980)

Beer, Gillian, *Forging the Missing Link* (Cambridge, 1992)

Bradley, A.C., *Shakespearean Tragedy* (1904)

— , *Oxford Lectures on Poetry* (1909)

Bristol, Michael D., *Shakespeare's America, America's Shakespeare* (1999)

Brown, Terence, 'Edward Dowden: Irish Victorian', in *Ireland's Literature* (Mullingar, 1988), pp. 29–48

Buckley, Reginald R., *The Shakespeare Revival and the Stratford-upon-Avon Movement* (1911)

Burnett, Mark Thornton, and Ramona Wray (eds), *Shakespeare and Ireland: History, Politics, Culture* (1997)

Carlyle, Thomas, *The French Revolution* (1837), ed. K.J. Fielding and David Sorensen (Oxford and New York, 1989)

— , *On Heroes, Hero-Worship and the Heroic in History* (1841), notes and intro. by Michael K. Goldberg (Berkeley, Los Angeles and Oxford, 1993)

Chatterjee, Sudipto, and Jyotsna G. Singh, 'Moor or less? The surveillance of *Othello*, Calcutta 1848', in *Shakespeare and Appropriation*, ed. Christy Desmet and Robert Sawyer (London and New York, 1999), pp. 65–84

Cooke, Katharine, *A.C. Bradley and his Influence in Twentieth-Century Shakespeare Criticism* (Oxford, 1972)

Curtis, L. Perry, Jr, *Apes and Angels: The Irishman in Victorian Caricature* (Newton Abbot, 1971)

[Dickens, Charles, and R.H. Horne], 'Shakspeare and Newgate', *Household Words*, 4 October 1851, in *The Uncollected Writings of Charles Dickens: Household Words 1850–1859*, 2 vols, ed. Harry Stone (1969), I, pp. 343–9

Dowden, Edward, *Shakspere: A Critical Study of His Mind and Art* (1975)

Emerson, Ralph Waldo, 'Shakspeare; or, the Poet', *Representative Men* (1850), in *Essays and Lectures*, Library of America (Cambridge, 1983), pp. 710–26

Foster, R.F., *Paddy and Mr Punch* (1993)

Foulkes, Richard, *The Shakespeare Tercentenary of 1864* (1984)

— , *Church and Stage in Victorian England* (Cambridge, 1997)

— , *Performing Shakespeare in the Age of Empire* (Cambridge, 2002)

Furtwangler, Albert, *Assassin on Stage: Brutus, Hamlet, and the Death of Lincoln* (Urbana and Chicago, 1991)

Griffiths, Trevor, '"This island's mine": Caliban and colonialism', *Yearbook of English Studies*, 13 (1983), 159–80

Hazelton, Nancy J. Doran, *Historical Consciousness in Nineteenth-Century Shakespearean Staging* (Ann Arbor, 1987)

Hunter, Robert E., *Shakespeare and Stratford-upon-Avon, ... together with A Full Record of the Tercentenary Celebration* (1864)

James, Henry, 'The Birthplace', in *The Better Sort* (1903)

— , 'Introduction to *The Tempest*' (1907), in *Literary Criticism: Essays on Literature, American Writers, English Writers*, ed. Leon Edel, Library of America (Cambridge, 1984), pp. 1205–20

Lewes, G.M., *The Life of Goethe* (3rd edn, 1875)

Loomba, Ania, 'Shakespearian transformations', in *Shakespeare and National Culture*, ed. John J. Joughin (Manchester and New York, 1997), pp. 109–41

Nilan, Mary M., '"The Tempest" at the turn of the century', *SS* 25 (Cambridge, 1972), pp. 113–23

Pater, Walter, *Appreciations: with an Essay on Style* (1889), Library Edition (1910; repr. Oxford and New York, 1967)

Rawlings, Peter (ed.), *Americans on Shakespeare 1776–1914* (Aldershot, 1999)

Rowell, George, *Queen Victoria Goes to the Theatre* (1978)

Rozmovits, Linda, *Shakespeare and the Politics of Culture in Late Victorian England* (Baltimore and London, 1998)

Ruskin, John, *The Complete Works*, 39 vols, ed. E.T. Cook and Alexander Wedderburn (1903–12)

Schlegel, A.W., *A Course of Lectures on Dramatic Art and Literature*, trans. John Black (1846)

Schoch, Richard W., *Shakespeare's Victorian Stage: Performing History in the Theatre of Charles Kean* (Cambridge, 1998)

Shaw, George Bernard, *Shaw on Shakespeare*, ed. Edwin Wilson (1962)

278 SHAKESPEARE AND THE VICTORIANS

Singh, Jyotsna, 'Different Shakespeares: the bard in colonial/postcolonial India',
    Theatre Journal, 41.4 (December 1989), 445–58

Taylor, Gary, *Reinventing Shakespeare: A Cultural History from the Restoration to the
    Present* (1989)

Vaughan, Alden T., and Virginia Mason Vaughan, *Shakespeare's Caliban: A
    Cultural History* (Cambridge, 1991)

Viswanathan, Gauri, *Masks of Conquest: Literary Study and the British Rule in India*
    (1989)

Wilson, Daniel, *Caliban: The Missing Link* (1873)

Yeats, W.B., 'At Stratford-on-Avon', in *Ideas of Good and Evil* (1903), later in
    Essays and Introductions (1961)

DUBLIN EPILOGUE

Allison, Jonathan, 'W.B. Yeats and Shakespearean Character', in *Shakespeare and
    Ireland: History, Politics, Culture*, ed. Mark Thornton Burnett and Ramona
    Wray (1997), pp. 114–35

Chothia, Jean, *English Drama of the Early Modern Period, 1890–1940* (1996)

Conrad, Joseph, *Lord Jim* (1900)

Ellmann, Richard, *James Joyce*, new and revised edn (Oxford, 1982)
    — , *Oscar Wilde* (1987)

Horne, Philip, '"Where did she get hold of that?": Shakespeare in Henry James's
    The Tragic Muse', in *Victorian Shakespeare: Literature and Culture*, ed. Gail
    Marshall and Adrian Poole (Basingstoke, 2003)

James, Henry, *The Wings of the Dove* (1902)

Joyce, James, *Ulysses* (1922)

Poole, Adrian, 'Henry James, war and witchcraft', *Essays in Criticism*, 41.4
    (1991), 291–307

Schwartz, Nina, 'The master lesson: James reading Shakespeare', *Henry James
    Review*, 12.1 (Winter 1991), 69–83

Shaw, George Bernard, *Shaw on Shakespeare*, ed. Edwin Wilson (1962)

Stapes, J.H., 'Shakespeare', in the *Oxford Reader's Companion to Conrad*, ed. Owen
    Knowles and Gene Moore (Oxford, 2000), pp. 340–6

Wilde, Oscar, 'The Truth of Masks', in *Intentions* (1891); *Collins Complete Works
    of Oscar Wilde*, Centenary Edition, ed. Merlin Holland (Glasgow, 1999)

Yeats, W.B., *Autobiographies* (1955)

INDEX